Know Your Body

Know Your Body

THE ATLAS OF ANATOMY

INTRODUCED BY Emmet B. Keeffe, M.D.
Professor of Medicine, Stanford University

Ulysses Press

Published by Ulysses Press
P.O. Box 3440
Berkeley, California 94703-3440
Tel: 510-601-8301; Fax: 510-601-8307
e-mail: ulysses@ulyssespress.com

Produced by Marshall Cavendish Books
an imprint of Times Media Private Limited
Times Centre, 1 New Industrial Road
Singapore 536196
Tel: (65) 2848844; Fax: (65) 2854871; e-mail: te@corp.tpl.com.sg

Library of Congress Catalog Card Number 98-88298
ISBN 1-56975-166-8
Printed in United Arab Emirates
10 9 8 7 6

Distributed in the United States by Publishers Group West and in Canada by Raincoast Books.

This book has been written and published strictly for informational purposes, and in no way should it
be used as a substitute for consultation with your own medical doctor or health care professional.

Contents

Introduction

As a physician, I have been fascinated for my entire career with how the human body is put together. This beautiful book captures my sense of excitement. With superb illustrations and clear, concise descriptions, *Know Your Body* provides a complete and technically accurate picture of our inner workings.

Most people, when asked to point to their liver, point to various locations over the entire torso and even the back. Only a few fingers point correctly to the right upper quadrant of the abdomen. This example is typical—most people do not know where in their bodies their organs are located.

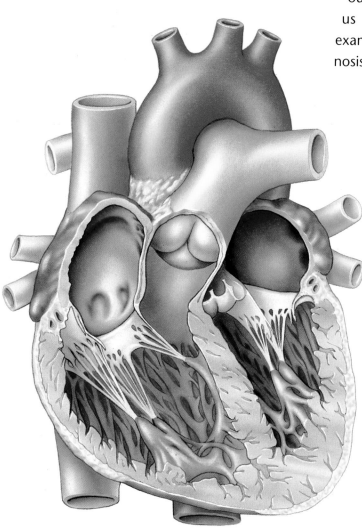

Knowledge of anatomy gives us important insights into our health. Knowing about our bodies also helps us communicate with physicians during routine exams, which can be crucial both for aiding diagnosis and for letting us be active participants in our own medical care. Without a reasonable understanding of our bodies, it becomes much harder to recognize new symptoms that might be important signals to underlying illness.

Know Your Body: The Atlas of Anatomy is a wonderfully illustrated and clearly written book that goes a long way toward educating people about the human body. By interspersing high-quality artwork with descriptive text, it captures just the right balance between medical thoroughness and brevity, presenting complex subjects in an engaging, accessible way.

The book shows all the systems of the body through clear schematic drawings, with a variety of views that highlight the three-dimensional nature of our anatomy. The illustrations of individual organs and their internal structures are particularly helpful in understanding how our bodies work. These drawings display the physiology and biochemistry that is important to many of our daily functions.

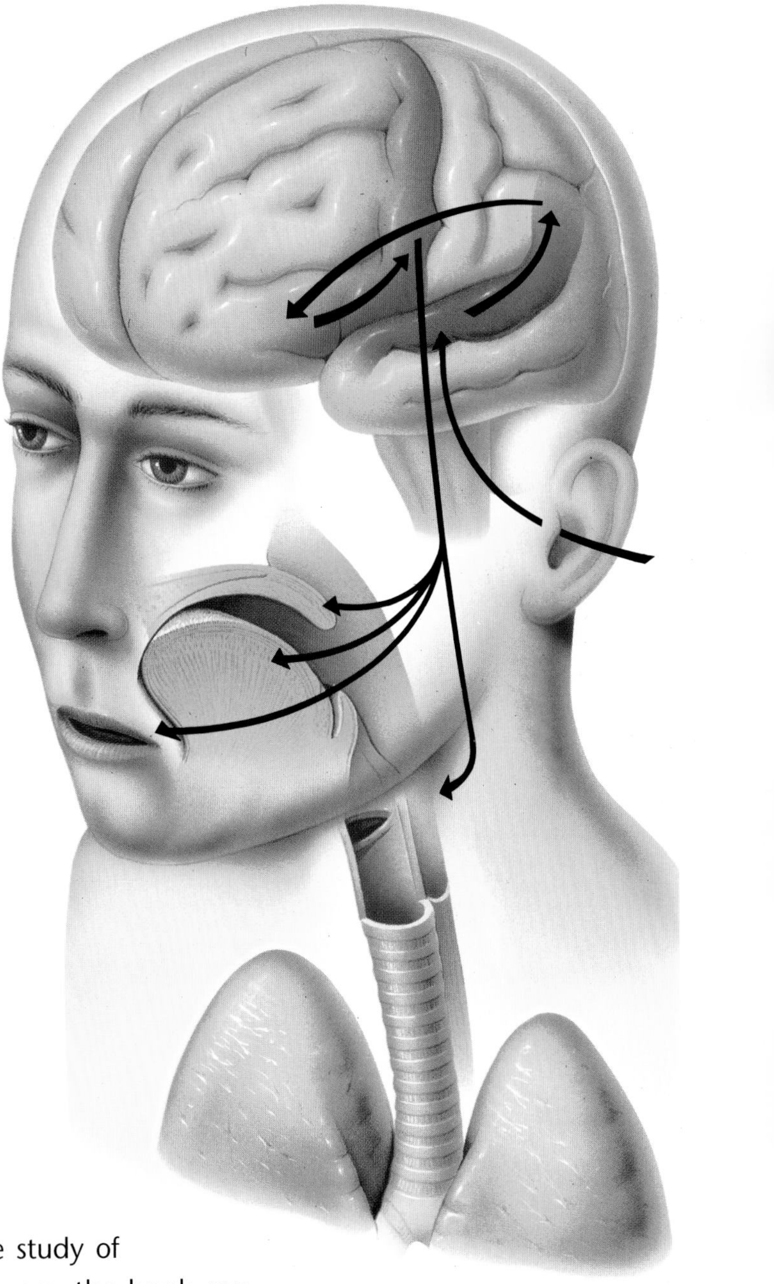

Significantly, *Know Your Body* goes beyond the topics usually found in anatomy texts, such as discussions of the major organs. There are essays that help unify understanding of the interrelated processes of the body—for example, immune response, biochemical homeostasis, and coordination. The discussions of cells, chromosomes and metabolism, which lead the reader from microcosm to gross anatomy, are particularly illuminating.

This book is of immense value as a family reference. It can serve as a tool for the general education of children at home and as a resource for identifying symptoms. *Know Your Body: The Atlas of Anatomy* can also be used in a classroom setting as an effective text for the study of human anatomy. When a new symptom appears, the book can help pinpoint its origin. When a question about the structure or function of the human body system arises, this fascinating book can provide the answer.

Emmet B. Keeffe, M.D.
Professor of Medicine
Stanford University

CHAPTER 1
BODY STRUCTURE

Human anatomy is generally studied by looking at the many and varied organs of the body. Most of these can be grouped together into different systems on the basis of those organs and their accompanying structures that work together to perform specific body functions. Ultimately, all the body systems — and the minute cells that are the basic components of all organs and tissues — are involved in maintaining health and keeping the body in a state of internal balance under constantly changing circumstances.

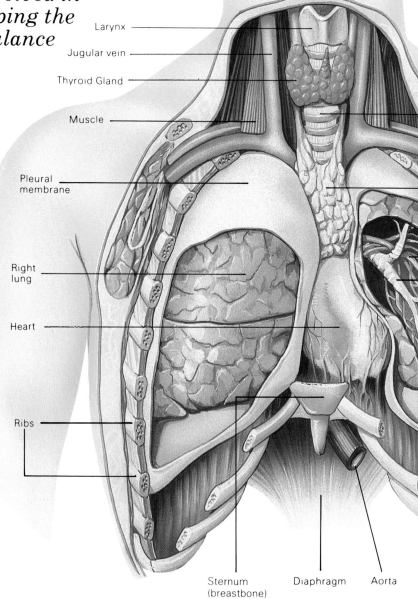

Larynx

Jugular vein

Thyroid Gland

Muscle

Pleural membrane

Right lung

Heart

Ribs

Sternum (breastbone)

Diaphragm

Aorta

The thoracic cavity extends from the bottom of the neck to the diaphragm which separates the thorax from the abdomen. The organs, which include the heart and the lungs, are protected and enclosed by the bones which make up the rib cage.

Organs

Structure means simply the way something is put together. In the case of the human body it is possible to talk about this enormously complicated structure by looking at its basic elements and considering how they fit together. This is essentially the concern of anatomy – it describes the form and arrangement of the parts of the body. An extension of anatomy, physiology is concerned with how the various parts of the body work. However, because the structure of an organ or other unit is closely related to its function (role), anatomy and physiology are very closely related. For example, a description of the structure of an organ such as the stomach inevitably involves learning about its specific role or function – in this case, the digestion of food.

An organ is a distinct unit composed of various tissues with a specific structure and function. It is, therefore, a convenient unit on which to base a

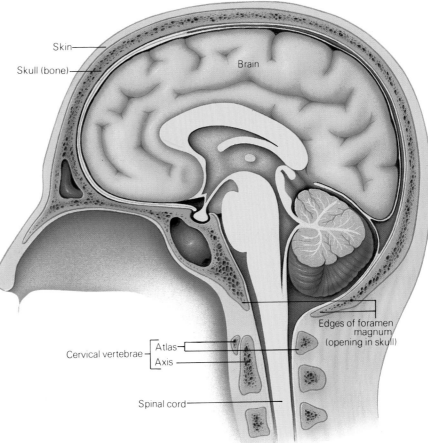

Skin

Skull (bone)

Brain

Cervical vertebrae — Atlas
Axis

Spinal cord

Edges of foramen magnum (opening in skull)

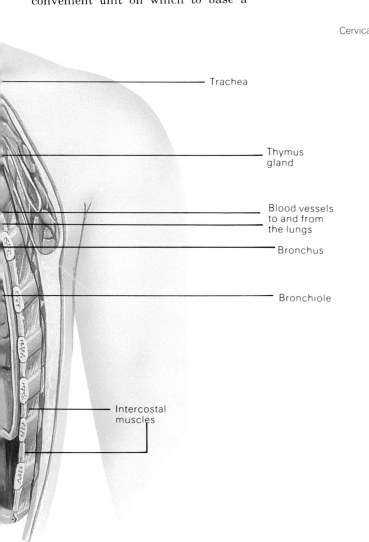

Trachea

Thymus gland

Blood vessels to and from the lungs

Bronchus

Bronchiole

Intercostal muscles

The soft tissues of the brain fill the cranial cavity, which is lined with a tough protective tissue called the dura mater (below). The spinal cord enters the bottom of the cranium through the foramen magnum and from there continues into the cavity as the brain stem.

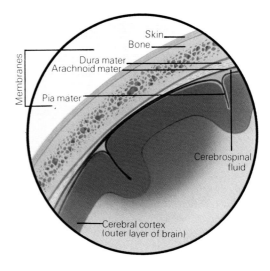

Skin

Bone

Dura mater
Arachnoid mater

Membranes

Pia mater

Cerebrospinal fluid

Cerebral cortex (outer layer of brain)

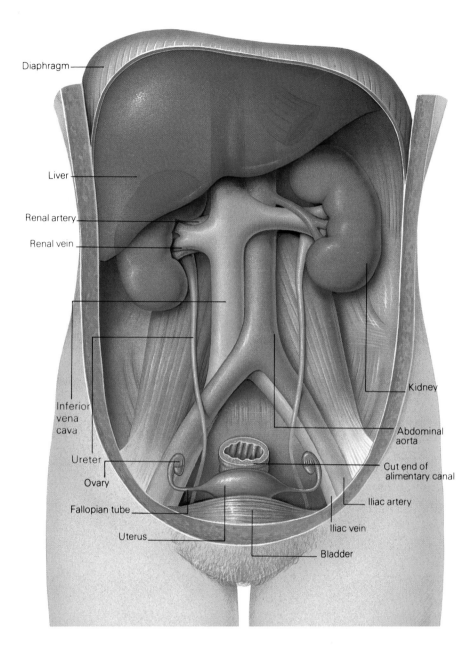

Diaphragm

Liver

Renal artery

Renal vein

Inferior vena cava

Ureter

Ovary

Fallopian tube

Uterus

Kidney

Abdominal aorta

Cut end of alimentary canal

Iliac artery

Iliac vein

Bladder

Contents of the female abdomen with the alimentary canal removed. Nearly all of the female organs of reproduction are found within the cavity, but take up relatively little space. Note the size of the uterus in relation to the liver.

study of the human body. As a preliminary to a more detailed study, it is worth looking at the body's major organs, which are contained in the three large cavities of the body: the cranium, thorax and abdomen.

Cranial cavity

The cranium, or skull, consists of two parts: the cranial cavity, which encloses the brain; and the face, which provides a framework for the eyes, nose and mouth.

The brain completely fills the cranial cavity. It is the growth of the brain that determines the shape of the skull. Initially the skull bones are joined together by cartilage, which permits the bones to move. The cartilage is gradually replaced by bone in the first 18-24 months of life, after which the skull becomes rigid.

The brain is comprised of a soft, jelly-like substance which is easily torn or crushed. It is wrapped in an extremely tough layer of tissue called the dura mater and it is this, and the bones of the skull, which protect the brain. However, if the brain is damaged and swells, its tissue can be further damaged by being crushed against the bony outer layer.

Smaller cavities in the skull include the nasal cavity and the much smaller sinuses, or air cavities, which lead off it. The jaws are usually considered as an appendage to the skull.

At the base of the skull there are several openings, enabling arteries, nerves and veins to pass through. The largest of these spaces, called the foramen magnum, is the outlet for the spinal cord.

Thoracic cavity

The thorax, or chest, is a bony cage that contains two of the most important organs in the body: the lungs and the heart. The basic function of these is to transfer oxygen from the air to the tissues, where it is essential for the continuation of life.

The rib cage is located just under the skin of the chest. It totally encloses the lungs and heart on all but their lowest surface, and resembles a bell in shape. It is attached to the spine at the back, and its base is sealed off by the diaphragm, which is the thick muscular sheet separating the contents of the chest from the abdomen.

In between the ribs there are further muscular sheets called the intercostal ('between the rib') muscles. The chest wall therefore consists of a bell-shaped muscular bag – having the ribs as struts – which by expanding and contracting is able to suck air in and out through the windpipe, or trachea, emerging from the chest into the neck.

The whole of the inside of the chest is lined with a membrane called the pleura. Similar membranes cover the lungs and the heart. When the pleura becomes inflamed this gives rise to the condition known as pleurisy.

The left and right lungs fill the bulk of the chest and are connected by their tubes, the main bronchi, to the trachea. Smaller tubes, or bronchia, then split off from the main bronchus of each lung in a tree-like fashion, carrying air to the air sacs in the lungs, where oxygen is extracted from the air and passed into the blood, and carbon dioxide – which is the body's waste product – moves in the reverse direction.

The heart lies between the two lungs at the front, inside its own membranous bag. The heart receives blood from the body through its right-sided pumping chambers (the right atrium and ventricle) and pumps it into the lungs. Blood returns full of oxygen to the atrium and ventricle on the left side of the heart from where it is pumped out into the main artery of the body – the aorta.

Apart from the heart and lungs, the chest contains the gullet, or oesophagus, which carries food from the mouth into the stomach, which lies just below the diaphragm. There is also a gland called the thymus, which lies at the top of the chest in front of the trachea. This is important in controlling the body's defence mechanisms.

Abdominal cavity

The abdomen is the largest cavity in the body, extending from underneath the diaphragm down to the groins. Bounded at the back of the body by the spine, and round its upper sides by the ribs, the front of the abdomen is covered by a thick sheet of muscle which can be felt just by 'pulling it in'. There are a great number of organs, often called the viscera, in the abdomen. Nearly all the alimentary canal lies inside the abdomen, starting with the stomach sited just under the diaphragm and ending with the rectum, which empties out via the anus. The alimentary canal is the body's food processing and excretory system – it breaks down food into substances that can be absorbed into the blood to be carried to all parts of the body, and ejects indigestible wastes. Backing up the alimentary canal are important abdominal glands such as the liver and pancreas, plus the spleen, which is part of the lymph-vascular system. A huge network of blood vessels serves all the abdominal organs and nerves.

Behind the alimentary canal lie the kidneys, each joined by a tube, called a ureter, to the bladder, which is in the lower part of the abdomen and in which urine is stored before it is released. Closely connected to the urinary system is the reproductive system. In women, nearly all the sex organs are inside the abdomen, but in men part of the sex organs descend to their permanent position outside the body before birth.

It might seem impossible for so many vital organs to be squeezed into such a comparatively small space, but the 10 m (33 ft) or so of gut are coiled and twisted to fit inside the abdomen. To keep everything in place, the abdomen is lined with a membrane called the peritoneum and the organs are attached to it by sheets or strings of tissue known as mesenteries.

The peritoneum covers all the organs contained within the abdomen. Thus, the liver, the stomach and the intestines are covered with peritoneum, as are the spleen, gall bladder, pancreas, uterus and appendix. The function of the peritoneum is to allow the various structures inside the abdomen to move about freely. While the peritoneum covers organs such as the stomach, it also lines the abdominal cavity. The former is known as the visceral peritoneum, and the latter as the parietal peritoneum. The parietal peritoneum has an extremely sensitive nerve supply, so that any injury or inflammation occurring in this layer is felt as an acute localized pain. The visceral peritoneum is not so sensitive and pain is only experienced if, for example, the intestine is stretched or distended.

Position of the peritoneum

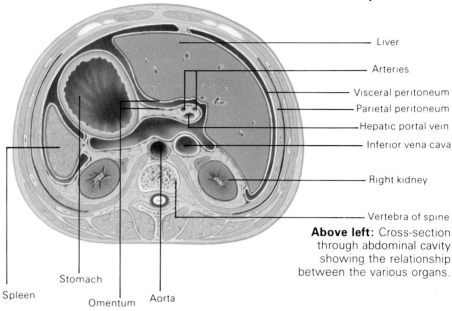

Spleen
Stomach
Omentum
Aorta
Liver
Arteries
Visceral peritoneum
Parietal peritoneum
Hepatic portal vein
Inferior vena cava
Right kidney
Vertebra of spine

Above left: Cross-section through abdominal cavity showing the relationship between the various organs.

Contents of the abdominal cavity

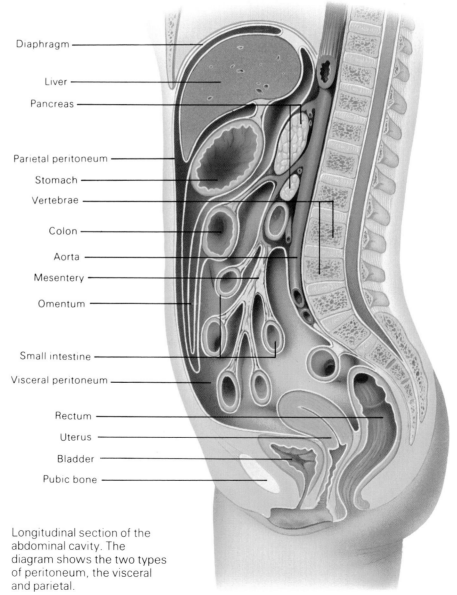

Diaphragm
Liver
Pancreas
Parietal peritoneum
Stomach
Vertebrae
Colon
Aorta
Mesentery
Omentum
Small intestine
Visceral peritoneum
Rectum
Uterus
Bladder
Pubic bone

Longitudinal section of the abdominal cavity. The diagram shows the two types of peritoneum, the visceral and parietal.

Body Systems

To understand how the different organs link up, the body is studied in systems – groups of organs that work together. One of the most familiar is the digestive system. The others are the skeletal system, the integument, or skin, the muscular system, lymph-vascular and cardio-vascular systems, the nervous system, respiratory system, excretory systems, endocrine or hormonal system and the reproductive system. Each of these is discussed individually in the following chapters.

The organs in a system are grouped together not only because they are interconnected, but also because they contain the same type, or types of tissue. There are four main types of tissue and each organ is made up of at least one of them.

Epithelial tissue, or epithelium, is tissue that covers or lines the body organs. Many of them secrete substances such as hormones.

Muscle tissue has the ability to contract, thus enabling movement of the whole body as well as the internal structures. The heart is composed almost entirely of muscular tissue.

Connective tissue, which includes bones and tendons, connects, supports and fills out body structures. This tissue is either loose – a support between or inside other tissues – or dense. Both tendons and ligaments are examples of dense tissues.

Nervous tissue is confined to the nervous system. It helps the body parts to work in harmony by providing a fast and efficient means of communication and control. Nervous tissue is made up of cells and their processes. Although other tissues, such as connective tissue, work with nervous tissue, they do not actually enter it.

System	Major organs and structures
Skeletal	All the body's bones, cartilage, joints and the ligaments that connect them
Muscular	The body's muscles, some under conscious control (skeletal or striped muscle), others working unconsciously (smooth or involuntary muscle)
Nervous	Brain, sense organs (eyes, ears, taste buds, smell and touch receptors), nerves, spinal cord
Endocrine	Hormone-producing glands: pituitary, thyroid, parathyroid, adrenals, pancreas, thymus, parts of testes and ovaries and small areas of tissue in the intestines
Respiratory	Lungs, bronchi (tubes to lungs), trachea (windpipe), mouth, larynx, nose, diaphragm
Cardio-vascular	Heart, arteries, veins, capillaries, blood
Lymph-vascular	Structures involved in the circulation of lymph and the body's defence against disease, including lymph nodes, lymph vessels, spleen, tonsils, adenoids, thymus
Digestive	Mouth, teeth, tongue, salivary glands, oesophagus, stomach, small intestine, liver, gall bladder, pancreas
Excretory	Organs and glands involved in the removal of waste matter from the body: sweat glands, large intestines and the urinary system (kidneys, ureters, bladder, urethra)
Reproductive	Male: testes, penis, prostate gland, seminal vesicles, urethra Female: ovaries, Fallopian tubes, uterus, cervix, vagina, vulva Male and female sex hormones influencing sexual growth and function and secondary sexual characteristics, i.e. menstruation in females.

Urinary system

Inferior vena cava
Kidney
Aorta
Ureter
Bladder
Urethra

Membranes

Membranes are simply layers of tissue which cover, line or divide. There are five main types of membrane.

Mucous membranes are principally found as the lining of tubes, as in the alimentary tract. Synovial membranes cover joint surfaces and tendons. Serous membranes surround organs in the chest and stomach. A special category, the meninges, cover the brain and spinal cord.

At a microscopic level, every one of the millions of cells from which our bodies are ultimately built, and the tiny compartments within those cells, are enclosed and divided by some type of membrane.

As the name suggests, mucous membranes contain specialized cells to secrete the slimy fluid properly called mucus. Among its several functions are fighting infection (it contains antibodies, the body's 'defence troops') and keeping our throats, nostrils and indeed the whole alimentary tract moist and pliable.

Some mucous membranes, notably those in the respiratory tract (the passages leading to the lungs) contain cells with additional functions. Sprouting from them are hair-like projections called cilia which move in concerted 'waves' to push harmful foreign bodies, such as dust, back upwards to the throat to be coughed out of the body.

The membranes lining the intestines are folded into finger-like projections, called villi, to increase the surface area available for digestion of food.

There are also mucous membranes in the sexual or reproductive systems, notably the endometrium, or lining of the uterus, which is shed each month during menstruation.

Synovial membranes occur at moving joints and take the form of bags or sacs containing the lubricating fluid called synovial fluid. Tendons, the tough bands of tissue that connect muscle to bone, are surrounded with a sheath of synovial membrane for protective and lubricating purposes. Serous membranes are coverings for organs in the chest and stomach, providing protection against disease and greatly reducing friction with neighbouring parts. In the chest cavity there are two serous membranes, called the pleura. In the abdomen, all organs are covered by the serous membrane known as the peritoneum.

At the beginning of every new life, membranes have a special, temporary function. The developing foetus is surrounded in the womb by a special, membranous bag called the amniotic sac. This contains fluid in which the foetus virtually floats – creating an ideal protective shock-absorbing system. Following the baby's delivery, it is expelled along with the placenta as the afterbirth.

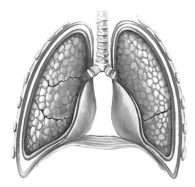

Serous membranes called the pleural membranes (purple) prevent friction between the lungs and the rib cage.

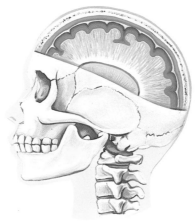

The meninges (orange) surround the delicate tissue and cushion it from the hard, bony skull.

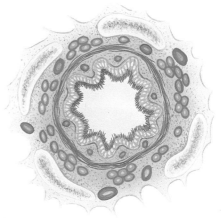

The mucous membrane lining the respiratory tract supports cilia (red) to waft foreign substances away from the lungs.

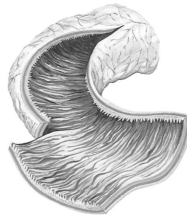

The villi of the mucous membrane (pink) lining the small intestine create an increased surface area for the digestion and absorption of food.

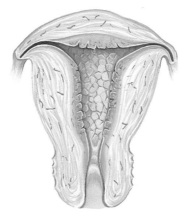

The mucous membrane (red) lining the uterus provides nutritive secretions and prevents friction.

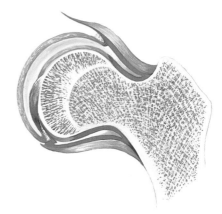

The synovial membrane (red) lining a joint capsule secretes fluid in order to lubricate all movements of the joint.

Cells and Chromosomes

Every adult body contains more than a hundred million cells, microscopic structures averaging only a hundredth of a millimetre in diameter. No one cell is capable of surviving on its own outside the body unless it is cultured (artificially bred) in special conditions.

The body cells vary greatly in shape, size and detailed structure according to the jobs they have to do. Muscle cells, for example, are long and thin and can contract and relax, thus allowing the body to move. Many nerve cells are also long and thin, but are designed to transmit impulses which compose the nerve messages, while the hexagonal cells of the liver are equipped to carry out a multitude of vital chemical processes. Doughnut-shaped red blood cells transport oxygen and carbon dioxide, while spherical cells in the pancreas make and replace the hormone insulin.

Despite these variations, all body cells are constructed according to the same basic pattern. Around the outside of every cell is a boundary wall or cell membrane enclosing a jelly-like substance, the cytoplasm. Embedded in this is the nucleus, which houses the chromosomes.

The cytoplasm, although between 70 and 80 per cent water, is far from inactive. Many chemical reactions take place between substances dissolved in this water, and the cytoplasm also contains many tiny structures called organelles, each with an important and specific task.

The cell membrane also has a defi-nite structure: it is porous and is rather like a sandwich of protein and fat, with the fat as the filling. As substances pass into or out of the cell, they are either dissolved in the fat or passed through the porous, semi-permeable membrane.

Some cells have hair-like projections called cilia on their membranes. In the nose, for example, the cilia are used to trap dust particles. These hairs can also move in unison to waft substances in a particular direction.

The cytoplasm of all cells contains microscopic sausage-shaped organs called mitochondria, which convert oxygen and nutrients into the energy needed for all the other actions of the cells. These 'power-houses' work through the action of enzymes, complex proteins which speed up chemical reactions in the cell, and are most numerous in the muscle cells.

Lysosomes — another type of microscopic organ in the cytoplasm — are tiny sacs filled with enzymes that make it possible for the cell to utilize its nutrients. The liver cells contain the greatest number.

Substances made by a cell which are needed in other parts of the body, such as hormones, are first packaged and then stored in further minute organs called the Golgi apparatus.

Many cells possess a whole network of tiny tubes which are thought to act as a kind of internal cell 'skeleton', but all cells contain a system of channels - endoplasmic reticulum.

Dotted along the reticulum are tiny spherical structures called ribosomes, responsible for controlling the construction of essential proteins needed by all cells. The proteins are required for structural repairs and, in the form of enzymes, for cell chemistry and the manufacture of complex molecules such as hormones.

Chromosomes

Each nucleus is packed with information coded in the form of a chemical called deoxyribonucleic acid (DNA) and organized into groups called genes which are arranged on thread-like structures, the chromosomes. Every chromosome contains thousands of genes, each with enough information for the production of one protein. This protein may have a small effect within the cell, and on the appearance of the body, but equally it may make all the difference between a person having brown or blue eyes, straight or curly hair, normal or albino skin.

Apart from mature red blood cells, which lose their chromosomes in the final stages of their formation, and the eggs and sperm (the sex cells), which contain half the usual number of chromosomes, every body cell contains 46 chromosomes arranged in 23 pairs. One of each pair comes from the mother and one from the father. The eggs and sperm have only half that number so that when an egg is fertilized the new individual is assured of having the correct number.

At the moment of fertilization, the genes start issuing instructions for the moulding of a new human being. The father's chromosomes are responsible for sex determination. The chromosomes are called X or Y, depending on their shape. In women both the chromosomes in the pair are X, but in men there is one X and one Y. If an X-containing sperm fertilizes an X egg, the baby will be a girl, but if a Y sperm fertilizes the egg, then the baby will be a boy.

Cell division

As well as being packed with information, the DNA of the chromosomes also has the ability to reproduce itself; without this, the cells could not duplicate themselves, nor could they pass on information from one generation to another.

The process of cell division in which the cell duplicates itself is called mitosis; this is the type of division that takes place when a fertilized egg grows first into a baby and then into an adult, and when worn out cells are replaced.

Parts of a cell

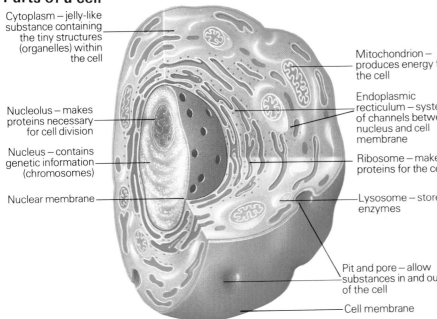

Cytoplasm – jelly-like substance containing the tiny structures (organelles) within the cell

Nucleolus – makes proteins necessary for cell division

Nucleus – contains genetic information (chromosomes)

Nuclear membrane

Mitochondrion – produces energy for the cell

Endoplasmic recticulum – system of channels between nucleus and cell membrane

Ribosome – makes proteins for the cell

Lysosome – stores enzymes

Pit and pore – allow substances in and out of the cell

Cell membrane

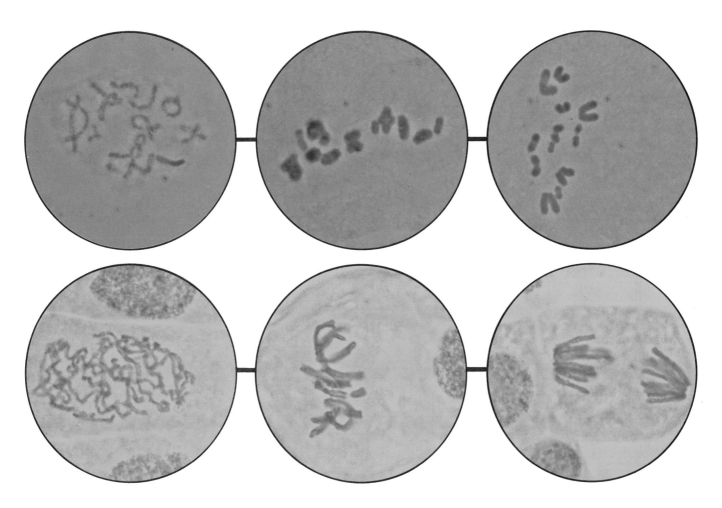

The main difference between the two methods of cell division can be seen above, greatly enlarged. In meiosis (top sequence), the chromosomes are duplicated and then they pair up and intertwine before pulling apart and dividing to produce sex cells containing half the genetic information needed to produce a human being; the remaining half is supplied during fertilization. In mitosis (bottom sequence), pairs of chromosomes separate and each half divides into two identical parts which arrange themselves so that when the respective parts move to opposite ends of the cell and the cell divides into two, each new cell will contain all the genetic information necessary to replace or duplicate existing body cells. The illustration (right) shows the structure of a chromosome in detail.

When the cell is not dividing, the chromosomes are not visible in the nucleus, but when the cell is about to divide the chromosomes become shorter and thicker and can be seen to split in half along their length. These double chromosomes then pull apart and move to opposite ends of the cell. Finally, the cytoplasm is halved and new walls form round the two new cells, each of which has the normal

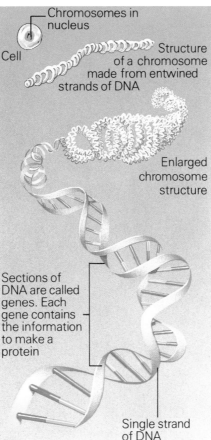

Chromosomes in nucleus

Cell

Structure of a chromosome made from entwined strands of DNA

Enlarged chromosome structure

Sections of DNA are called genes. Each gene contains the information to make a protein

Single strand of DNA

number of 46 chromosomes.

Every day a huge number of cells die and are replaced by mitosis; some cells are more efficient at this than others. Once formed, the cells of the brain and nerves are unable to replace themselves, but liver, skin and blood cells are completely replaced several times a year.

Making cells with half the usual chromosome number in order to determine inherited characteristics involves a different sort of cell division called meiosis. In this, the chromosomes first become shorter and thicker as in mitosis and divide in two, but then the chromosomes pair up so the one from the mother and the other from the father lie side by side.

Next, the chromosomes become very tightly intertwined so that when they eventually pull apart, each new chromosome contains some of the mother's genes and some of the father's. After this, the two new cells divide again so that each egg or sperm contains the 23 chromosomes it needs. The interchange of genetic material during this process of meiosis explains why children do not look exactly like their parents and why everyone except identical twins has a unique genetic make-up.

Metabolism

The complex processes that help keep our bodies functioning normally are efficiently controlled by body chemicals called enzymes and hormones. Enzyme activity influences chemical conversions so that necessary substances are made available to body cells, while hormones control activities such as growth and the utilization of energy reserves.

Metabolism refers to all the chemical processes that occur within the body, enabling it to grow, survive and reproduce. It is the product of two quite distinct and complementary processes, called catabolism and anabolism. Catabolism consists of the breakdown of carbohydrates, fats and proteins and a number of waste products, such as dead cells and tissues, for energy. The energy released by catabolism is converted into useful work through muscle activity, and a certain amount is lost as heat. Anabolism involves the constructive processes by which food materials are adapted by the body to be stored as energy or used for the purposes of growth, reproduction and

defence against infections and disease.

In a growing child or adolescent, the energy input derived from the breakdown of food outweighs the energy output, to provide for the energy requirements of growth. In adults any excess of energy intake will be converted into fat: conversely, too much energy expenditure will result in weight loss.

Carbohydrate breakdown

Much of our energy requirement is provided by the breakdown of carbohydrates, found in foods such as bread and potatoes, into sugars. The most common sugars obtained from food are glucose, fructose and galactose. These are first transported to the liver, where fructose and galactose are converted into glucose. (See Chapter 9 page 104).

Cells obtain energy from glucose by breaking it down into a substance called pyruvic acid. The energy released by this process is temporarily stored as a high energy compound, ATP.

Fat and protein breakdown

Fats and proteins are an important part of the food we eat, and if carbohydrate intake is low, fats and proteins may be used as an energy source.

When carbohydrate sources of energy run out, the fat molecules are split up again into glycerol and fatty acids which are catabolized separately. Glycerol is converted in the liver into glucose and thus enters the pathway of glucose metabolism.

Proteins contained in the diet are broken down into amino acids which are required for growth, and also the enzymes needed to accelerate each cell's metabolic processes.

Many metabolic disorders are caused by a deficiency of enzymes at birth and this can result in the accumulation of poisons in the body.

Disturbances in hormone production are another common cause of metabolic disorder. Diabetes, for example, is caused by decreased production of the hormone insulin by the pancreas. Without insulin, body cells cannot absorb and break down glucose.

How food is used in the body

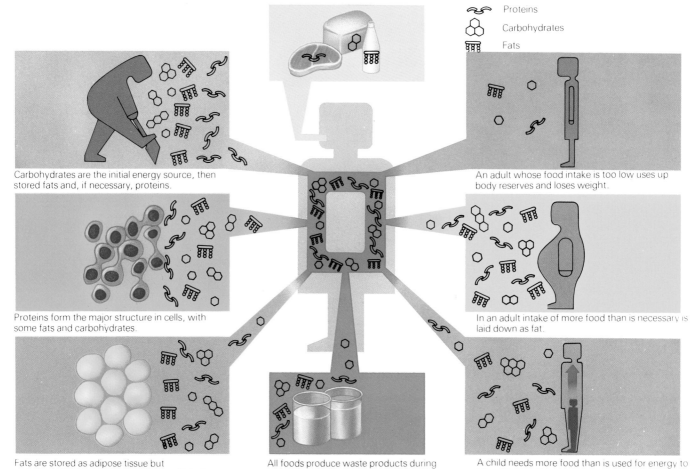

Proteins
Carbohydrates
Fats

Carbohydrates are the initial energy source, then stored fats and, if necessary, proteins.

An adult whose food intake is too low uses up body reserves and loses weight.

Proteins form the major structure in cells, with some fats and carbohydrates.

In an adult intake of more food than is necessary is laid down as fat.

Fats are stored as adipose tissue but carbohydrates or proteins can be turned into fat.

All foods produce waste products during metabolism that must be excreted.

A child needs more food than is used for energy to allow for growth.

Homoeostasis

To remain healthy, our bodies must be regulated in a constant state of internal balance, under ever-changing conditions. The term used to describe this process is homoeostasis. Many of the mechanisms involved in this interplay between ourselves and our environment can be thought of as separate and individual control systems, each with its own specific job to do, and which together form one overall system that is responsible for all our bodily functions.

For example, all the cells of the body are bathed in fluid which supplies their nourishment and carries away waste products. The characteristics of this extracellular (outside the cell) fluid must remain nearly constant to enable the cells to live and work properly. Homoeostasis is, therefore, a state of co-ordination which maintains the normal functions of the body until one or more of its systems gets out of balance. When this happens, all the cells of the body suffer, and disease or ill-health is the result.

A healthy body is able to resist disease and to repair and adapt itself to compensate for injury or stress, but in illness this control is lost. Susceptibility to flu, for example, is largely determined in this way, which explains why not everyone who is exposed to the illness will ultimately come down with it.

It is easy to imagine homoeostasis in engineering terms. All the control and regulating systems of the body act by a process of 'negative feedback', in which the 'output' of a given process is monitored by some other element. When the 'output' rises or falls beyond the desired limits, a part of it is diverted back to the source to act as a control.

A familiar domestic example is the thermostat which controls a central heating system. If the temperature of the room falls below the setting on the thermostat, an electrical circuit is completed which switches on the boiler and pump to circulate hot water through the system. When the desired temperature is reached, the thermostat switches everything off again. However, unlike the central heating system, the body always has several different mechanisms available to perform similar tasks in diffent ways, thus providing 'fail-safe' back-up systems.

There are several thousand control systems in the body which are co-ordinated to regulate virtually every function. The most vital regulators through the body are the nervous

When dehydration occurs, the hypothalamus registers a change in water level in the blood. It then triggers the posterior pituitary to release antidiuretic hormone (ADH) thus decreasing the amount of water lost through the kidneys and bladder. The adrenals are also stimulated to produce more aldosterone enabling more salt to be retained — and with it, water — in the kidneys. Water, drunk to quench thirst felt by a dry mouth and throat, replenishes water in the body. The hypothalamus resisters the change and causes a decrease in ADH and aldosterone.

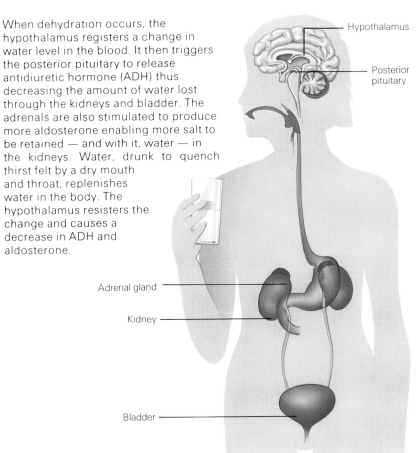

Hypothalamus

Posterior pituitary

Adrenal gland

Kidney

Bladder

system and the endocrine system. Because they are so closely interrelated, and each is necessary for the function of the other, they are sometimes referred to jointly as the neuro-endocrine system.

The part of the nervous system primarily concerned in homoeostasis is known as the autonomic nervous system. This is involved with the automatic regulation of such organs as the heart, lungs, stomach, intestines, bladder, sex organs and blood vessels.

The endocrine system is much slower to react to a situation, but its effects last for some time, whereas the autonomic nervous system produces rapid responses, which are only sustained as long as necessary. Sometimes they work independently of each other, and often they work together, depending on the nature and severity of the problem. One example of homoeostasis which makes use of several systems, is the regulation of the volume of water in the body.

The body is made up of approximately 70 per cent water, with certain tissues - such as the grey matter in

the brain - containing up to 85 per cent, and other tissues - such as fat layers - only 25 per cent. It is also the basic substance of the body's major transport system, blood, which is 80 per cent water. Under certain circumstances the amount of water in the body falls. Fortunately, the body has the necessary machinery to tell us when we need water. Thirst is a basic human drive; when we feel thirsty, the body is signalling its need for water. The volume of water we then drink in order to satisfy the body's needs is dependent on how much water the body has lost.

The main control centre for our sense of thirst is deep in the brain, in the hypothalamus, the control centre of the autonomic nervous system. Small groups of nerve cells in this gland are sensitive to the amount of water in the blood. If the amount of water in the blood compared to the amount of salts and other substances diminishes, these cells are stimulated and, in addition to producing hormones which make the kidneys conserve water (see page 126), produce the sensation of thirst.

CHAPTER 2
SKELETAL SYSTEM AND SKIN

The support structure of the human body is a marvel of complex engineering, designed to give maximum strength and mobility. Each bone is a particular shape because it has a specific role. In those parts of the skeleton where more flexibility is required, cartilage takes over from bone, but it is the joints and their ligaments that make the skeleton a highly articulated piece of machinery. The external covering of the body, the skin, is in fact an organ — the largest in the body — that not only protects the internal structures from injury but also helps to regulate body temperature.

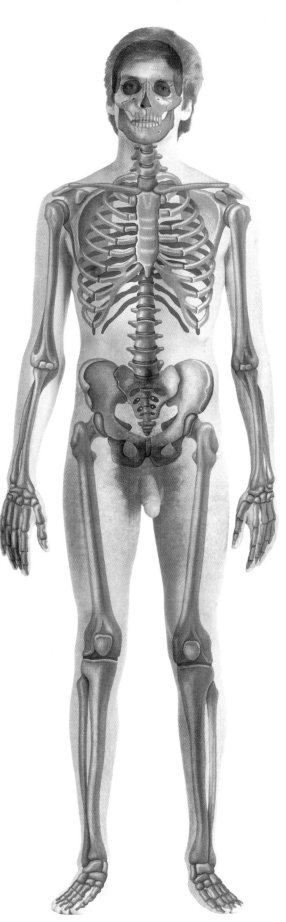

Right: Men and women have the same number of bones – about 206 – but in general the female skeleton is lighter and smaller. In order to accommodate the growing foetus during pregnancy a woman's pelvis is more boat-shaped and broader, giving her hips their characteristic shape. Her shoulders, however, are relatively narrow. In a man the proportions are reversed, broad shoulders and slim hips.

Bones and Cartilage

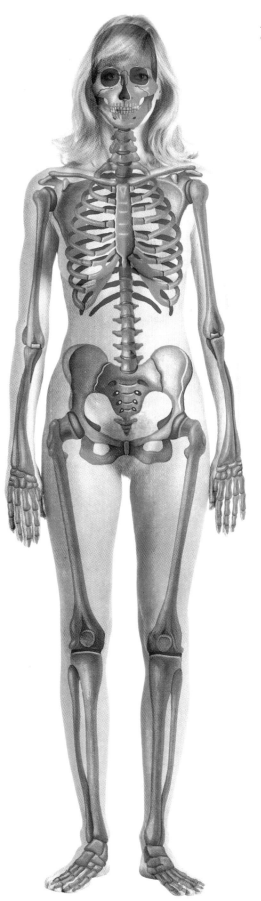

About 206 bones make up the skeleton of the average adult. The bones have a hard, thick, strong outer layer and a soft middle, or marrow. They are as strong and tough as concrete and can support great weights without bending, breaking or being crushed. Linked together by joints and moved by muscles which are attached at either end, they provide cages to protect the soft and delicate parts of the body while still allowing for great flexibility of movement. In addition, the skeleton is the framework or scaffolding on which the other parts of the body are hung and supported.

Like everything else in the body, bones are made up of cells. These are of a type which creates what is technically called a fibrous tissue framework, a relatively soft and pliable base material. Within this framework, there is a network of harder material, which gives a result something like concrete, with lots of 'stones' (i.e. the hard material) providing strength to a 'cement' base of fibrous tissue. The end product is an extremely strong structure, with considerable flexibility.

The growth of bones

When bones begin growing they are completely solid. Only at a secondary stage do they start to develop hollow centres. Hollowing out a tube of material only very slightly reduces its strength, while very much reducing the weight. This is a basic law of structural engineering of which nature takes full advantage in the design of bones. The hollow centres contain the marrow, in which the manufacture of blood cells takes place.

Surprising as it may seem, a newborn baby has more bones in its body than an adult. At birth, around 350 bones make up the tiny frame; over the years some of these fuse together into larger units. A baby's skull is a good example of this, during the birth process, it is squeezed through a narrow canal. Were the skull as inflexible as an adult's it would simply not be possible for the baby to pass through the mother's pelvic outlet. The fontanelles, or gaps between the various sections of the skull, allow it to be moulded sufficiently to accommodate itself to the birth canal. After the

Below: The 14 bones of the face protect the vulnerable sensory organs of the head – the delicate eye mechanism and the smell and hearing receptors. The bones also provide a stable frame for the facial muscles so we can move our face while chewing, speaking or expressing emotions.

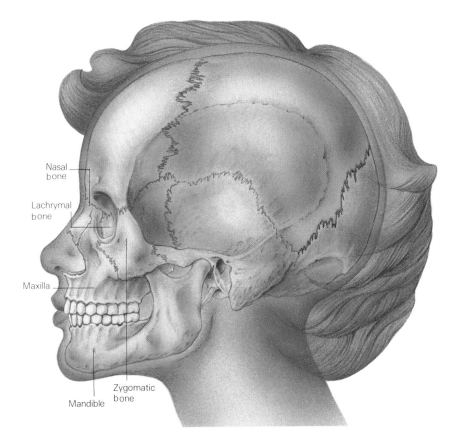

Nasal bone

Lachrymal bone

Maxilla

Zygomatic bone

Mandible

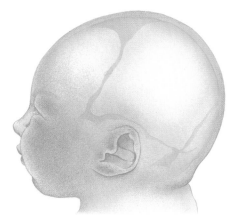

Fontanelles are membraneous gaps in the skull which make it pliable, allowing it to move during birth.

birth these fontanelles gradually close.

The skeleton of a child is made not only of bone, but also of cartilage which is much more flexible. As the body grows this gradually hardens into bone – a process known as ossification which continues well into adulthood.

Growth takes place by an increase in length of the bones of the arms, legs and back. The long bones of the limbs have a growth plate at each end, and this is where growth comes about. This growth plate is made of cartilage rather than bone and for this reason the area of the growth plate does not show up on an X-ray. Once the growth plate has been turned into solid bone there can be no further increase in bone length. The growth plates turn into solid bond or fuse in all the various bones of the body in a set order. It is not until the age of about 20 that full skeletal maturity is reached.

The proportions of the human skeleton change quite dramatically as the skeleton matures. The head of a six-week-old embryo is as long as its body; at birth the head is still large in proportion to the body but the mid-point has shifted from the baby's chin to the navel. In an adult the mid-line of the body runs through the symphysis pubis, or just above the genitals.

In general, a woman's frame is lighter and smaller than a man's. Her pelvis is proportionately wider and it allows room for the growing foetus during pregnancy. The male shoulders are broader and the rib cage longer, but, contrary to popular belief, men and women have the same number of ribs.

An important and remarkable feature of bones is their ability to grow into the right shape. This is especially important for the long bones which support the limbs. They are wider at each end than at the middle, and this provides extra solidarity at the joint

where it is most needed. This shaping, technically known as modelling, is specially engineered during growth and goes on all the time afterwards.

Different shapes and sizes

There are several different types of bone, each designed to perform in varying ways. Long bones, forming the limbs, are simply cylinders of hard bone with the soft, spongy, marrow interior. Short bones, found, for example, at the wrist and ankle, have basically the same form as long bones, but are more squat to allow a great variety of movement without loss of strength.

Flat bones consist of a sandwich of hard bone with a spongy layer between. They are flat to provide protection (as in the skull) or a particularly large area for the attachment of certain muscles (as with the shoulder blades).

The final bone type, irregular bone, comes in several different shapes designed specifically for the job it does. The bones of the spine, for example, are box-shaped to give great strength and plenty of space inside for the marrow. And the bones that make up the structure of the face are hollowed out into air-filled cavities to create extra lightness.

Cartilage

Cartilage, or gristle, is a smooth, tough but flexible part of the body's skeletal system. In adults it is found mainly in joints and covering the ends of bones, and at other strategic points in the skeleton where its toughness, smoothness and flexibility are most needed.

The structure of cartilage is not the same throughout the skeleton. Its make-up varies according to the speci-

Structure of a long bone

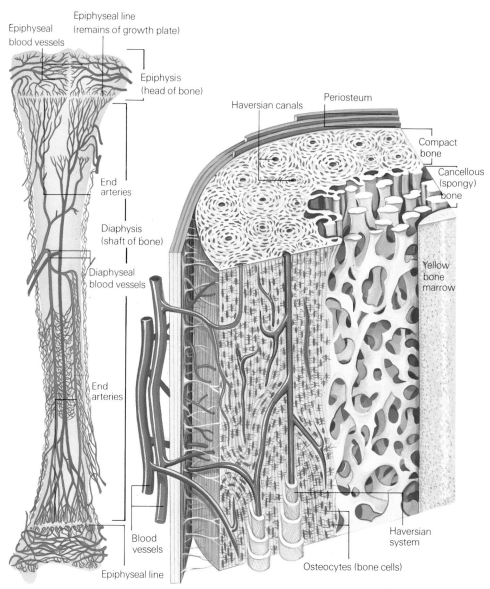

Position of cartilage in the larynx

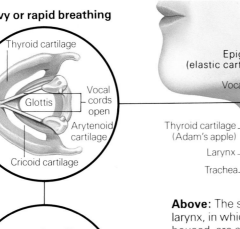

Heavy or rapid breathing

Thyroid cartilage
Glottis
Vocal cords open
Arytenoid cartilage
Cricoid cartilage

Making a high-pitched sound

Vocal cords almost closed

Epiglottis (elastic cartilage)
Vocal cords
Thyroid cartilage (Adam's apple)
Larynx
Trachea

Above: The supporting structures of the larynx, in which the vocal cords are housed, are composed of cartilage. The epiglottis is made up of elastic cartilage but the other three parts – thyroid, cricoid and arytenoid – are hyaline cartilage. The vocal cords are made of fine elastic fibres.

Below: Hyaline cartilage cells in the growth plate multiply, move down the bone and produce a calcified matrix. The cells die, leaving spaces. Osteoblast cells produce bone to fill the spaces and replace the matrix.

the end of the nose, and also the stiff but flexible rings surrounding the windpipe and the larger tubes (bronchi) leading to the lungs. At the end of the ribs, bars of hyaline cartilage form the connections between the ribs and the breastbone and play their part in enabling the chest to expand and contract during breathing.

In the larynx, or voice box, hyaline cartilages are involved not only in support, but also in the production of the voice. As they move, they control the amount of air passing through the larynx and, as a result, the pitch of the note which is emitted.

Fibrocartilage

Fibrocartilage, the second type, is composed of many bundles of the tough substance collagen which makes it both resilient and able to withstand compression. Both these qualities are much in demand at the site in which fibrocartilage is most plentiful, namely between the bones of the spinal column.

In the backbone, each bone or vertebra is separated from its neighbour by a disc of fibrocartilage. The discs cushion the backbone against jarring and help make it possible for the human frame to be held upright. Each

fic job it has to do. All cartilage is composed of a ground structure, or matrix, in which there are embedded cells, plus fibres made up of proteins called collagen and elastin. The consistency of the fibres varies in different sorts of cartilage, but all cartilage is alike in that it contains no blood vessels. Instead, it is nourished by nutrients that diffuse through the covering (perichondrium) of the cartilage, and lubricated by synovial fluid which is made by membranes lining the joints.

According to their different physical properties, the various types of cartilage are known as hyaline cartilage, fibrocartilage and elastic cartilage.

Hyaline cartilage

Hyaline cartilage is a bluish-white translucent tissue, and of the three types, has the fewest cells and fibres. What fibres there are all consist of collagen.

This cartilage forms the embryo skeleton and is capable of the immense amount of growth that allows a baby to grow from only about 45 cm (18 in) into a man 1.8 m (6 ft) tall. After growth is complete, hyaline cartilage remains in a very thin layer only 1-2 mm (1/32 in) across on the ends of the bones where it lines the surfaces of bones in the joints.

Hyaline cartilage is also abundant in the respiratory tract, where it forms

How long bones lengthen

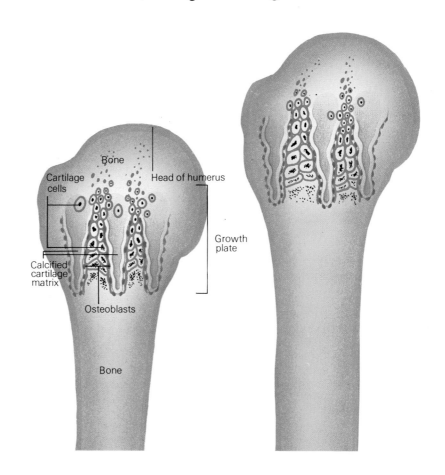

Bone
Cartilage cells
Head of humerus
Growth plate
Calcified cartilage matrix
Osteoblasts
Bone

The arm bones consist of the humerus of the upper arm and the radius and ulna of the lower arm. The elbow which joins the lower and upper arms together is a combined joint; a hinged joint connects the humerus and ulna, and a ball and socket joint connects the humerus to the radius.

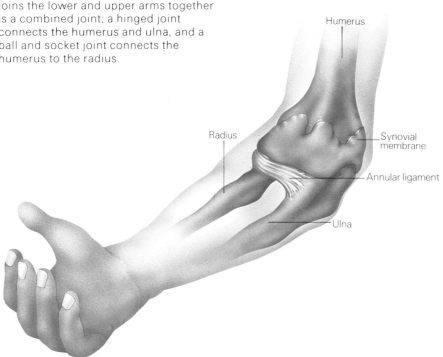

Humerus

Radius

Synovial membrane

Annular ligament

Ulna

bone, it is also very flexible. This enables us to bend down and touch our toes and to hold ourselves stiff and upright. The vertebrae also protect the delicate spinal cord which passes through the middle. The bottom end or tip of the spinal column is called the coccyx. In some animals, such as the dog and cat, it's very much longer and forms a tail.

The spine is made up of a chain of small bones called vertebrae, classified according to their position in the body. Those illustrated here are found in the lumbar region (small of the back). Each vertebra is cushioned by a disc, which is rather like a small bubble of jelly.

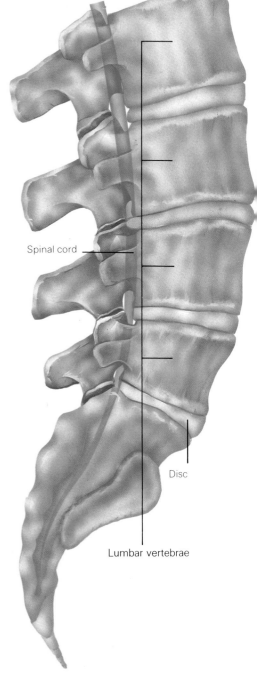

Spinal cord

Disc

Lumbar vertebrae

disc is made up of an outer coating of fibrocartilage surrounding a thick, syrupy fluid. The cartilaginous part of the disc, which has a lubricated surface, prevents the bones being worn away during movement, while the fluid acts as a sort of natural shock absorber.

Fibrocartilage also serves as a tough form of connection between bones and ligaments; in the hip girdle, it joins the two parts of the hips together at the joint known as the symphysis pubis. In women this cartilage is particularly important because it is softened by the hormones of pregnancy to allow the baby's head to pass through.

Elastic cartilage

The third, elastic type of cartilage gets its name from the presence of fibres of elastin, as well as collagen, within its make-up. The elastin fibres give elastic cartilage a distinctive yellow colour. Strong but supple, elastic cartilage forms the flap of tissue called the epiglottis, which snaps down over the entrance to the airway as food is swallowed.

Elastic cartilage also makes up the springy part of the outer ear, and also supports the walls of the canal leading to the middle ear and the Eustachian tubes which link each ear with the back of the throat. Along with hyaline cartilage, elastic cartilage also helps make up the supporting and voice-producing parts of the larynx.

Structure of the skeleton

Each of the different parts of the skeleton is designed to do a particular job. The skull or cranium protects the brain and also the eyes and ears. Of the 29 bones in the skull, 14 form the basic framework for the eyes, nose, cheek bones and upper and lower jaw. A look at the skull shows how the vulnerable features of the face are protected by these bones. The deep eye sockets, overhung by the forehead, shelter the complex and delicate eye mechanisms. Likewise, the smell-detecting part of the olfactory area is tucked away high up behind the central nose hole in the upper jaw or maxilla.

A striking feature of the skull is the size of the mandible or lower jaw. Hinged for movement, it forms the ideal crushing instrument as it comes in contact, via the teeth, with the maxilla. When the facial bones are covered with muscle, nerves and skin, it is not so noticeable how efficiently the jaws are constructed. Another example of good design is that the facial area is stronger around the eye and nose to prevent the facial bones being driven either backwards under the skull or upwards.

The backbone or spine is made up of a chain of small bones, rather like cotton reels, called vertebrae, and forms the central axis of the skeleton. It has enormous strength, but because it is a rod made up of small sections, instead of being one solid piece of

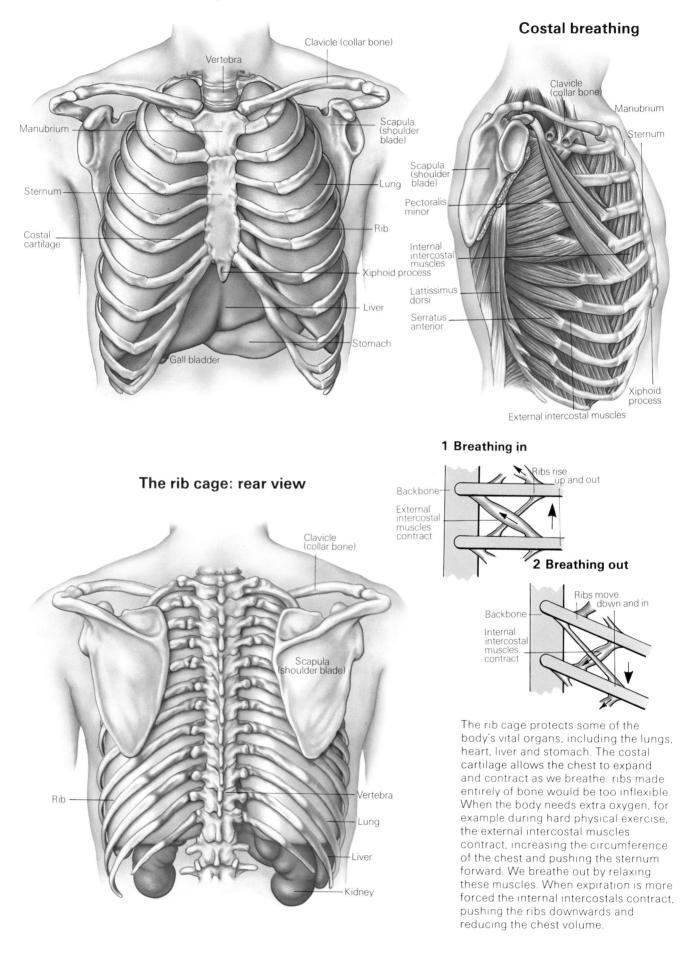

The rib cage: front view

Clavicle (collar bone)

Vertebra

Manubrium

Scapula (shoulder blade)

Sternum

Lung

Costal cartilage

Rib

Xiphoid process

Liver

Stomach

Gall bladder

Costal breathing

Clavicle (collar bone)

Manubrium

Sternum

Scapula (shoulder blade)

Pectoralis minor

Internal intercostal muscles

Lattissimus dorsi

Serratus anterior

Xiphoid process

External intercostal muscles

The rib cage: rear view

Clavicle (collar bone)

Scapula (shoulder blade)

Rib

Vertebra

Lung

Liver

Kidney

1 Breathing in

Ribs rise up and out

Backbone

External intercostal muscles contract

2 Breathing out

Ribs move down and in

Backbone

Internal intercostal muscles contract

The rib cage protects some of the body's vital organs, including the lungs, heart, liver and stomach. The costal cartilage allows the chest to expand and contract as we breathe: ribs made entirely of bone would be too inflexible. When the body needs extra oxygen, for example during hard physical exercise, the external intercostal muscles contract, increasing the circumference of the chest and pushing the sternum forward. We breathe out by relaxing these muscles. When expiration is more forced the internal intercostals contract, pushing the ribs downwards and reducing the chest volume.

The rib cage is made up of the ribs at the sides, the spinal column at the back and the breastbone, or sternum, in front. The ribs are fixed to the spine by special joints which allow movement during breathing. At the front they are attached through a piece of cartilage to the sternum. The two lowest ribs (the 11th and 12th) are attached only at the back and are too short to be joined to the sternum. These are usually known as floating ribs and have little connection with breathing. The first and second ribs are closely connected with the collar bone, or clavicle, and form the root of the neck near which several large nerves and blood vessels pass on their way to the arms. The rib cage is designed to protect the heart and lungs which lie inside it, since damage to these organs could prove fatal.

The bones of the leg are the longest and heaviest in the body. The femur, or thigh bone, fits into the hip socket, the acetabulum, in the iliac bone of the pelvic girdle. The acetabulum faces outwards so that the legs are kept far enough away from the mid-line of the body for effective balance and walking.

Leg and hip bones

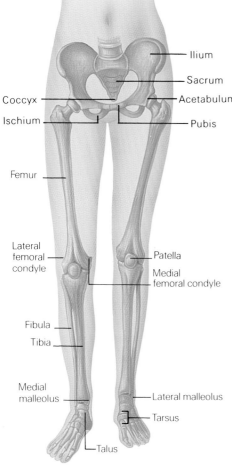

Structure of the wrist and hand

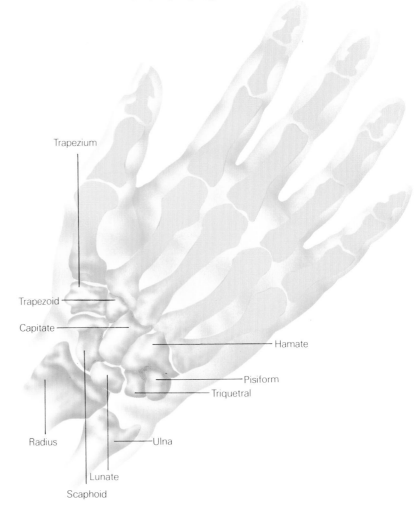

The limbs and pelvis

The arms are joined on to the central axis of the spinal column by the shoulder girdle which is made up of the scapula (shoulder blade) and the clavicle (collar bone). The large bone of the upper arm is called the humerus and is joined at the elbow to the two bones of the forearm: the radius and ulna. The hand is made up of a large number of small bones. This makes it possible for us to grip things and to carry out delicate, complicated movements in which each of the many parts of the hand moves in a different, but highly co-ordinated way.

The legs are attached to the spine by the pelvis, which is constructed from a group of immensely strong bones. The back of the pelvis is made up of the sacrum. Joined to each side of the sacrum is a massive hip bone, or ilium, whose curved top can easily be felt at the body surface. The vertical sacroiliac joints between sacrum and ilium are toughened with fibres and bound with a criss-cross series of ligaments. In addition, the surfaces of

the bones are slightly notched, so that they fit together like a loosely connected jigsaw, thus giving extra stability.

About two-thirds of the way down each ilium is a deep socket, the acetabulum, which is perfectly shaped to accommodate the ball at the end of the femur, or thighbone, the longest bone in the body. Below this socket, the hip bone curves around towards the front of the body. This part of the pelvis is the pubis and it is supplemented by a loop of bone known as the ischium which forms the basis of the buttock. At the front of the body, the two pubic bones come together at the symphysis pubis, explained above. Padding the junction between the two bones is a disc of cartilage, the interpubic disc. More ligaments bind the joint and also run from the top of it to the ilium to help keep the pelvis stable.

There are two bones in the lower leg – the shin bone or tibia and the much thinner fibula. The foot, like the hand, is made up of a complicated arrangement of small bones. This enables us to both stand firmly and comfortably and also to walk and run without falling over.

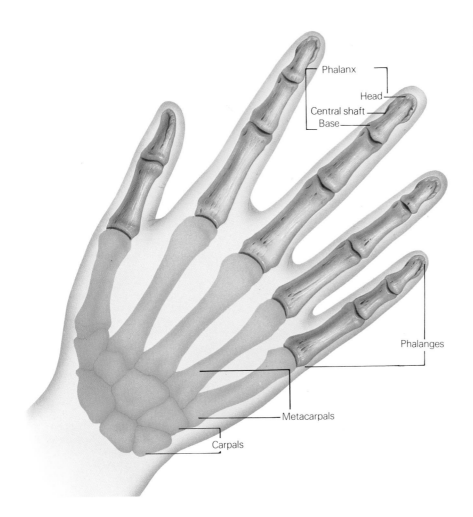

Phalanx
Head
Central shaft
Base

Phalanges

Metacarpals

Carpals

Left: The hand has 14 phalanges (finger bones, or in the case of the foot, toe bones). There are three in each finger and two in the thumb. Movement of these bones is brought about by joints and muscles.
Far left: The wrist is made up of no less than eight separate bones called carpals, arranged in two rows. The carpals sit between the metacarpals of the hand and the radius and ulna of the arm. The only one of the wrist carpals that can be seen below the skin is the pisiform, which is visible as the bumpy wrist bone.

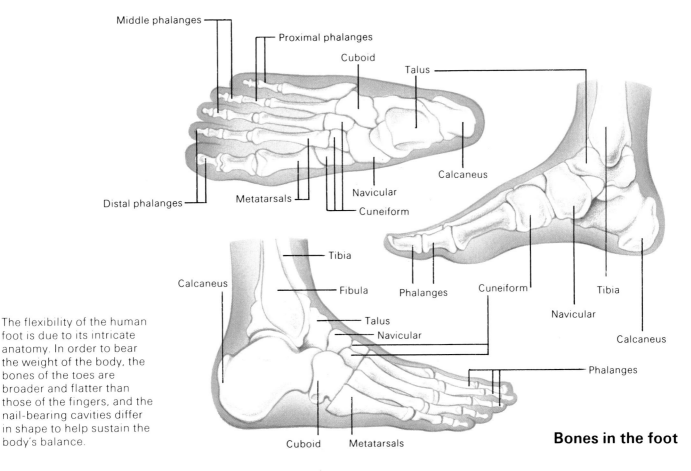

Middle phalanges
Proximal phalanges
Cuboid
Talus

Distal phalanges
Metatarsals
Navicular
Cuneiform

Calcaneus

Talus

Phalanges
Cuneiform
Tibia
Navicular

Calcaneus

Calcaneus
Tibia
Fibula
Talus
Navicular

The flexibility of the human foot is due to its intricate anatomy. In order to bear the weight of the body, the bones of the toes are broader and flatter than those of the fingers, and the nail-bearing cavities differ in shape to help sustain the body's balance.

Cuboid
Metatarsals

Phalanges

Bones in the foot

Joints and Ligaments

The bones of the skeleton are linked together by joints. While bones must be joined securely, at the same time some of them must be able to move very extensively in relation to one another. It is these joints that give us our full range of movements and make the skeleton a highly articulated piece of machinery.

Joints are divided into two main types – mobile, or synovial, and fixed, or fibrous. Synovial joints are designed to allow a large range of movements and are lined with a slippery coating called synovium. Fibrous joint movement is limited by fibrous tissue. In addition to these two types, some joints in the body are formed between bone and cartilage. Because cartilage is very flexible it allows a good deal of movement without the need for synovium. The joints between the ribs and the breastbones are examples of cartilagenous joints.

Synovial joints

The synovial joints can be sub-divided again depending on the range of movement of which they are capable. Hinge jonts, such as the ones at the elbow and knee, allow bending and straightening movements: gliding joints allow sliding movements in all directions because the opposing bone surfaces are flattened or slightly curved. Examples of gliding joints are found in the spinal bones, the wrist and the tarsal bones of the feet. Pivot joints in

the neck at the base of the skull and at the elbow between the humerus and ulna, are special types of hinge joints which rotate around the pivot. The pivot joint in the neck allows the head to turn and the one in the elbow allows twisting of the lower arm to enable movements such as turning a doorknob or a screwdriver. Joints which can be moved in any direction, such as the hip and shoulder, are called ball and socket joints.

The joints in the fingers are typical examples of hinged synovial joints. The bone ends are covered in a tough elastic material known as articulating cartilage. The entire joint is enclosed in a very strong coating of tough gristle called the joint capsule. This holds the joint in place and so prevents any abnormal movement.

Lining the inside of the joint but not running over the articulating cartilage is the synovium. This is a layer of tissue sometimes only one cell thick which provides fluid which oils the joint and prevents it drying up. It is not absolutely essential for the normal functioning of the joint and in certain conditions where the synovium becomes diseased, such as rheumatoid

The hand contains numerous synovial joints; it is easy to see how, in severe cases of rheumatoid arthritis, deterioration of the affected joints can result in crippling deformities of the fingers and wrist.

arthritis, it may be removed without damaging the joint in the short term. However, a healthy synovial membrane is probably essential to help prevent wear and tear of the joint.

The knee joint

The knee joint is a much more complicated hinged joint. The end of the femur is smoothly rounded off, and rests comfortably into the saucer-shaped top of the tibia. The surfaces of the bones are covered with cartilage.

In order to stabilize the joint further, yet still allow flexibility of movement, two leaves of cartilage lie in the joint space on either side of the knee. These are the bits of cartilage which get torn in sports injuries and may be removed in a cartilage operation on the knee. Without them the knee can still function, but wear and tear seems to be increased so that arthritis may set in later in life.

To lubricate the joint, the surfaces are bathed in synovial fluid. There are also additional bags of fluid, called bursae, which lie in the joint and act as cushions against severe stresses.

Strength and stability are provided by the fibrous bands called ligaments. Without hindering the hinge movement of the knee, these ligaments lie on both sides and in the middle of the joint and hold it firmly in place.

The movements of the knee joint are governed by muscles in the thigh. Those at the front pull the knee

Wrist and hand section showing synovial joints

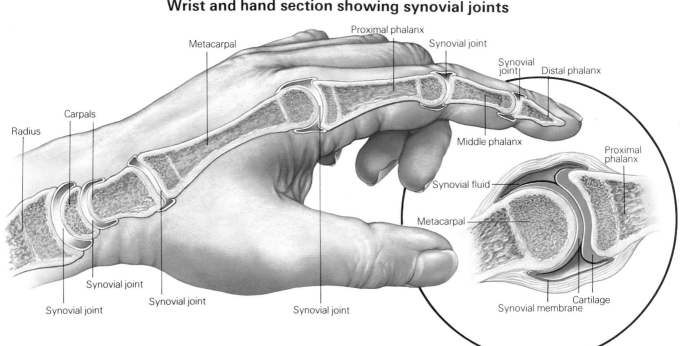

Structure of the knee

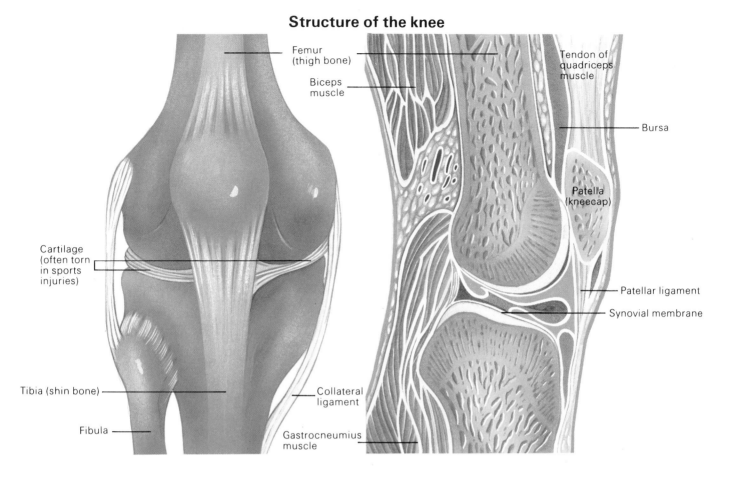

Front view (left) shows the bones, ligaments and cartilage of the knee joint. The section (right) shows the structure in detail, including the bursae (sacs of fluid) and the synovial membrane.

straight and those at the back hinge it backwards. At the top, these muscles are attached to the hip and the top of the femur. Further down the leg, they condense into fibrous tendons which cross over the knee and are then attached to the tibia. (See Chapter 3.)

To prevent the tendon at the front from rubbing the joint as it moves, a bone has been built into the tendon. This bone is the kneecap, or patella, and lies in the tendon itself, unattached to the rest of the knee. It runs up and down the bottom of the femur in a cartilage-lined groove and is lubricated by synovial fluid. There are also two further bursae which act as the shock absorbers for the kneecap.

The knee is important principally for locomotion. At every step it bends to allow the leg to be brought forwards without striking the ground – otherwise the leg would have to be swung outwards by tilting the pelvis, as in the typical stiff leg walk. Once forwards, the knee is straightened and the foot brought back to the ground by movement at the hip.

Fibrous joints
The fibrous joints include those of the back, the sacrum, the skull and some of the joints in the ankle and the pelvis. These joints have no synovium; the bones are joned by tough, fibrous tissue, permitting little or no move-

ment in this type of joint. The joints of the spine are a special exception, as they are flexible enough to allow some movement but at the same time maintain their role of supporting the spinal column.

Ligaments
The bones at a joint are moved by muscles. These are joined to the bones by tendons, which cannot stretch. Ligaments, which can stretch very slightly, join the two bones that form the joint and keep them in place by restricting the amount of movement they can make. Without ligaments the bones would become dislocated very easily.

Ligaments are also found in the abdomen where they hold in place organs such as the liver and uterus, while at the same time allowing a degree of movement which is necessary for different postures and for the changes that accompany eating, digestion and pregnancy. There are also ligaments made up of very fine strands of fibre in the breasts which support

the weight of the breasts and prevent them sagging.

We are not usually aware of the existence of ligaments until we injure one. A sprained or strained ligament makes its presence felt in no uncertain way and can be just as painful as a broken bone.

Structure
Ligaments are a form of connective tissue. The connective tissue in ligaments is made up mainly of the tough white protein collagen, with some of the yellowish and more elastic protein, elastin. In most ligaments this tissue is arranged in bundles of fibres.

These bundles of fibres run in definite directions depending on the type of movement they resist. In ligaments arranged in a cylindrical shape as a long cord the fibres run longitudinally down the length of the cord and resist stretching along the length. Others which are meant to prevent joints moving sideways are arranged as a flat band of criss-cross fibres preventing movement through the band.

Between the fibres there are specialized cells called fibroblasts which are responsible for the creation of new collagen fibres and the repair of damaged ones. Between the fibre bundles there is a spongy tissue carrying blood and lymph vessels and providing space for nerves to pass through.

Ligaments are attached to the bones they unite by fibres which penetrate the outer covering of the bone (the periosteum). The periosteum is supplied with nerves and blood vessels so that it can nourish the bone as well as providing attachment for the ligaments and muscles. The ligament and periosteum grow together so perfectly that the periosteum is often affected if a ligament is injured.

Specialized ligaments exist for each of the various different types of joints in the body. In major joints such as the knees, hip, elbows, fingers and spinal joints, parts of the joint capsule are especially thickened for strength and are known as intrinsic (capsular) ligaments. In addition, there are other ligaments either inside or outside the joint capsule which play individual roles in restricting particular types of movement. These are known as extrinsic (accessory) ligaments.

Purpose

The variety of movements the body can make depends on two things – the shape and design of the bone surfaces at the joint (the articulating bone surfaces) and the ligaments.

In some joints the bones are the most important factor. In the elbow joint the ulna forms the lower half of the joint and is a hook-like shape which allows only simple backwards and forwards movement (like a hinge).

Here the ligaments serve only to prevent side to side rocking and a specialized ligament (the annular ligament) fits like a collar around the head of the radius (the outer bone in the forearm) to attach it to the ulna while still allowing rotation.

In the knee joint, however, the shapes of the bones offer no resistance to movements of joints. So, although the knee is also a hinge joint, it is controlled by specialized (cruciate) ligaments which prevent the knee from bending backwards and help to lock the joint while a person is standing still.

The muscles at the joints work in groups, some contracting while others relax, to enable the bones to move. The ligaments work in concert with these muscles, preventing them making excessive movement.

Ligaments have no ability to contract, and they function as static and passive structures in the body. They can be stretched slightly by movement in the joint and as this happens they gradually become tighter and tighter until no more movement is possible.

There are also ligaments which pass between two points on the same bone and are unaffected by any movement. They protect or hold in position important structures such as blood vessels or nerves.

Each movement that a trained athlete makes depends on the interplay of joints, muscles, tendons and ligaments. Shown below are the most important ligaments needed for actions involving the shoulder, and below right, those needed for actions involving the elbow, when Olympic medal winning athlete Daley Thompson goes into action.

Humerus
Annular ligament
Ulnar collateral ligament

Coracoacromial ligament
Muscle
Humerus
Clavicle
Scapula
Coracoclavicular ligament
Coracohumeral ligament

Structure of the skin

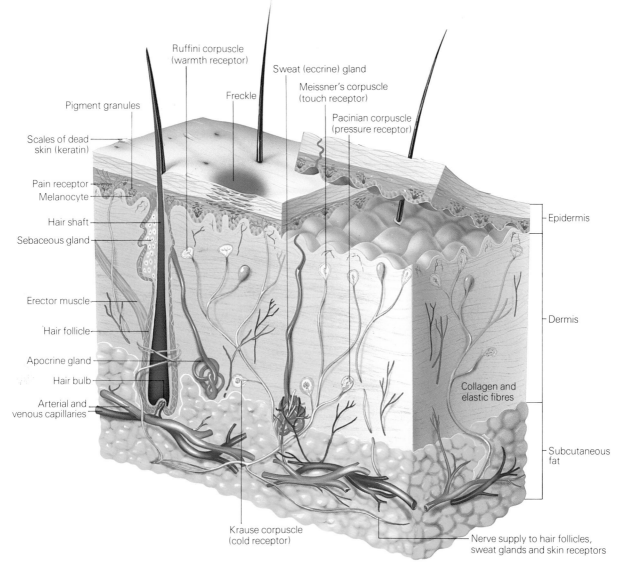

Ruffini corpuscle (warmth receptor)

Sweat (eccrine) gland

Freckle

Meissner's corpuscle (touch receptor)

Pigment granules

Pacinian corpuscle (pressure receptor)

Scales of dead skin (keratin)

Epidermis

Pain receptor
Melanocyte

Hair shaft

Sebaceous gland

Erector muscle

Dermis

Hair follicle

Apocrine gland

Hair bulb

Collagen and elastic fibres

Arterial and venous capillaries

Subcutaneous fat

Krause corpuscle (cold receptor)

Nerve supply to hair follicles, sweat glands and skin receptors

Skin

The skin, or integument, is much more than a simple wrapping around our bodies. It is an active and versatile organ which is waterproof so that we do not dry up in the heat or melt in the rain, and it protects us from the damaging radiation of sunlight. It is tough enough to act as a shield against injury, yet supple enough to permit movement. It conserves heat or cools the body as required, thus keeping our internal temperature constant.

Structure of the skin
The skin is made of two main parts. The outermost part – the epidermis – consists of several layers of cells, the lowest of which are called the mother cells. Here the cells are constantly dividing and moving up to the surface, where they flatten, die and are transformed into a material called keratin

which is finally shed as tiny, barely visible scales. It takes three to four weeks for a cell in the lowest layer to reach the skin surface.

This outer protective layer is firmly attached to an underlying layer called the dermis. Tiny, finger-like bulges from the dermis fit into sockets in the epidermis, and this waviness at the junction of the two layers of skin gives rise to ridges, which are most obvious at the fingertips and give us our fingerprints. The dermis is made up of bundles of collagen and elastin fibres. Embedded in the dermis are sweat, sebaceous and apocrine glands, hair follicles, blood vessels and nerves. The nerves penetrate the epidermis but the blood vessels are confined to the dermis. The hairs and ducts from the glands pass through the epidermis to the surface.

The skin is made up of two different layers of tissue: the dermis and epidermis. Both layers contain nerve endings which transmit sensations of pain, pressure, heat and cold. The sweat glands are vital in regulating the body's temperature, while the sebaceous glands lubricate the skin and hair. The apocrine glands develop at puberty and are a sexual characteristic. The pigment-producing cells, called melanocytes, can cause freckles.

Each sweat gland is formed of a coiled tube of epidermal cells which leads into the sweat duct to open out on the skin surface. The sweat glands are controlled by the nervous system and are stimulated to secrete either by emotion or by the body's need to lose heat. (See page 129.)

Structure of the scalp

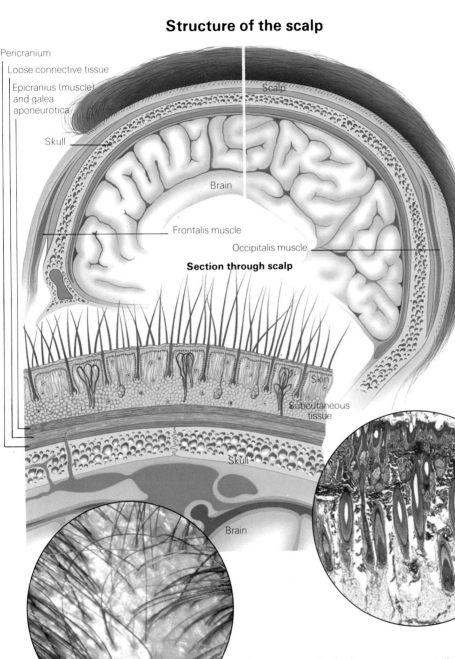

Pericranium

Loose connective tissue

Epicranius (muscle) and galea aponeurotica

Skull

Scalp

Brain

Frontalis muscle

Occipitalis muscle

Section through scalp

Skin

Subcutaneous tissue

Skull

Brain

A detailed view of the scalp shows the several layers that make up this unusual part of the skin. It is the loose connective tissue that enables the scalp muscles to move or 'wiggle' the scalp. Hair follicles on the outside (inset left) and the inside (inset right) are responsible for production and growth of hair.

Bottom: The nail is produced by living cells in the skin in the area around the nail root, but the body of the nail itself is a dead structure. However, the nail is responsive to touch as the skin beneath it contains many nerve endings.

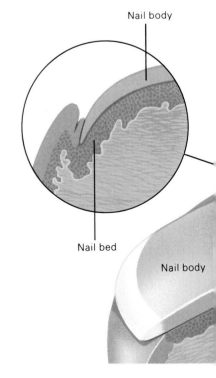

Nail body

Nail bed

Nail body

The sebaceous glands open into the hair follicles and are made up of specialized epidermal cells which produce grease, or sebum. They are most numerous on the head, face, chest and back. Their function is to lubricate the hair shaft and surrounding skin and they are controlled by sex hormones.

The apocrine glands develop at puberty and are found in the armpits, breasts and near the genitals. They are odour-producing and are a sexual characteristic. When they begin to function they secrete a thick milky substance.

There is a fine network of nerve endings in both layers of skin, and they are particularly numerous at the fingertips. They transmit pleasurable sensations of warmth and touch, as well as cold, pressure, itching and pain which may evoke protective reflexes.

Hair and nails

Hair and nails are both specialized forms of keratin. Although nails are produced by living skin cells the nail itself is dead and will not hurt or bleed if it is damaged. The visible part of the nail is called the nail body and its shape is partly determined by genetic factors. The bottom part of the nail, which is implanted in a groove in the skin, is called the root. Overlapping this root are the cuticles (eponychia). These outer layers of skin cover the white crescent, or lunula, found towards the base of the nail. The lunula, which is usually most clearly visible on the thumb, is slightly thicker than the rest of the nail and looks white because it obscures the blood beneath.

The lowest layer of cells in the skin composing the nail folds is known as the general matrix. The cells of the matrix divide and the upper ones become thickened and toughened with keratin. When the cells die they become part of the nail itself. If the matrix is seriously damaged the whole nail is lost.

Hair is formed by cells in the hair follicles and there are two types: fine, downy hair which is found over most of the body except the palms of the hands and soles of the feet, and thick, pigmented hair which is present on the scalp, eyebrows, beard and genital areas.

The visible part of a hair is called the shaft: it is formed from keratin and is composed of dead tissue. The shaft is rooted in a tube-like depression in the skin called the follicle. The hair develops from a root, the dermal papilla, which is at the bottom of the follicle, and is nourished by the bloodstream. If the root is damaged, hair growth stops and it may never regrow.

The follicle also contains a sebaceous gland, and arrector pili muscles. When a person is cold, afraid or alarmed, these muscles contract, making the hair stand on end and bunching the skin around the shaft to form what are known as goose pimples.

Adults have about 120,000 hairs on their head: redheads have fewer, blondes more. Hair type varies according to structure: there are fine, soft baby hairs which grow on portions of the body; long hairs which grow on the scalp; and short, stiff hairs which compose the eyebrows. Blonde hair is the finest; black the coarsest.

The type of hair shaft determines whether hair is straight or curly. A cylindrical hair shaft produces straight hair, and an oval shaft produces curly or wavy hair, and a flattened or kidney-shaped shaft produces woolly hair.

The cells that make keratin for hair are among the most rapidly dividing of the body. Scalp hair grows an average of 1.25 cm (½ in) a month. Hair growth is not continuous, and every five or six months the hair goes into a resting phase, during which no growth takes place. The roots of resting hair become club-shaped – hence their name, club hairs – and lose their normal pigmentation. Up to ten per cent of our scalp hairs are in the resting phase at any one time. It is the club hairs that seem to come out in handfuls when we wash our hair. No damage is done to the follicles, and when the root has finished its rest, normal hair growth begins again.

Skin colour
Skin colour is due to the black pigment melanin. Melanin is also found in the hair and in the iris of the eye. It is formed in melanin-making cells, called melanocytes, situated in the basal layer of the skin.

Irrespective of racial type, the same number of melanocytes are found in the skin of every human being. The amount of melanin produced by these cells, however, varies greatly. In dark-skinned races, the melanocytes are larger and produce more pigment. Melanin's function is to protect the skin from the harmful rays of the sun; the darker the skin the less likely it is to suffer from sunburn.

The complex chemical process of the body which converts the amino acid, tyrosine, into melanin, takes place on the outer part of each melanocyte. Once formed, the pigment moves to the centre of the cell to cloud over, and thereby protect, the highly sensitive nucleus. Exposure to ultraviolet light, either from artificial sources or sunlight, stimulates melanin production by the normal process of tanning. Melanin is formed, the cells expand and the skin darkens in colour. Response varies from individual to individual, but all persons except albinos can eventually become pigmented when exposed to enough sunlight.

Other factors contributing to skin colour are the blood in the blood vessels of the skin and the natural yellowish tinge of the skin tissue. The state of the blood within the blood vessels can greatly change skin colour. Thus we become 'white' with fear when small vessels close off, 'red' with anger due to an increased blood flow, and 'blue' with cold when most of the oxygen in the blood moves out to the tissues as the flow slows down.

Differences in skin colour are due to different levels of melanin. Melanin granules are produced in the epidermis by cells called melanocytes. Sunlight speeds up the action of the melanocytes.

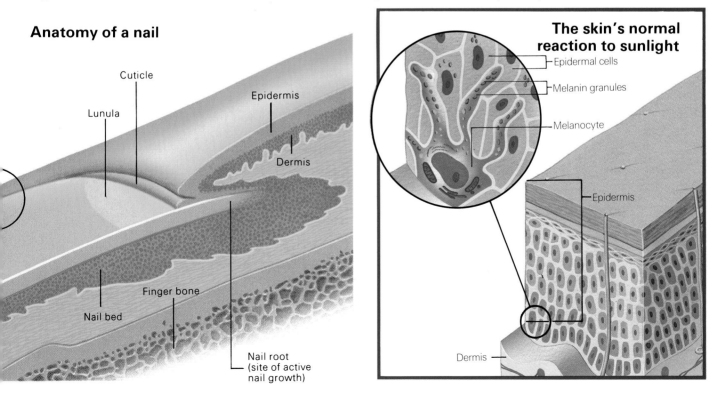

Anatomy of a nail

Cuticle

Lunula

Epidermis

Dermis

Nail bed

Finger bone

Nail root
(site of active
nail growth)

The skin's normal reaction to sunlight

Epidermal cells

Melanin granules

Melanocyte

Epidermis

Dermis

CHAPTER 3
MUSCULAR SYSTEM

Every movement of the body, from the blink of an eyelid to a leap into the air, is made possible by muscles and tendons — the muscle extensions that play a crucial role in transmitting power from a muscle to the bone it moves. Behind their activities lie sophisticated mechanisms that make even an apparently simple action, such as turning the head, a complicated procedure involving the brain, nerves and the sense organs.

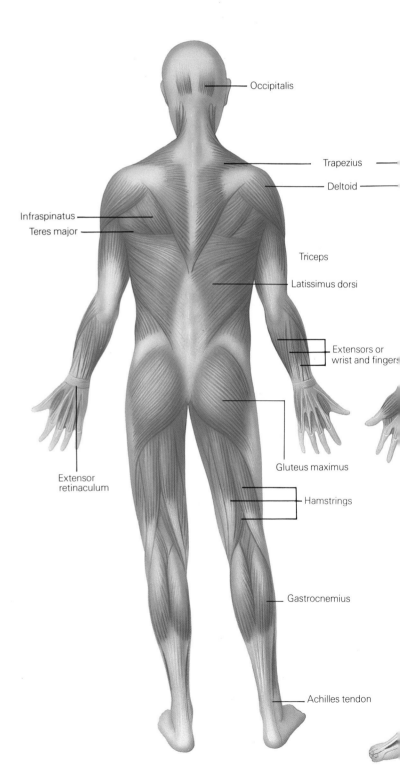

Occipitalis

Trapezius

Deltoid

Infraspinatus

Teres major

Triceps

Latissimus dorsi

Extensors or wrist and fingers

Extensor retinaculum

Gluteus maximus

Hamstrings

Gastrocnemius

Achilles tendon

Right: The body's voluntary muscles work with the bones and tendons to provide the movements which are under conscious control. They are also responsible for those automatic reactions to stimuli, such as the knee jerk reflex, that are known as reflex actions.

Muscles

There are three different kinds of muscle in the body. The first is skeletal, or voluntary muscle. Together with the bones and tendons it is responsible for all forms of conscious movement, such as running up a flight of stairs, and is also involved in the automatic reactions known as reflexes. The second is smooth muscle (so called because of the way it looks under the microscope), which is concerned with the involuntary movement of internal organs such as the guts and bladder. The third is cardiac muscle which makes up the main bulk of the heart.

Voluntary muscles are also called striated (striped) muscles because the arrangement of the fibres which form them gives them a striped appearance under the microscope. They produce their effect by shortening in length, a process called contraction. They have to be able to produce sudden, explosive contractions of the kind that the muscles of the legs make when someone jumps into the air, and to maintain a constant contraction to keep the body in a particular posture.

Voluntary muscles are distributed throughout the body, making up a very large proportion of its weight –

up to 25 per cent, even in a newborn baby. They are rather like springs attached at various points to the skeleton, and control the movement of different bones, from the tiny stapedius muscle which works on the stapes, a minute bone in the inner ear, to the huge gluteus maximus which forms the bulk of the buttock and controls the hip joint.

In smooth, or involuntary muscle, each fibre is a long, spindly cell. Smooth muscle is not under the conscious control of the brain, but is responsible for the muscular contractions required in processes such as digestion where the rhythmic squeezing of the intestines (peristalsis), which moves food, is caused by smooth muscle contraction.

Cardiac muscle has a structure very similar to voluntary muscle, but the

Below: The heart is the only structure in the body that is made up of cardiac muscle. Contractions of the heart are the result of pulses that are controlled by pacemaker tissues within the heart, which enable it to squeeze blood into the blood vessels.

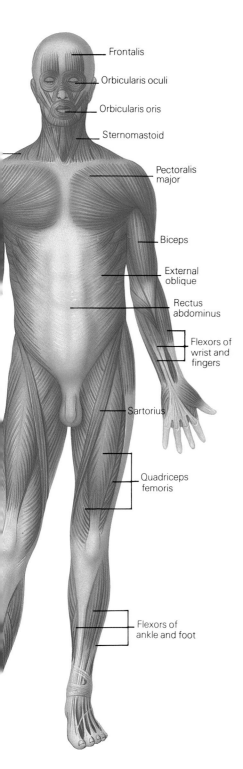

Frontalis
Orbicularis oculi
Orbicularis oris
Sternomastoid
Pectoralis major
Biceps
External oblique
Rectus abdominus
Flexors of wrist and fingers
Sartorius
Quadriceps femoris
Flexors of ankle and foot

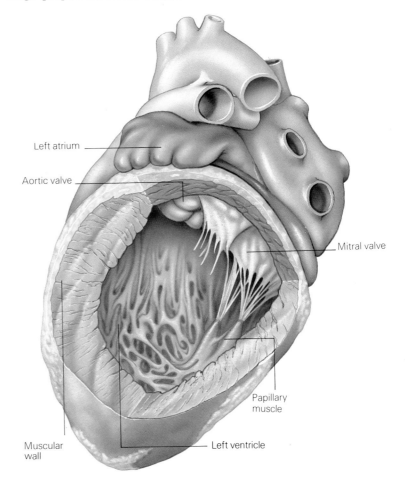

Left atrium
Aortic valve
Mitral valve
Papillary muscle
Muscular wall
Left ventricle

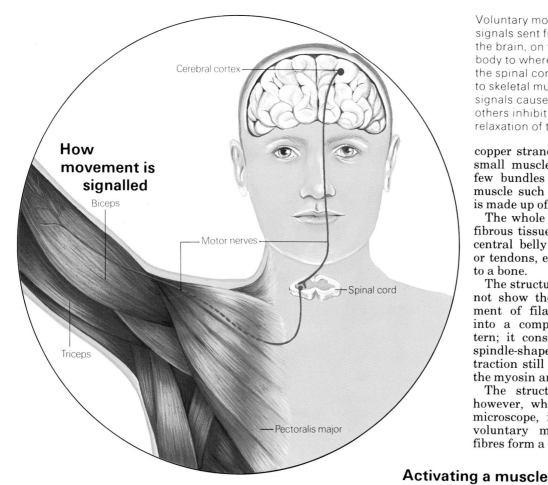

How movement is signalled

Cerebral cortex

Biceps

Motor nerves

Triceps

Spinal cord

Pectoralis major

Voluntary movement is initiated by signals sent from the cerebral cortex of the brain, on the opposite side of the body to where movement occurs, down the spinal cord and along motor nerves to skeletal muscles. Some of these signals cause muscles to contract, others inhibit motor nerves and ensure relaxation of the antagonistic muscles.

copper strands of an electric cable. A small muscle may consist of only a few bundles of fibres, while a huge muscle such as the gluteus maximus is made up of hundreds of bundles.

The whole muscle is contained in a fibrous tissue covering. It has a thick central belly and two tapering ends, or tendons, each of which is attached to a bone.

The structure of smooth muscle does not show the same orderly arrangement of filaments and fibres, built into a complicated geometrical pattern; it consists of loosely arranged spindle-shaped cells, although its contraction still depends on the action of the myosin and actin filaments.

The structure of cardiac muscle, however, when it is seen under the microscope, is the same as that of voluntary muscle, except that the fibres form a criss-cross pattern.

fibres are short and thick and form a dense mesh.

The structure of muscles

Voluntary muscle can be visualized as a series of parallel fibre bundles gathered to make up a complete unit. The smallest of these fibres – and the basic working unit of the muscle – are the actin and myosin filaments, so tiny that they can only be seen with the aid of an electron microscope. They are made of protein and are sometimes known as the contractile proteins. A muscle shortens when the myosin and actin filaments are pulled together along their length.

These filaments are gathered into bundles called myofibrils. Between them are the deposits of muscle fuel in the form of glycogen (the carbohydrate that is commonly called starch), and the normal energy factories of the cell, the mitochondria, where oxygen and food-fuel are burned to make energy.

The myofibrils are gathered into further bundles called muscle fibres. These are really the muscle cells, with cell nuclei along their outside edge. Each one has a nerve fibre coming to it to trigger it into action when necessary. The muscle fibres themselves are grouped together in bundles, in an envelope of connective tissue, rather like the insulation surrounding the

Activating a muscle

At the motor end plate, the electrical impulse bursts a number of vesicles containing acetylcholine. This activates the muscle.

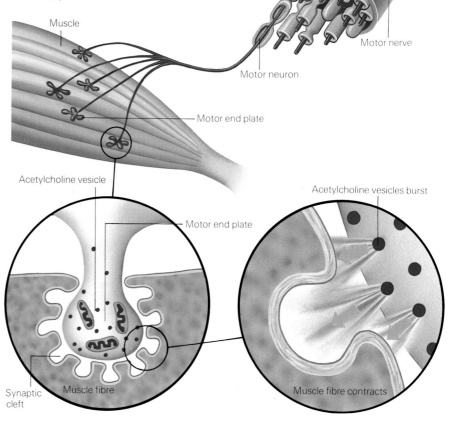

Muscle

Motor nerve

Motor neuron

Motor end plate

Acetylcholine vesicle

Motor end plate

Acetylcholine vesicles burst

Synaptic cleft

Muscle fibre

Muscle fibre contracts

The structure of voluntary muscle

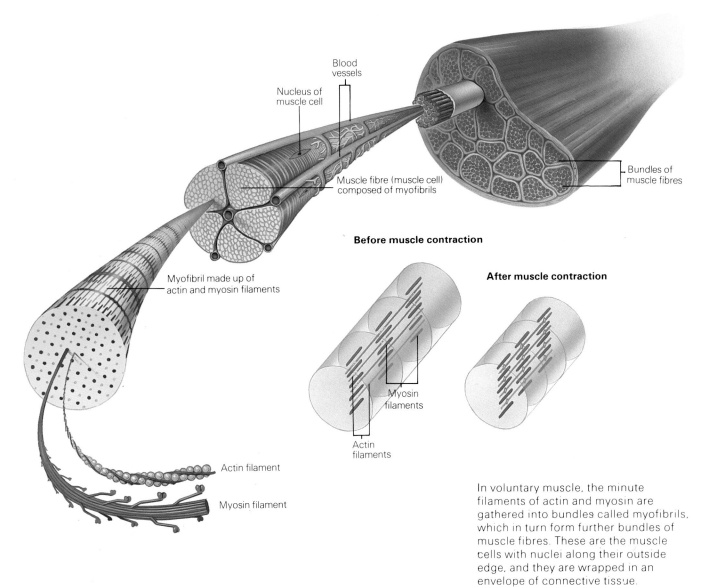

Blood vessels

Nucleus of muscle cell

Bundles of muscle fibres

Muscle fibre (muscle cell) composed of myofibrils

Myofibril made up of actin and myosin filaments

Actin filament

Myosin filament

Before muscle contraction

After muscle contraction

Myosin filaments

Actin filaments

In voluntary muscle, the minute filaments of actin and myosin are gathered into bundles called myofibrils, which in turn form further bundles of muscle fibres. These are the muscle cells with nuclei along their outside edge, and they are wrapped in an envelope of connective tissue.

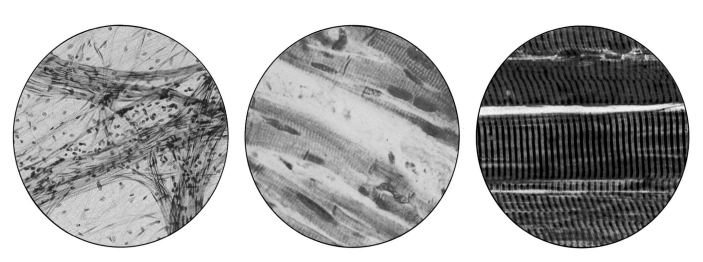

Involuntary, or smooth-muscle is composed of long, spindly cells.

Cardiac muscle is made up of fibres in an orderly criss-cross pattern.

The actin and myosin fibres in voluntary muscle meet like two sets of comb teeth.

How muscles work

Skeletal, or voluntary, muscles are activated by motor nerves in the spinal cord – the bundle of nerve fibres that runs down from the brain through a channel in the spinal column. These motor nerves split into several strands, where they enter, or innervate, a voluntary muscle. Each strand then makes contact with a different muscle cell. An electrical impulse runs down the nerve from the brain and on reaching the tip of the nerve allows a tiny amount of the chemical acetyl choline, to be shed from granules where it is stored. The short distance between the nerve endings and the muscle is crossed by the acetyl choline where it alights on special areas of the muscle surfaces known as receptors. Once the receptor is occupied by the acetyl choline the muscle then contracts and remains in this state as long as the chemical is in touch with the receptor. In order to ensure that the muscles can relax, an enzyme that neutralises acetyl choline comes into action.

The simplest reflex movements happen through direct activation of motor nerves by signals arriving at the spinal cord from sensory receptors, the nerves that receive sensations. For example, in the 'knee-jerk' reflex, a tap just below the knee cap is sensed by receptors inside one of the tendons that runs across the knee joint. These receptors send signals to the spinal cord, and in turn activate motor nerves running from the spinal cord to the thigh muscles. As a result, the thigh muscle rapidly contracts, and the lower part of the leg jerks forward.

Conscious movements of the voluntary muscles, in contrast, are set off by signals sent down the spinal cord from the brain. Some of these signals act to stimulate particular motor nerves, and others act to dowse them so a pattern is worked out which will cause some muscles to contract, and others to relax.

The activities of the myosin and actin filaments during muscular contraction is a complicated process, in which a series of chemical bonds between them is continually formed and broken. This requires energy, provided by the burning of oxygen and food-fuel in the mitochondria, and stored and transferred as a compound called ATP (adenosine triphosphate), which is very rich in high energy phosphate. The process of muscular contraction is started by a flow of calcium (one of the common minerals of the body) into the muscle cells through a whole series of little tubes running between the myofibrils, called the microtubules.

At any given time, several cells in a muscle will be contracting, giving the muscle a degree of tension, or tone. When enough muscle fibres contract, the whole muscle shortens, reducing the distance between its attachment points, so that two or more bones move in relation to others.

Individual muscles can act only to shorten, and not to lengthen, the distance between two attachment points – they can pull but not push. For movement in the opposite direction, another muscle must be activated. For example, the biceps in the upper arm can flex the elbow, but extension of the arm is brought about by another muscle, the triceps, on the underside of the upper arm. Muscles such as

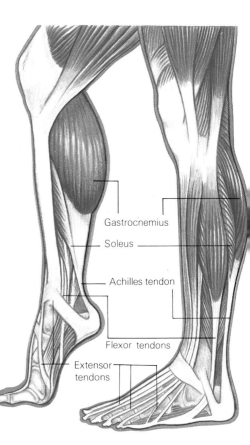

Above: Muscles of the lower leg and foot. When walking, the body is thrown forward by the powerful muscles in the lower leg – the gastrocenmius and soleus. These muscles pull on the ankle joint, which is used as a lever. The extensor muscles in the foot bend the toes for the final thrust forward.

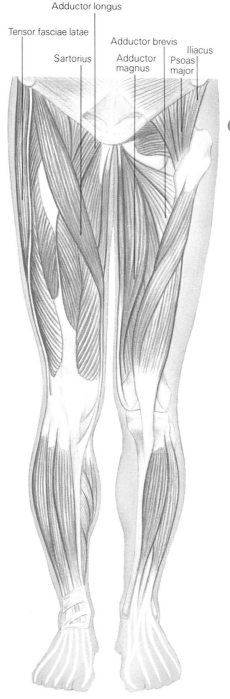

Left: Moving the leg forwards from the hip involves the tensor fascia lata, which joins the pelvis with the femur, and the sartorious, the longest muscle in the body, which runs from the pelvic girdle to the knee. The three adductor muscles — brevis, magnus and longus — pull the leg back into its original position.

biceps and triceps are called antagonistic – they 'work against each other'.

Smooth muscle is also supplied with motor nerves. However, instead of one motor nerve stimulating one muscle cell, stimulation spreads in a wave over several of the cells. This wavelike action helps, for example, in moving food through the intestines.

Contraction of cardiac muscle is not brought about by motor nerves but by pulses from a special pulsemaker tissue within the heart. These pulses pass over the heart about 72 times every minute, causing the heart to contract and to squeeze out blood.

Tendons

Tendons, or sinews, play an important part in a wide variety of movements. Basically, a tendon joins the active section or body of a muscle to the part – usually a bone – which it is intended to move. The force of the contracting muscle fibres is concentrated in and transmitted through the tendon, achieving traction on the part concerned and thus making it move.

Tendons are specialized extensions or prolongations of muscles and they are formed by the connective tissue, which binds the bundles of muscle fibres together, joining and extending beyond the muscle as a very tough, inelastic cord. They have very few nerve endings and, being essentially inactive tissues, little in the way of a blood supply. At one end they are formed from the belly of the muscle and at the other they are very firmly tethered to the target bone, some of their fibres being actually embedded in the bone structure.

Several tendons are located close to the surface of the body and can easily be felt. For instance, the hamstring tendons, controlling knee bending, are at the back of the knee. Tendons are also often found where there are a large number of joints to be moved in a relatively small space, since they take up much less room than 'meaty' muscles. Thus both the backs and the fronts of the hands and feet contain a whole battery of different tendons. The muscles working these tendons are sited well back in the arms and legs.

An unusual tendon is found in connection with the muscle tissue that forms the wall of the heart and brings about its pumping action. Here strips of thickened, fibrous connective tissue form tough strips within the heart muscle which both give it a firmer structure and form firm supporting rings at the points where the great blood vessels join the heart.

Tendon sheaths

In order that they can move smoothly and without friction or the danger of abrasion, tendons at the ankle and wrist are enclosed in sheaths at the points where they cross or are in close contact with other structures. The tendon sheath is a double-walled sleeve designed to isolate, protect and lubricate the tendon so that the possibility of damage from pressure or friction is reduced to a minimum. The space between the two layers of the tendon sheath contains fluid so that these

Tendons and tendon sheaths

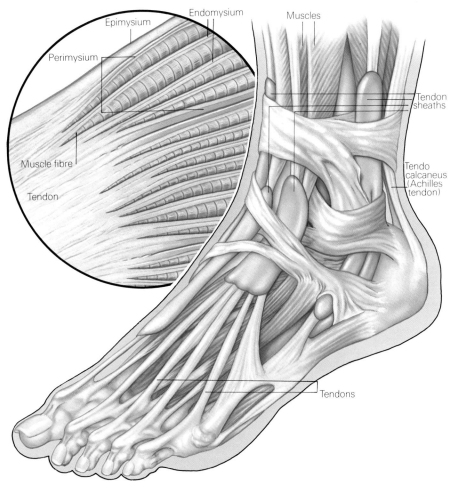

Endomysium
Epimysium
Muscles
Perimysium
Tendon sheaths
Muscle fibre
Tendo calcaneus (Achilles tendon)
Tendon
Tendons

Above: Tendon sheaths protect tendons from rubbing against other structures. A tendon (inset) is formed by membranes that join together at the end of a muscle.

Extensor tendons

Flexor tendons

Extensor tendons

Extensor tendons in the hand enable us to straighten the fingers.

layers slide over each other easily.

But the human machine cannot sustain repeated movements of the same sort without sustaining damage in the form of inflammation. This is because rest periods are necessary for the lubricating fluid to be replenished. If this does not happen, and the system is run without adequate lubrication, the two layers of the tendon sheath begin to rub against each other and chafe. Continued movement will then both be painful and cause a creaking sound called crepitus. This is the basis of the condition called tenosynovitis – inflammation of the tendon sheath. Sudden, unaccustomed use of a particular set of muscles is especially likely to give rise to tenosynovitis.

CHAPTER 4

NERVOUS SYSTEM

The nervous system is essential to sensory perception, the perception of pain and pleasure, control of movements and the regulation of body functions such as breathing. The body's most important and complex network, it is also vital for the development of language, thought and memory. At its centre are the brain and the spinal cord which ultimately control all the nervous tissue in the other parts of the body.

Arrangement of the central and peripheral nervous system

Cerebrum

Cerebellum

Cervical nerves (8 pairs) supplying neck, shoulders and arms

Thoracic nerves (12 pairs) supplying trunk and arms

Lumbar nerves (5 pairs) supplying legs and lower back

Sacral nerves (5 pairs) supplying legs and genitals

Coccygeal nerves (1 pair) supplying vestigial 'tail'

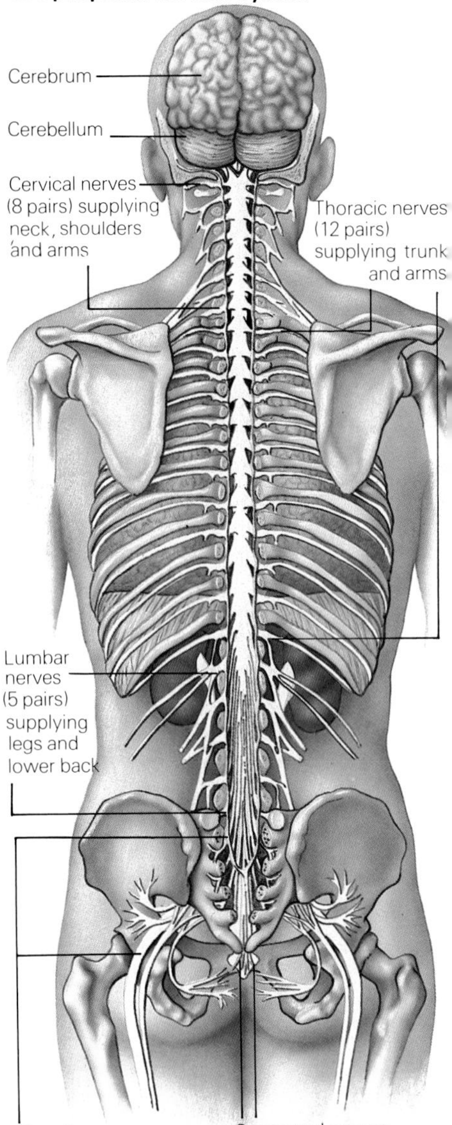

Anatomy of a neurone (nerve cell)

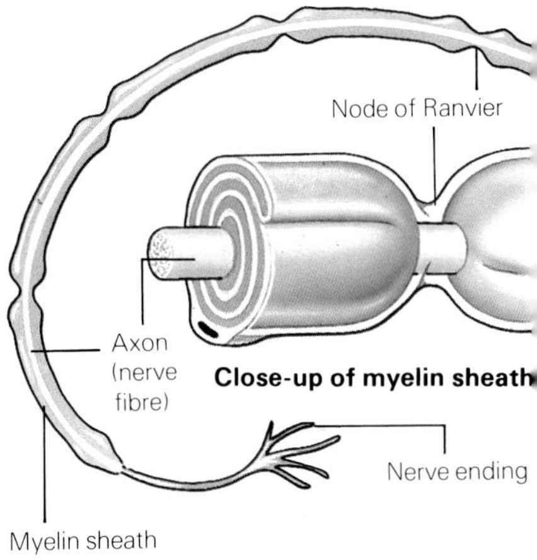

Node of Ranvier

Axon (nerve fibre)

Close-up of myelin sheath

Nerve ending

Myelin sheath

A rear view of the interconnecting brain, spinal cord and peripheral nervous system (above right). Their interplay is extremely complex (far right, above) with nerves of the somatic system linked to those of the autonomic via the ganglia, and both with common pathways out of, and into, the spinal cord. A cut-away of the spine (far right) shows how well the cord is protected. The neurone (right) is shown with its myelin sheath; the nodes of Ranvier aid the transmission of electrical impulses.

Nerve Cells

The working parts of the nervous system are millions of interconnected nerve cells called neurones. Their function is rather similar to the wires in a complex electrical machine: they pick up signals in one part of the nervous system and send them to another, where they may be relayed on to other neurones or bring about some action, (e.g. contraction of muscle fibres).

Neurones are divided into three types, according to their function: sensory neurones, which convey information from the body's sense organs to the central nervous system; integrative neurones (interneurones) which process the information received; and motor neurones, which initiate voluntary and involuntary actions.

Structure of a neurone

Neurones come in various shapes and sizes, but they all have the same basic structure. Like all cells, they have a nucleus, or centre, which is contained in a roughly spherical part of the neurone called the cell body. A number of fine, root-like fibres project from the cell body. These are called dendrites. Also projecting from the cell is a single, long fibre called the axon, the main conducting fibre in a nerve. At its far end, the axon divides into a number of branches, each ending in a number of tiny knobs.

Each knob is in close proximity to, but not actually touching, a dendrite from another neurone. This gap is called a synapse, across which messages are transmitted by chemicals called nerve transmitter substances.

Every neurone is bounded by a thin semi-permeable wall called the neuronal membrane, which plays an important part in the transmission of signals. Signals are always started by the excitation of one or more of the neurone's dendrites, and are first carried towards the cell body. They are then transmitted away from the cell body along the axon. To speed the transmission of signals, many axons have a covering called myelin.

When a signal reaches the knobs at the end of the axon, it may, under certain circumstances, jump across the synapse to the dendrite of an adjacent neurone and so continue its journey.

Neurones are not the only type of cell found in the nervous system. Cells known as neuroglia, or glia, are present in large numbers in the central nervous system, and Schwann cells are found in the peripheral nervous system. Both types bind, protect and nourish and also provide support for the neurones.

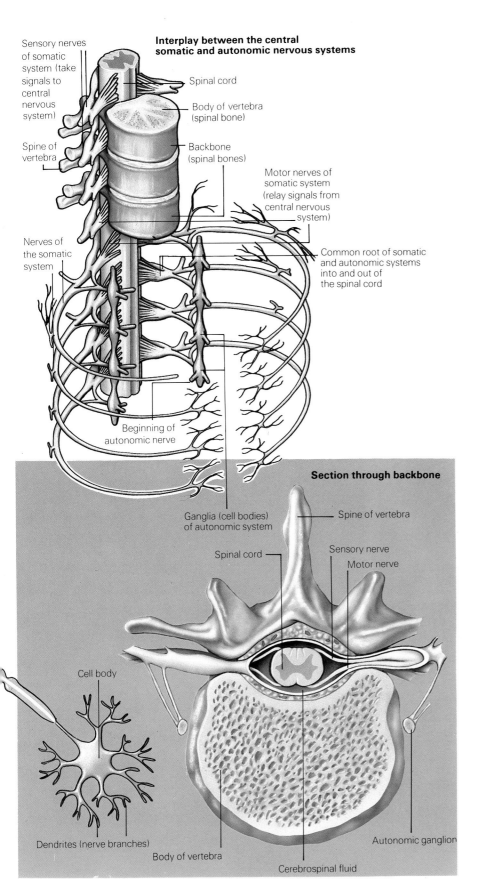

Sensory nerves of somatic system (take signals to central nervous system)

Spine of vertebra

Nerves of the somatic system

Interplay between the central somatic and autonomic nervous systems

Spinal cord

Body of vertebra (spinal bone)

Backbone (spinal bones)

Motor nerves of somatic system (relay signals from central nervous system)

Common root of somatic and autonomic systems into and out of the spinal cord

Beginning of autonomic nerve

Ganglia (cell bodies) of autonomic system

Section through backbone

Spine of vertebra

Spinal cord

Sensory nerve

Motor nerve

Cell body

Dendrites (nerve branches)

Body of vertebra

Cerebrospinal fluid

Autonomic ganglion

The Peripheral Nervous System

The main components of the peripheral nervous system are nerves, which connect the central nervous system to all other parts of the body, and ganglia, groups of nerve cells which are sited at various points in the nervous system.

A nerve is a bundle of motor and sensory fibres, together with connective tissue and blood vessels. The major nerves, of which there are 43, actually arise in the central nervous system: 12 pairs emerge from the underside of the brain (cranial nerves) and 31 pairs from the spinal cord (spinal nerves).

The cranial nerves mainly supply sense organs and muscles in the head, although a very important cranial nerve, the vagus, supplies the digestive organs, heart and air passages in the lungs. Some cranial nerves, such as the optic nerve to the eye, contain only sensory fibres.

The spinal nerves emerge at intervals from the spinal cord and always contain both motor and sensory fibres. They supply all areas of the body below the neck. Each spinal nerve is attached to the spinal cord by means of two roots, one of which carries motor fibres, and the other sensory fibres. It is just beyond the roots that the sensory and motor fibres come together to form the nerve, although each acts independently of the other, like two wires in an electrical lead. (While cranial nerves are also attached to the underside of the brain by roots, the sensory and motor fibres form separate nerves.)

At a short distance from the spinal cord each spinal nerve splits into branches which in turn split into numerous smaller ones, forming a network that radiates all over the body.

Both sensory and motor fibres are just part of the sensory and motor neurones. The motor and sensory fibres of the peripheral nervous system are merely the longest fibres of their respective neurones. For example, a motor fibre from a neurone in the spinal cord may extend without interruption to a muscle in the foot.

Somatic and autonomic

The peripheral nervous system has two main divisions: the somatic nervous system which is under our conscious control, and the autonomic system, which is under unconscious control.

The somatic system has a dual role. First, it collects information about the outside world from sensory organs, such as the eyes, which contain special receptor cells. Signals from these receptors are then carried towards the central nervous system, in the sensory nerve fibres. Second, it transmits signals through motor fibres from the central nervous system to the skeletal muscles, thus initiating movement.

The autonomic system is mainly concerned with keeping up the automatic functions, without deliberate mental or other effort on our part, of organs such as the heart, lungs, stomach, intestine, bladder, sex organs and blood vessels. It consists entirely of motor nerves arranged in relays from the spinal cord to the various muscles.

The autonomic nervous system is divided into two parts, known as the sympathetic and parasympathetic. Each uses a different chemical transmitter where the nerve fibre reaches its target organ, each is built differently, and each has a different effect on the organ it serves. For example, parasympathetic nerves serving the bronchial airways leading to and from the lungs, make them constrict, or grow narrow. The sympathetic nerves leading to the same area cause widening, that is, dilating of the bronchial passages.

The whole of the autonomic system is controlled by an area of the brain called the hypothalamus. This receives information about any variations in, for instance, the body's chemical make-up and adjusts the autonomic system to bring the body back to the right balance. If, for example, oxygen levels fall due to exercise, the hypothalamus instructs the autonomic nervous system to increase the heart rate in order to supply more oxygenated blood.

Below: Diagram illustrating how the peripheral nervous system controls the heartbeat. Sensory nerves send information to the cardioregulatory centre in the spinal cord. The heartbeat is then adjusted by the sympathetic or the parasympathetic system. A major parasympathetic nerve is the vagus, which inhibits the rate of the heartbeat.

Controlling the heartbeat

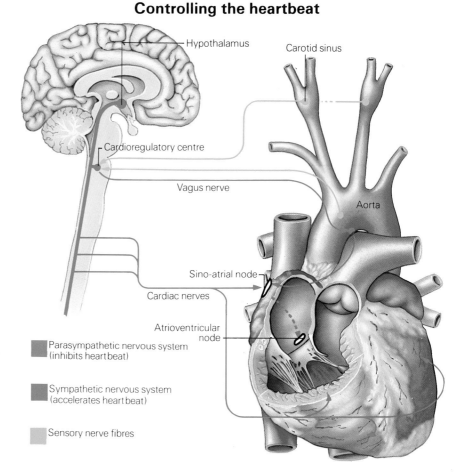

Hypothalamus

Carotid sinus

Cardioregulatory centre

Vagus nerve

Aorta

Sino-atrial node

Cardiac nerves

Atrioventricular node

■ Parasympathetic nervous system (inhibits heartbeat)

■ Sympathetic nervous system (accelerates heartbeat)

■ Sensory nerve fibres

The peripheral nervous system

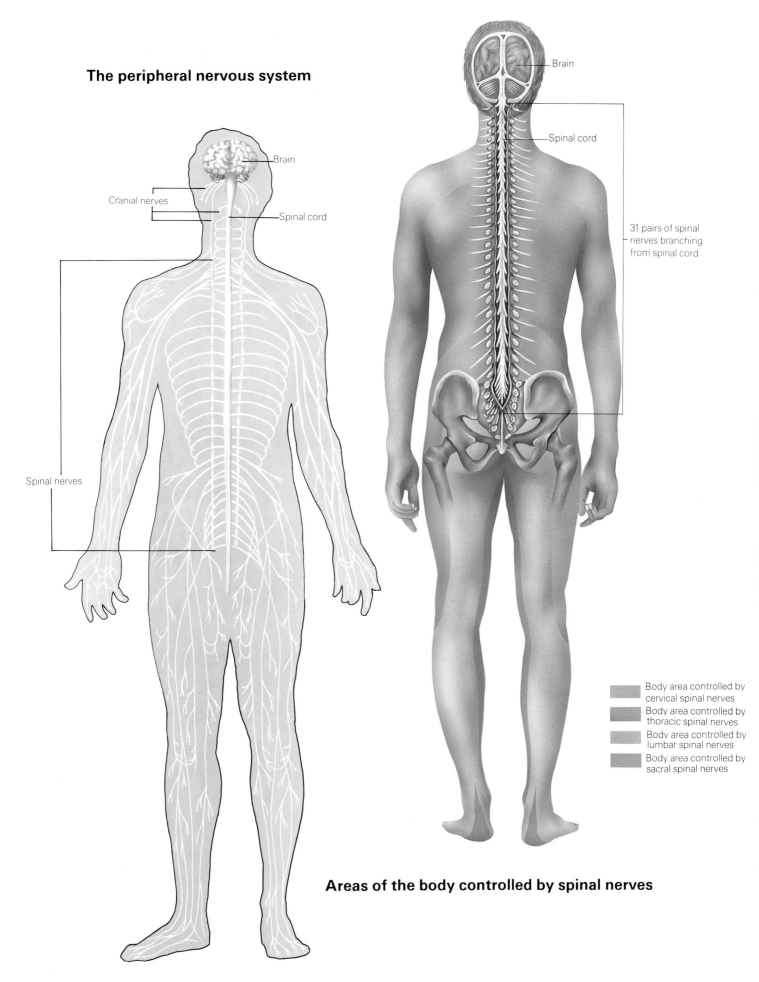

Brain

Cranial nerves

Spinal cord

Spinal nerves

Brain

Spinal cord

31 pairs of spinal
nerves branching
from spinal cord

Body area controlled by
cervical spinal nerves

Body area controlled by
thoracic spinal nerves

Body area controlled by
lumbar spinal nerves

Body area controlled by
sacral spinal nerves

Areas of the body controlled by spinal nerves

Central Nervous System

The peripheral nervous system acts only to relay sensory and motor messages between the central nervous system and the body's muscles, glands and sense organs. It plays virtually no part in the analysis of sensory signals, or the initiation of motor signals. Both these activities, and much else besides, occurs in the central nervous system.

The brain and spinal cord form the central processing unit of the nervous system. They receive messages via the sensory fibres from the body's sense organs and receptors, filter and analyse it, then send out signals along the motor fibres which produce an appropriate response in the muscles and glands.

The analytical, or processing aspect, may be relatively simple for certain functions carried out in the spinal cord, but analysis in the brain is usually highly complex, involving the participation of thousands of different neurones. Although many sensory neurones terminate, and many motor neurones originate in the brain, the majority of the brain's neurones are interneurones, whose job is to filter, analyze and store.

The whole central nervous system has to be maintained with a plentiful supply of blood which provides oxygen and nutrients. It is also protected by two kinds of covering. The first is bone: the skull enclosing the brain, and the backbone enclosing the spinal cord. The second consists of three membranes of fibrous tissue called the meninges. These cover the whole of the brain and spinal cord.

Cerebrospinal fluid is a clear, watery fluid that flows round the meninges and spinal cord, and through the brain's ventricles (cavities). The fluid has a cushioning effect and so helps to protect the vital brain tissue from injury.

The fluid is made continuously from the blood by specialised cells of the choroid plexus in the brain ventricles. Unlike the heart ventricles which have names, the brain ventricles have numbers. The numbering goes from the topmost to the bottom, and the first and second ventricles (known as the lateral ventricles) are the largest.

The fluid flows from the lateral ventricles, through a narrow hole into the small third ventricle and then through an even narrower channel, the cerebral aqueduct, into the slightly wider fourth ventricle. From here it escapes through holes in the roof of the ventricle into the fluid-filled spaces (cisterns) which surround the brain stem at the base of the brain. Then the fluid flows up over the top of the brain (the cerebral hemispheres) and is reabsorbed by special outgrowths, called arachnoid villi, on the arachnoid membrane, one of the three meninges.

The spinal cord
The spinal cord is a roughly cylindrical column of nerve tissues, about

Major divisions of the brain

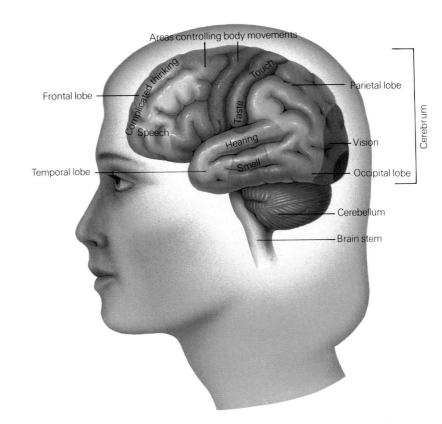

Areas controlling body movements
Complicated thinking
Frontal lobe
Speech
Touch
Taste
Parietal lobe
Hearing
Vision
Cerebrum
Temporal lobe
Smell
Occipital lobe
Cerebellum
Brain stem

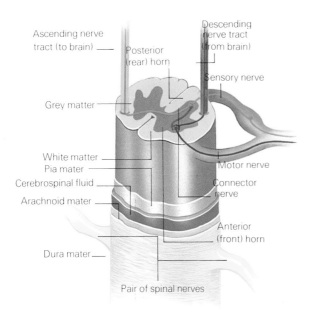

Ascending nerve tract (to brain)
Posterior (rear) horn
Descending nerve tract (from brain)
Sensory nerve
Grey matter
White matter
Pia mater
Cerebrospinal fluid
Arachnoid mater
Motor nerve
Connector nerve
Anterior (front) horn
Dura mater
Pair of spinal nerves

A cross-section of the cord shows sensory and motor pathways carrying messages to and from the brain. Reflex action occurs when messages cross the connector nerve.

Internal structures of the brain

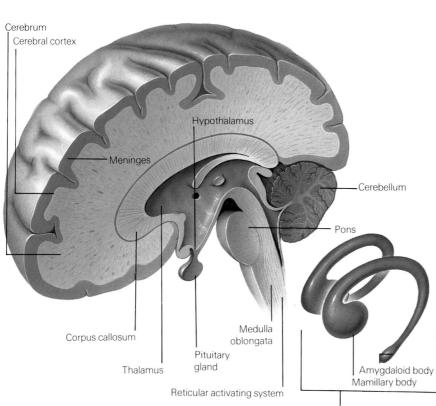

- Cerebrum
- Cerebral cortex
- Hypothalamus
- Meninges
- Cerebellum
- Pons
- Corpus callosum
- Medulla oblongata
- Pituitary gland
- Thalamus
- Amygdaloid body
- Mamillary body
- Reticular activating system
- Limbic system

cell bodies of sensory and motor neurones belonging to the peripheral nervous system. Messages can be transmitted across the synapses, between the peripheral neurones and the spinal neurones.

The second function of the spinal cord is to control simple reflex actions. This is achieved by neurones whose fibres extend short distances up and down the spinal cord, and by interneurones, which relay messages directly between the sensory and motor neurones.

If, for example, you accidentally put your hand on a hot stove, pain receptors in the skin send messages along sensory fibres to the spinal cord. Some of these messages are relayed immediately by neurones to motor neurones that control the movements of the arms and hand muscles, and the hand is quickly, and automatically, withdrawn. Other messages travel up the spinal cord and are relayed by interneurones to the motor neurones that control the neck's movements. In this

Left: This cross-section highlights the major structures of the brain. The limbic system (inset) located within the thalamus is chiefly concerned with memory, learning and emotions.

Position of the basal ganglia

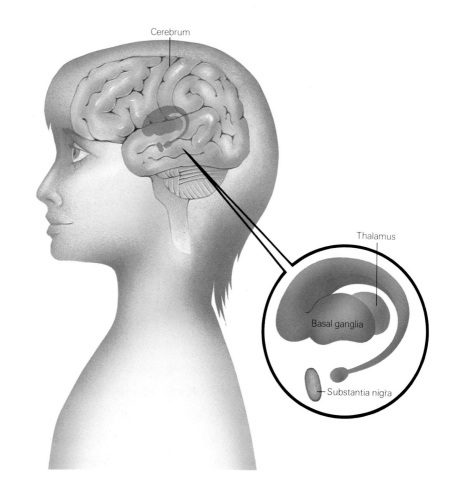

- Cerebrum
- Thalamus
- Basal ganglia
- Substantia nigra

40cm (16in) long, which runs inside the backbone from the brain to the lower back. It is composed of collections of neurones and bundles of nerve fibres. The grey matter – which is what the nerve cell collections are called – is H-shaped in cross-section, with a posterior (rear) and anterior (front) horn (protruberance) in each half. The anterior is composed of motor neurones, while the posterior horn contains cell bodies of connector neurones and sensory neurones.

The grey matter is surrounded by the white matter. This white matter is divided into three columns and contains ascending and descending nerves which connect the brain and the spinal cord in both directions. The descending nerves send motor impulses from the brain to the peripheral nervous system, while the ascending nerves channel sensory impulses to the brain.

Functions of the spinal cord

The spinal cord has two main functions. First, it acts as a two-way conduction system between the brain and the peripheral nervous system. This is achieved by means of sensory and motor neurones whose fibres extend in long bundles from parts of the brain. They run varying distances down the spinal cord, and at their ends furthest from the brain they come into contact with the fibres or

way, the head is automatically turned towards the source of the pain. Further messages are carried all the way up to the brain and cause the conscious sensation of heat and pain.

The brain

Basically the brain can be divided into three different regions: hindbrain, midbrain and forebrain. Each of these regions is in turn divided into separate areas responsible for quite distinct functions, all intricately connected to other parts of the brain.

The largest structure in the hindbrain is the cerebellum. This is the area that is concerned mainly with motor activities. It sends out signals which produce unconscious movements in muscles so that posture and balance are maintained, and it acts in concert with the motor areas of the cerebrum to co-ordinate body movements.

The brain stem, which links the brain with the spinal cord, comprises part of the hindbrain, all of the midbrain and part of the forebrain. It is here in the brain stem that all incoming and outgoing messages come together and cross over, for the left side of the body is governed by the right-hand side of the brain and vice-versa.

The various structures in the brain stem - including those known as the medulla oblongata and pons of the hindbrain and the reticular formation (sometimes termed the reticulating activating system) of the midbrain - are in charge of life itself. They control heart rate, blood pressure, swallowing, coughing, breathing and unconsciousness.

Controlling the level of consciousness is one of the brain's most important functions. It is the reticular formation that sifts through the mass of incoming information and decides which is important enough to alert the brain. Nerve routes from around the body branch out to the reticular formation and feed it a constant stream of electrical signals that arise in the nerve cells. This action, in turn, causes the reticular formation to fire off signals to targets all around the brain, to the appropriate centres where the signals are gathered, collated and acted upon.

If this driving force slows down, or is prevented from occurring, the part of the brain known as the cerebral cortex becomes inactive and the person becomes unconscious.

Cerebrum and hypothalamus

The largest part of the entire brain is the cerebrum, which is located in the forebrain. It is more developed in humans than in any other animal and is essential to thought, memory, consciousness and the higher mental processes. This is where the other parts of the brain send incoming messages for a decision.

The cerebrum is divided right down the middle into two halves known as the cerebral hemispheres. They are joined at the bottom by a thick bundle of nerve fibres called the corpus collosum. Although the two hemispheres are mirror images of each other, they have completely different functions and work together through the corpus callosum.

At the centre of the cerebral hemispheres there is a collection of grey matter (nerve cells) known as the basal ganglia. These cells form a complex control system that co-ordinates the muscle activity which allows the body to perform specific types of movement freely and unconsciously. This sort of muscle activity is involved in the swinging of the arms during walking, in facial expression and in the positioning of limbs before standing or walking.

The hypothalamus lies at the base of the brain, under the two cerebral hemispheres. It is immediately below another important structure in the forebrain, the thalamus, which acts as a telephone exchange between the spinal cord and the cerebral hemispheres.

The hypothalamus is actually a collection of specialized nerve centres, which connect up with other important areas of the brain, as well as with the pituitary gland. It is the region of the brain concerned with the control of such vital functions as eating, sleeping and temperature control. It is also linked closely with the endocrine (hormone) system. (See Chapter 5.)

The sleep/wakefulness centre is located in the brain-stem. Stimulated by information including physical sensations, it passes messages to the cerebral cortex which determine whether we fall asleep or stay awake. It also responds to signals from the cerebral cortex, so that a worrying thought can keep us tossing and turning. Equally a quiet mind, warmth, certain drugs – and even monotony – will induce sleep. The brain waves change as we become drowsy, sleep and awake refreshed.

How the brain controls sleep

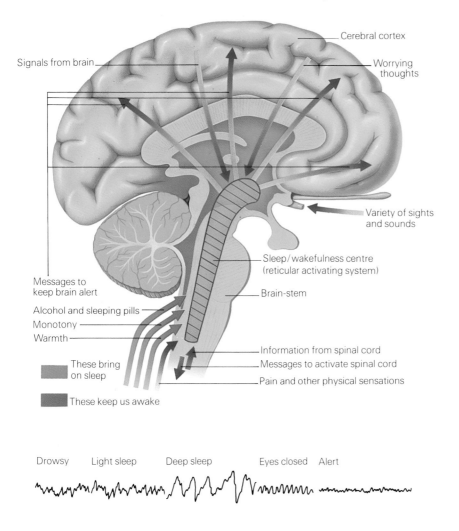

Signals from brain

Cerebral cortex

Worrying thoughts

Variety of sights and sounds

Sleep/wakefulness centre (reticular activating system)

Brain-stem

Messages to keep brain alert

Alcohol and sleeping pills
Monotony
Warmth

These bring on sleep

These keep us awake

Information from spinal cord
Messages to activate spinal cord
Pain and other physical sensations

Drowsy   Light sleep   Deep sleep   Eyes closed   Alert

How shivering occurs

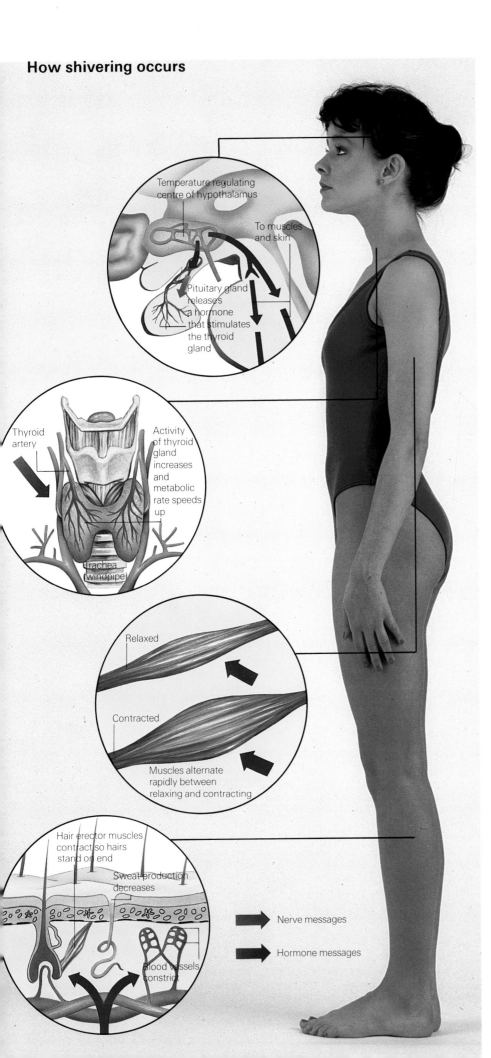

Temperature regulating centre of hypothalamus

To muscles and skin

Pituitary gland releases a hormone that stimulates the thyroid gland

Thyroid artery

Activity of thyroid gland increases and metabolic rate speeds up

Trachea (windpipe)

Relaxed

Contracted

Muscles alternate rapidly between relaxing and contracting

Hair erector muscles contract so hairs stand on end

Sweat production decreases

Nerve messages

Hormone messages

Blood vessels constrict

The hypothalamus has nervous pathways which connect with the limbic system, which is closely connected with the smell centres of the brain. This portion of the brain also has connections with areas involved with other senses, behaviour and the organization of memory.

The cerebral cortex

The cerebral cortex is the 3mm- (⅛in) thick wrinkled layer of grey matter folded over the outside of the cerebrum. This part of the brain has become so highly developed in humans that it has had to fold over and over in order to fit inside the skull. Unfolded, it would cover an area 30 times as large as when folded.

Among all the folds there are certain very deep grooves which divide each of the two hemispheres of the cortex into four areas called lobes. Each of the lobes serves one or more specific functions. The temporal lobes are involved with hearing and also smell, the parietal lobes with touch and taste, the occipital lobes with sight and the frontal lobes with movement, speech and complicated thinking.

Within each of these lobes there are specific portions devoted to receiving the sensory messages from one area of the body. For example, the sense of touch has a tiny area in the parietal lobe devoted to nothing but sensation from the knee, and a large area for the thumb. This is why areas like the thumb are more sensitive than areas like the knee. And the same principle applies to the other sensory parts of the cortex and to the motor parts as well.

It is in the cerebral cortex, therefore, that information received from the five senses – sight, hearing, touch, taste and smell – is analyzed and processed so that other parts of the nervous system can act on the information if necessary. In addition, the premotor and motor areas of the cerebral cortex work with other areas of the central and peripheral nervous systems to bring about co-ordinated movements which are vital to every conscious activity the body performs.

How shivering occurs. Shivering is governed by four mechanisms. The hypothalamus, at the base of the brain, senses that the temperature is too low, and sends messages to the thyroid gland, telling it to speed up the metabolic rate. The body muscles then alternately contract and relax rapidly, thus producing heat. The nerves then send messages to the skin and the skin pores narrow, ensuring that the heat is conserved within the body.

The Eyes

The eye is usually likened to a superbly designed camera, when people want to explain how we can see. However, to understand fully how the outside world can be viewed inside the tiny chamber of the eye, one has to go back to basics.

The best way to think of light is as a transmitting medium. From whatever source, it bounces off objects in all directions, carrying with it the possibility of the objects being seen.

The other important thing to understand about light is that although it usually travels in straight lines, it can be bent if it passes through certain substances, such as the specially shaped glass of a camera lens, or the lens made of tissue in a human eye.

Moreover, the degree of bending can be precisely controlled by the shape in which a lens is made. Light can, in fact, be bent inwards, or concentrated, to form tiny, but perfect images of much larger objects.

The cornea

When a ray of light strikes the eye, the first thing it encounters is a round, transparent window called the cornea, which is the first of the eye's two lenses. The cornea forms the powerful, fixed-focus lens of the eye. The optical power of the cornea accounts for about two thirds of the total eye power. Yet the cornea is only half a millimetre thick at the centre and one millimetre thick where it joins the white of the eye, called the sclera.

The cornea consists of five layers. On the outside is a five-cell layer called the epithelium, which corresponds to body skin. Underneath this is an elastic, fibre-like layer known as Bowman's layer. Next comes the tough stromal layer made up of collagen. This stromal layer is the thickest part. The stroma helps to keep the cornea free from infection, for in this layer there are various infection-fighting antigens: the stroma is also thought to help control inflammation in the cornea.

After the stroma comes a layer called the endothelium which is only one cell thick. This thin layer keeps the cornea transparent and maintains a balance of water flow from the eye to the cornea. Once formed, the cells of this layer cannot regenerate and so injury or disease to the endothelium can cause permanent damage to sight. The final layer, which is called Descemet's membrane, is an elastic one.

A tear film covers the epithelium. Without tears, the cornea would have no protection against bacterial micro-

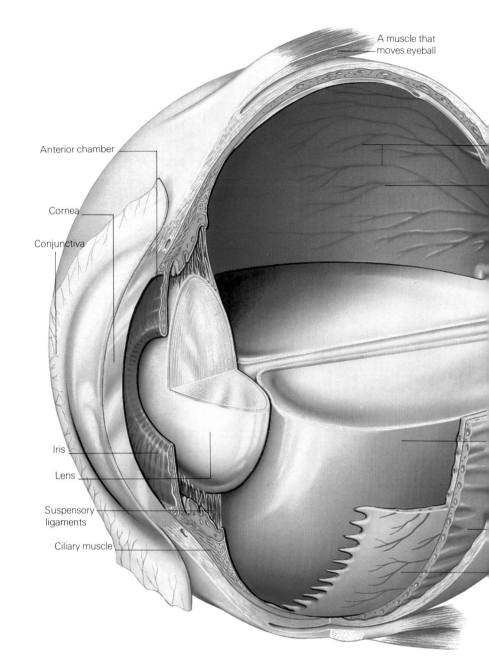

A muscle that moves eyeball

Anterior chamber

Cornea

Conjunctiva

Iris

Lens

Suspensory ligaments

Ciliary muscle

organisms, pollution or dust. The tear film also provides the optical layer and without tears the epithelium would lose its transparency and become opaque.

After passing through the cornea, the ray of light enters the outer of two chambers within the eye, properly called the anterior chamber. This is filled with a watery fluid called the aqueous humour that is constantly drained away and replaced.

The uvea

The uvea is the name given to the area that is comprised of three distinct structures located in the centre of the eyeball: the choroid, the ciliary body and the iris of the eye, which together are sometimes called the uveal tract.

The choroid is a thin sheet of membrane between the outer protective sclera and the retina. This membrane is full of blood vessels which supply the retina and form an intricate lattice throughout most of the eye. In this lattice there are supporting tissues which contain a varying amount of pigment; this prevents light bouncing around the back of the eye giving confusing images.

The ciliary body consists of a ridged-up area of the uveal tract right at the front of the eye. Its role is to alter the shape of the lens through movement of the ciliary muscle – allowing us to

Structure of the eye

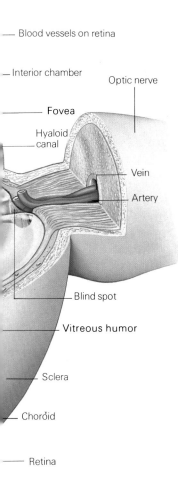

— Blood vessels on retina

— Interior chamber

Optic nerve

— Fovea

Hyaloid canal

Vein

Artery

— Blind spot

— Vitreous humor

— Sclera

— Choroid

— Retina

Right: A cross-section of the eye, in which the sclera has been 'rolled back', shows the blood vessels in the choroid.

If too strong a light falls on it, the pupil grows smaller, without our having to make any conscious effort. In dim light, it grows larger. Excitement, fear and the use of certain drugs also make the pupil widen or contract.

Just behind the iris is the soft, elastic, transparent lens. It is a relatively minor part because most of the work is done by the cornea.

Vitreous humour and retina

Behind the lens is the main, interior chamber of the eye.

This is filled with a substance called the vitreous humour which has a jelly-like texture, and makes the eye feel firm and rubbery. Running through its centre is the hyaloid canal, the remains of a channel which carried an artery during foetal development.

The curved inside of the ball is lined, all round the back chamber, with a light-sensitive 'coat', or layer, which is called the retina. This is actually made up of two different types of light-sensitive cells, called rods and cones because of their shapes.

Rods are sensitive to light of low intensity and do not interpret colour, which is 'picked up' by the cones. These are also responsible for clarity and are most plentiful at the back of

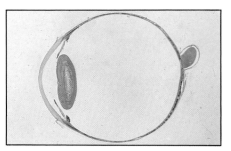

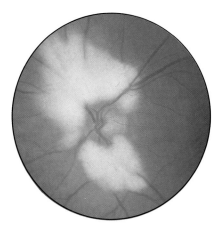

Top: A vertical section through a human eye, showing the optic nerve.
Above: Close-up of the 'blind spot', the retinal area covered by the optic nerve.

Uveal blood supply

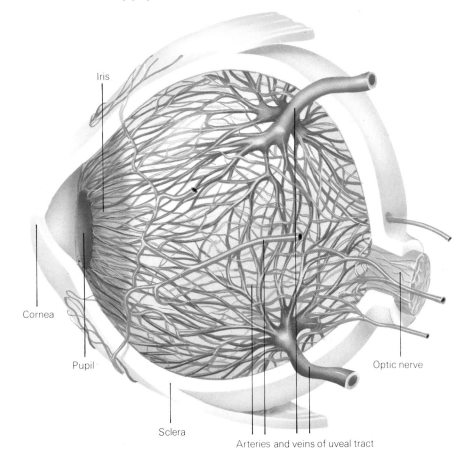

Iris

Cornea

Pupil

Sclera

Arteries and veins of uveal tract

Optic nerve

focus on near objects – and also to make the aqueous humour, the fluid which circulates in the chamber between the lens and the inner surface of the cornea.

Attached to the ciliary body is the third specialised area, the iris, which forms the back of the anterior chamber. This is the part of the eye whose pigment gives the eye its colour. It acts like the aperture stop of a camera, its muscle fibres dilating or contracting the pupil and thus controlling the intensity of light reaching the retina.

Focusing

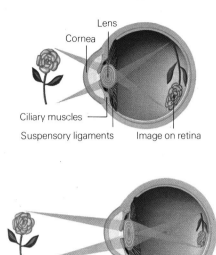

The mechanics of seeing

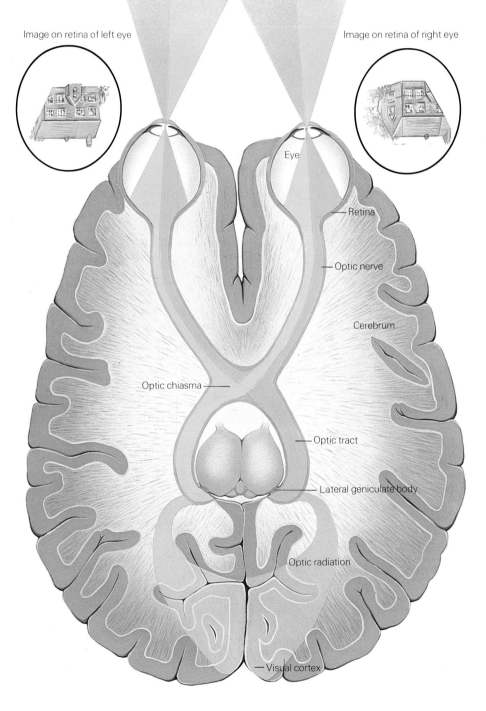

Image on retina of left eye

Image on retina of right eye

Eye

Retina

Optic nerve

Cerebrum

Optic chiasma

Optic tract

Lateral geniculate body

Optic radiation

Visual cortex

Above: Light rays from a near object diverge and the surface of the lens becomes more curved (top) to focus them. From a distant object, light rays are almost parallel and the lens (above) has less focusing to do.

the eye in an area known as the fovea, or macula. Here the lens also happens to focus its sharpest image, and this is where our vision is best.

Surrounding the fovea, or macula, the retina still registers images with clarity, but out towards its edges is what is known as peripheral vision – all that area which we 'half see'.

Together, this central and peripheral vision make up a complete view of the outside world.

The optic nerve

Every light-sensitive cell in the retina is connected by a nerve to the brain, where information about pattern, colours and shapes is computed. All these nerve fibres collect together at the back of the eye to form one main cable known as the optic nerve. This runs back from the eyeball through a bony tunnel in the skull and emerges inside the skull bone just beneath the brain in the region of the pituitary gland; here it is joined by its fellow optic nerve.

Left: The right and left eyes have slightly different fields of vision. Each visual field is split into a right and left side. When light rays reach the retinas they are transposed and inverted. These rays travel down the optic nerves to the optic chiasma, where a crossover takes place. All the information from the left side of each eye travels down the optic tract through the lateral geniculate body and the optic radiation to the right visual cortex and vice versa. Later, the images are combined and interpreted by the brain.

How the eyeball moves

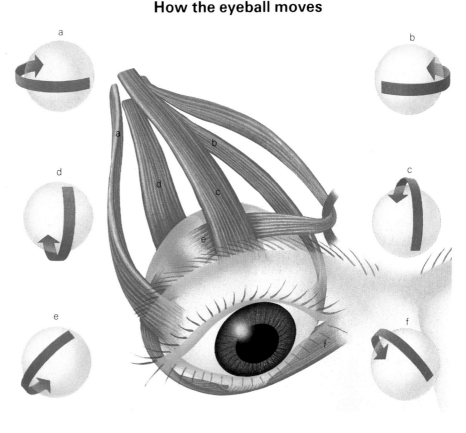

Right: Six main muscles move the eyeball. Muscle (a) swivels it away from the nose; (b) towards the nose; (c) rotates it upward; (d) downwards; (e) moves it down and outwards and (f) moves it upwards and outwards.

The nerves from each side then cross over so that some information from the left eye is passed to the right side of the brain and vice versa. Nerves from the temporal (near the temples) side of each retina do not cross over and so stay on the same side of the brain whereas those fibres from the part of the eye which does most of the seeing run to either side of the brain.

The optic nerve is nothing more than a bundle of nerve fibres carrying minute electrical impulses down tiny cables, each of which is insulated from the next by a layer of myelin. At the centre of the main cable is a larger artery which runs its entire length. This is known as the central retinal artery. This artery emerges at the back of the eye and the vessels from it spread over the surface of the retina. There is a corresponding vein which runs back down the optic nerve alongside the central retinal artery which drains the retina.

Nerves emerging from the retina are sensory; unlike motor nerves which only have one connection on their way to the brain, optic nerves make more than one connection. The first of these lies just behind the point where the sensory information from each eye is swapped. This cross-over point is known as the optic chiasma and lies very close to the pituitary gland. Immediately behind this cross-over is the first connection or cell station known as the lateral geniculate body. Here, information from left and right is swapped again across the midline.

The function of this connection is linked with the reflexes of the pupils.

From the lateral geniculate body the nerves fan out on each side around the temporal part of the brain forming the optic radiation. They turn slightly and collect together to pass through the main exchange, the internal capsule, where all the motor and sensory information supplying the body is concentrated. From there the nerves pass to the back of the brain to the visual cortex.

Below: The most common cause of short sight (1) is an eyeball which is too 'long', so that light rays form an image in front of the retina. It is corrected (2) by a concave lens. In long sight (3), the eyeball is 'short', so the image cannot be formed within the eye. A convex lens (4) focuses the image on the retina. (The brain turns it the right way round.)

Short sight

Long sight

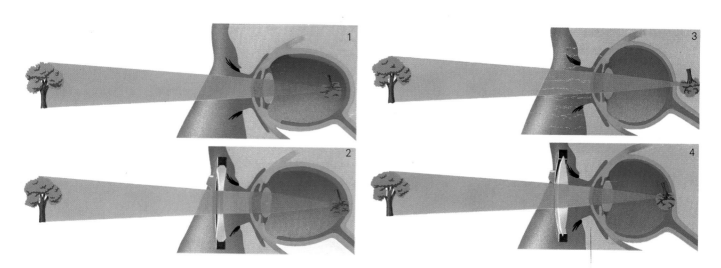

The Ears

The ear not only provides us with our sense of hearing, it also gives us the sense of balance. It is a complex organ that is divided into three parts: the outer ear, which gathers sound like a radar scanner; the middle ear, whose gear-like assembly of bones amplify the sounds they receive; and the inner ear, which converts sound vibrations into electrical impulses and works out the position the head is in.

The resulting messages are transmitted to the brain along a pair of nerves which lie side by side: the vestibular nerve for balance and the cochleal nerve for sound. The outer and middle ears are concerned mainly with hearing, but the inner ear structures which interpret head position and sound are separate, even though they are found together in the same organ.

Hearing

What we hear are sound waves which are produced by the vibrations of air molecules. The size and energy of these waves determines loudness, which is measured in decibels (dB). The number of vibrations or cycles per second make up frequency; the more vibrations, the higher the pitch of the sound. Sound frequency is expressed in terms of cycles per second, or hertz (Hz).

In young people, the range of audible frequencies is approximately 20 to 20,000 Hz per second, though the ear is most sensitive to sounds in the middle range of 500 to 4,000 Hz. As we get older, or if we are exposed to excessively loud noise over a period of time, our hearing becomes less acute in the higher frequencies. In order to measure the extent of hearing loss, normal hearing levels are defined by an international standard. A person's level of hearing is the difference in decibels between the faintest pure note perceived, and the standard note generated by a special machine called an audiometer.

The ear acts as a receiver (outer ear), an amplifier (middle ear) and a transmitter (inner ear).

The receiver is formed by the fleshy part of our ears called the pinna. At the centre of the pinna is a bony canal leading to the ear-drum. A waxy substance is secreted from the walls of the canal in order to prevent the skin from drying up and flaking.

The amplifier is formed by a system of gears consisting of three bones called the ossicles. These are the malleus, which is attached to the ear-drum; the stapes, which is a stirrup-like bone attached to the inner ear; and the incus, a small bone which connects the two. This gearing arrangement amplifies movement of the ear-drum 20 times.

From the middle ear a narrow tube, called the Eustachian tube, opens be-

The outer ear receives sounds, the middle ear amplifies them and the inner ear transmits messages to the brain.

Structure of the ear

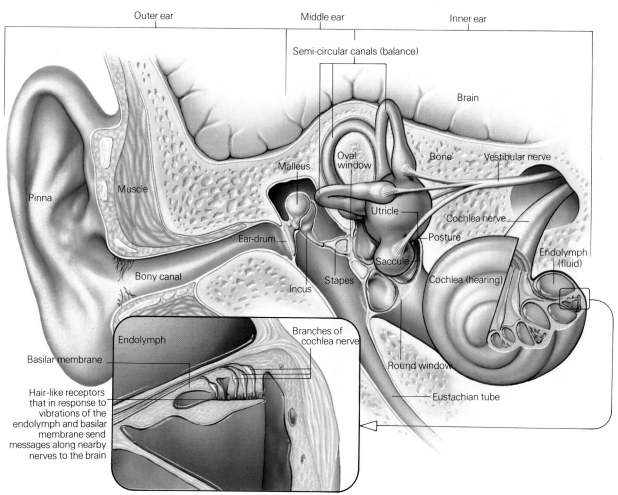

Organ of Corti (contains the receptors for hearing)

Position and structure of the mastoids

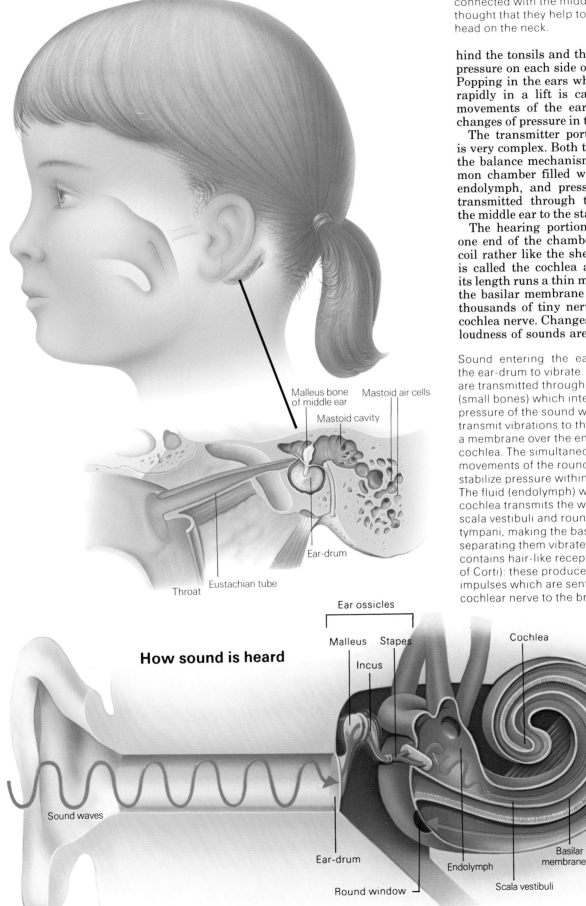

Left: The mastoids are the projections that lie behind the ear. They are connected with the middle ear and it is thought that they help to balance the head on the neck.

hind the tonsils and this equalizes air pressure on each side of the ear drum. Popping in the ears when we descend rapidly in a lift is caused by small movements of the ear-drum through changes of pressure in the middle ear.

The transmitter portion of the ear is very complex. Both the hearing and the balance mechanisms form a common chamber filled with fluid called endolymph, and pressure waves are transmitted through this fluid from the middle ear to the stapes.

The hearing portion is situated at one end of the chamber and forms a coil rather like the shell of a snail. It is called the cochlea and throughout its length runs a thin membrane called the basilar membrane which supplies thousands of tiny nerve fibres to the cochlea nerve. Changes in the pitch or loudness of sounds are sensed by tiny

Sound entering the ear canal causes the ear-drum to vibrate. The vibrations are transmitted through the ossicles (small bones) which intensify the pressure of the sound waves and transmit vibrations to the oval window, a membrane over the entrance to the cochlea. The simultaneous pulsating movements of the round window stabilize pressure within the inner ear. The fluid (endolymph) which fills the cochlea transmits the waves along the scala vestibuli and round into the scala tympani, making the basilar membrane separating them vibrate. This membrane contains hair-like receptor cells (organs of Corti): these produce nervous impulses which are sent along the cochlear nerve to the brain.

Malleus bone of middle ear

Mastoid air cells

Mastoid cavity

Ear-drum

Eustachian tube

Throat

How sound is heard

Ear ossicles

Malleus

Incus

Stapes

Cochlea

Cochlear nerve

Sound waves

Ear-drum

Endolymph

Scala vestibuli

Basilar membrane

Hair-like receptor cells

Scala tympani

Round window

How the body balances

When the body moves, the endolymph fluid in the semicircular canals causes the hairs in the galatinous mass to bend. These are connected to the vestibular nerve, which alerts the brain to re-balance the body.

Starting and stopping
Jutting out just above the utricle of the ear are three fluid-filled semi-circular canals. At the base of each canal is an oval mass of jelly. Encased in this jelly are the tips of sensitive hairs, which become bent by movements of fluid in the canals as the head moves.

The semi-circular canals pick up information about when the head starts and stops moving – particularly important during quick, intricate movements.

As the head begins to move one way, the fluid in the canals tends to stay still, making it push against the sensitive hairs. The hairs then send messages to the brain, which can take action.

But when the head stops moving, particularly when it stops turning round and round, the fluid goes on moving inside the semi-circular canals for up to a minute or more making you feel dizzy.

Control centre
The part of the brain most responsible for directing the action of the muscles in keeping the body balanced is the cerebellum. The eyes, too, have a very special part to play in balance, for they provide vital information about the body's relation to its surroundings. The eyes also have an important link-up with the semi-circular canals. When the head begins to move to the left, for example, the movement of fluid in the semi-circular canals makes the eyes move to the right. But the balance mechanism then makes them move to the left to adjust to the same position as the head.

This eye movement explains in part why people are more likely to be sick if they try to read while travelling during a journey in a moving vehicle, such as a car or bus. The reading tends to counteract these natural eye movements, which helps to trigger off those unpleasant attacks of nausea and vomiting which constitute travel sickness.

Learning to balance
This is a long process that takes up almost the first two years of a baby's life, with another year to master the art of standing on one leg. Before perfect balance can be achieved, both brain and muscles must be mature enough to provide the necessary strength and co-ordination.

hairs on the basilar membrane through pressure waves transmitted in the endolymph passing up and down the length of the cochlea. The cochleal nerve runs to a specialized part of the brain called the auditory or hearing centre.

The way in which waves are turned into electrical energy and interpreted by the brain is not understood. The current theory is that the cells of the cochlea measure pressure waves in the endolymph and turn them into electrical impulses. It is also not clear how the ear distinguishes between loudness and pitch.

Balance
As an organ of balance, the ear is responsible for moment-by-moment monitoring of the position and movements of the head. And if the exact position of the head is correctly monitored, then the body can adjust itself to stay balanced.

Well protected by the bones of the skull, the delicate organs of balance lie in the innermost part of the ear, appropriately called the inner ear. Here there exists a maze of tubes filled with fluid, all at various levels and at differing angles. Of these tubes, the ones directly involved in balance

are called the utricle, the saccule and the semi-circular canals.

The utricle and the saccule are concerned with detecting the position of the head. Each of these two cavities contains a pad of cells overlaid with a jelly-like substance in which are embedded small granules of chalk.

When the body is upright, gravity causes these granules to press against sensitive hairs in the jelly. The hairs then send nerve signals to the brain that say 'upright'.

When the head leans forwards, backwards or sideways, the chalk granules push against the hairs, bending them in a different way. This fires off new messages to the brain, which can then, if necessary, send out instructions to the muscles to adjust the position of the body.

The utricle is also in action when the body starts to move forwards or backwards. If a child, for example, starts to run, the chalk granules are pushed back against the hairs as though the child were falling backwards. As soon as the brain receives this information it sends signals to the muscles, which make the body lean forwards, restoring its balance. All these reactions are reversed if the child tips backwards off a chair.

Smell and Taste Receptors

The sense of smell is probably the oldest and the least understood of our five senses. During evolution it has kept its connections with the parts of the brain which grew to be the sorting house for our emotional responses, intimately linking the odours of things to our emotions.

Our sense of smell also plays an important role in sexual attraction, although this has become considerably muted during human evolutionary development. Its most important roles are those of a warning system and information gatherer: warning us of danger and giving us valuable information about the outside world.

The close link between the sense of taste and the sense of smell is something we are not always aware of. Only when we have a cold do we realize that not only can we not smell things, but the taste of food has also vanished.

Smell

As with many organs in the body the smelling apparatus is duplicated, each circuit acting independently.

The sensory receptors for smell are found in the roof of the nasal cavity, just beneath the frontal lobes of the brain. This is called the olfactory area and is tightly packed with millions of small cells, the olfactory cells. Each olfactory cell has about a dozen fine hairs – cilia – which project into a layer of mucus. The mucus keeps the cilia moist and acts as a trap for odorous substances, while the cilia effectively enlarge the area of each olfactory cell and so increase our sensitivity to smells.

It is not clearly understood how the minute amounts of chemical substances which give us smells trigger off the olfactory cells, but it is thought that these substances dissolve in the mucous fluids, stick on to the cilia and then cause the cells to fire off electrical signals.

Olfactory nerve fibres channel these signals across the bone of the skull to the two olfactory bulbs in the brain, where the information is gathered, processed and then passed through a complicated circuitry of nerve endings to the cerebral cortex. Here the message is identified and the smell becomes a conscious fact.

The exact molecular mechanism of the sense of smell is still largely unknown. Quite how the receptor cells can detect thousands of different odours and distinguish minute differences between them remains a mystery.

What is it we smell?

To be smelly a substance must give off particles of the chemical of which it is made. This type of substance is, in general, chemically complex. Simple chemical substances – such as salt – do not have a smell, or have only a faint trace.

The particles of a substance must remain in the air in gas form in order to be swept into the nostrils and to the mucus surrounding the cilia. Once there, they must be able to dissolve in the mucus for the smelling apparatus to detect them.

Those substances that give off gas easily – such as petrol – are usually very smelly as high concentrations of the chemicals are able to reach the cells.

Wetness also heightens smells. As the water evaporates from the substance, it carries particles of the sub-

Gaseous substances are dissolved in the mucus surrounding the cilia. A chemical reaction then takes place which stimulates the olfactory cells into electrical activity. These messages are passed across ethmoidal bone via sensory nerve fibres, and into the olfactory bulb. Here, the information is processed and then passed along the complex circuitry of the olfactory nerves to the cerebral cortex. At this point we become aware of the smell.

The sense of smell

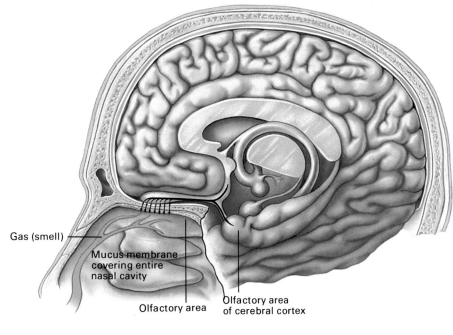

Gas (smell)

Mucus membrane covering entire nasal cavity

Olfactory area

Olfactory area of cerebral cortex

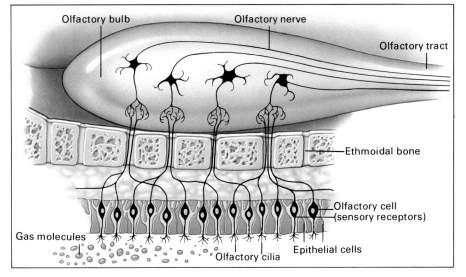

Olfactory bulb

Olfactory nerve

Olfactory tract

Ethmoidal bone

Olfactory cell (sensory receptors)

Gas molecules

Olfactory cilia

Epithelial cells

stance into the air. Perfumes are structured in such a way that they are chemically complex and give off gas easily.

Smell, emotions and memory

The part of the brain that analyzes messages coming from the receiver cells in the nose is closely connected with the limbic system, that part of the brain that deals with emotions, mood and memory. It is called the primitive brain, sometimes even the 'smelling brain'. The connection explains why smells are richly endowed with emotional significance. The smell of fresh rain on a summer's day usually makes people feel happy and invigorated; it may also evoke pleasant memories. The smell of fresh-baked bread may bring on instant pangs of hunger, while the scent of perfume may bring anticipation of sexual pleasure.

Conversely, unpleasant smells – such as rotten eggs – produce revulsion, and even nausea. But there are exceptions. The extremely unpleasant smell of a ripe Gorgonzola cheese actually attracts fervent fans; the smellier the better!

Certain smells will bring memories of long forgotten special occasions flooding back. This is because we tend to remember those things which have special emotional significance, since the areas of the brain which process memories and which are essential in their recall, are also closely linked to the limbic system, and which, in turn, is linked to the centres in the brain for the sense of smell.

Taste

The sense of taste is the crudest of our five senses. It is limited in both range and versatility and presents us with less information concerning the world about us than any other sense. In fact, this sense's exclusive role is that of selector and appreciator of food and drink, a role that is considerably aided by the more sensitive sense of smell. This sense adds colour to the four basic tastes which our taste buds can recognize. Consequently, the loss of the sense of taste – for whatever reason – is less of a problem than the loss of the sense of smell.

Taste buds

Like smell, the taste mechanism is triggered by the chemical content of substances in food and drink. Chemical particles are picked up in the mouth and converted into nerve impulses which are transmitted by nerves to the brain, where they are then interpreted.

The taste buds are at the heart of this system. Studding the surface of

the tongue are many small projections, called papillae. Inside these are the taste buds. An adult has about 9000 taste buds, mainly on the upper surface of the tongue, but there are also some on the palate and even the throat.

Each taste bud consists of groups of receptor cells, and each of these has fine hair-like projections – called microvilli – sticking out into the surface of the tongue through fine pores in the surface of the papilla. At the opposite end to this, the receptor cells link up with a network of nerve fibres. The design of this network is complex, as there is a great deal of interlinking between nerve fibres and receptor cells. Two different nerve bundles, which make up the facial nerve and the glossopharyngeal nerve, carry the impulses to the brain.

The taste buds respond to only four basic tastes: sweet, sour, salt and bitter; and the receptor sites for these tastes are located on different parts of the tongue. The buds that respond to sweet are at the tip of the tongue, while those specializing in salt, sour and bitter are located progressively further back.

Quite how the taste buds respond to the chemicals in the food and initiate the nerve impulses to the brain is not fully understood, but in order to be tasted, the chemicals must be in liquid form. Dry food gives very little immediate sensation of taste, and only acquires its taste after being dissolved in saliva.

At present, it is believed that the chemicals in the food alter the electrical charge on the surface of the receptor cells, which in turn cause a nerve impulse to be generated in the nerve fibres.

The analysis of taste

The two nerves carrying taste impulses from the tongue (the facial nerve or the glossopharyngeal nerve) first pass to the specialized cells in the brain stem. This area of the brain stem also acts as the first stop for other sensations coming from the mouth. After initial processing in this brain stem centre, the taste impulses are transferred in a second set of fibres across to the other side of the brain stem and ascend to the thalamus. Here, there is another relay, where further analysis of the taste impulses is carried out before information is passed to the part of the cerebral cortex participating in the actual conscious perception of taste.

The cortex also deals with other sensations - such as texture and temperature - coming from the tongue. These sensations are probably mixed with the basic taste sensations from the tongue, and so produce the subtle

The sense of taste

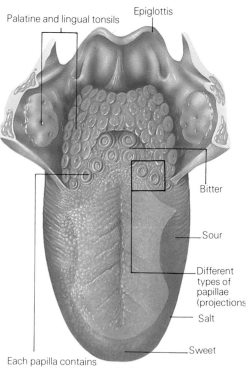

Each papilla contains one to two hundred taste buds

The papillae on the tongue increase the area in contact with food and except for those in the centre, they contain numerous taste buds. These, in turn, contain taste receptors which are distributed so that different parts of the tongue are sensitive to different tastes: sweet, salt, sour or bitter.

sensations with which we are familiar when we eat.

This analysis, carried out in the lower part of the parietal lobe in the cortex, is further influenced by smell information being analyzed in the nearby temporal lobe. Much of the refinements of taste sensation are due to smell sensations.

Compared to other sensations (in particular smell) our taste sense is not very sensitive. It has been estimated that a person needs 25,000 times as much of a substance in the mouth to taste it as is needed by the smell receptors to smell it. However, despite this, the combination of the four types of taste buds responding to the basic tastes of salt, sour, bitter or sweet enable a wide range of sensations to be determined as the brain analyzes the relative strength of the basic flavours. Some of the stronger tastes, such as the 'hot' flavour of spicy food come about through stimulation of pain-sensitive nerve endings in the tongue.

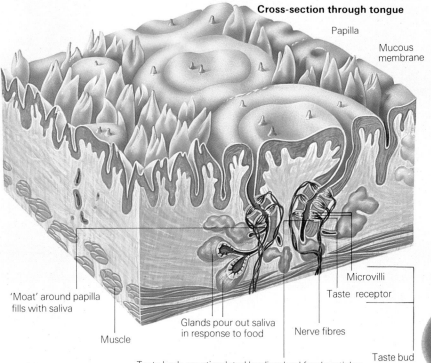

Cross-section through tongue

Papilla

Mucous
membrane

Microvilli

Taste receptor

'Moat' around papilla
fills with saliva

Glands pour out saliva
in response to food

Nerve fibres

Taste bud

Muscle

Taste buds are stimulated by dissolved food particles

If we were to lose our
sense of smell, almost
all taste sensation
would be lost as well.
Eating oysters, for
instance, where the
smell is so important
to the enjoyment,
would become a dull
and totally 'tasteless'
experience.

Touch Receptors

Wrapped around the base of the fine hairs of the skin are the free nerve endings which respond to any stimulation of the hair. These touch receptors are the least sophisticated in structure and rapidly stop firing if the hair continues to be stimulated. Receptors found in greater numbers in the hairless part of the skin, for example on the fingertips and lips, are formed into tiny discs. Because the nerve fibres are embedded within these discs they respond more slowly to pressure and continue to fire when the pressure is maintained. Other more structurally complicated receptors are formed by many membranes being wrapped around a nerve ending like an onion skin, and give responses to more maintained pressure. In addition, all the receptors tend to be influenced as to what information they send into the nervous system by the temperature at which they are operating. This explains why our sense of touch tends to be impaired in cold weather.

Nerve pathways

Some of the fibres conveying touch information pass into the spinal cord and, without stopping, go straight up to the brainstem. These fibres deal mainly with sensations of pressure, particularly a specific point of pressure. They therefore need to send their messages rather directly to the higher centres of the brain, so that this well-localized sensation can be assessed without confusion from any analysis in the spinal cord.

Other nerve fibres bringing information of more diffuse touch enter the grey matter of the spinal cord, and there meet a network of cells which perform an initial analysis of their information. This is the same area which receives messages from the pain receptors in the skin and elsewhere. The meeting in the spinal cord of messages dealing with both touch and pain allows for the mixture of these two sensations.

This spinal cord analysis filters the sensations which are then sent upwards to the brain. The grey matter of the spinal cord here acts as an electronic gate, so that pain information can be suppressed by the advent into the cord of certain types of touch impulse, limiting the amount of trivial information that must be transmitted.

This division of the touch pathways to the brain into two streams – one of which goes fairly directly up to the brain stem and the other which is first analyzed by the cells of the spinal cord – enables the fine discriminating aspects of touch to be preserved. We can, therefore, estimate accurately the amount of pressure in a touch and its position, but if the pressure is too great or too sharp, the pain analyzers become involved through the connections in the spinal cord.

The sensory sorting house

Whether the touch sensations from the skin have come by the more direct route or after analysis in the spinal cord, they eventually end in the compact knot of grey matter deep in the thalamus, where the pieces of information from various different types of receptor in the skin are assembled and co-ordinated. This enables the brain's highest centres in the cerebral cortex to put together a picture of the sensations of touch of which we become conscious. From the thalamus, the raw data is projected to a narrow strip in the front of the parietal lobes.

This primary sensory area of the cortex processes the information before passing it on to the secondary and tertiary sensory areas. In these latter areas the full picture of the site, type and significance of the touch sensations we feel is produced and correlated along with memories of previous sensations, as well as sensory stimuli coming via the ears and eyes.

The touch sensations are also, and very importantly, co-ordinated at this point with the sensations of what position our limbs, joints and digits are in: this is of importance since it enables us to determine an object's size and shape and helps us to distinguish one object from another.

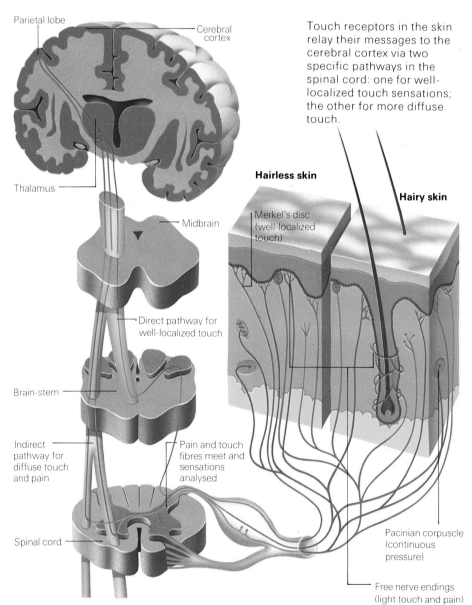

Touch receptors in the skin relay their messages to the cerebral cortex via two specific pathways in the spinal cord: one for well-localized touch sensations; the other for more diffuse touch.

Parietal lobe

Cerebral cortex

Thalamus

Midbrain

Direct pathway for well-localized touch

Brain-stem

Indirect pathway for diffuse touch and pain

Pain and touch fibres meet and sensations analysed

Spinal cord

Hairless skin

Merkel's disc (well-localized touch)

Hairy skin

Pacinian corpuscle (continuous pressure)

Free nerve endings (light touch and pain)

Speech

Speech is one of the most complex and delicate operations that the body is asked to undertake. Ultimately, all speech, talking and comprehension are controlled and co-ordinated by the brain. It is in the cerebral cortex that there are areas called the speech centres where words are deciphered and signals and instructions are sent out to the hundreds of muscles in the lungs, throat and mouth that are involved in producing speech.

The whole of the respiratory system and the entire structure of the muscles from the abdomen to the nose play some part in the production of speech sounds, but of these, the larynx, tongue, lips and soft palate are most important.

The larynx

The larynx is the body's voice box, containing the vocal cords, which vibrate to produce speech. As such, it is an extremely delicate instrument, but it also has a less complex function – a valve guarding the entrance to the lungs.

When we eat or drink, the larynx closes tightly, making food or liquids slide over it down into the oesophagus, which leads into the stomach. When we need to breathe in or out, it is, of course, open.

The larynx is placed at about the centre of the neck, at the top of the windpipe or trachea, out of sight around the 'corner' of the back of the throat. It is essentially a specialized section of the windpipe with an external sheath of cartilage. Positioned over it is the epiglottis, the flap-valve which comes down to cover the opening from the back of the throat into the larynx, known as the glottis.

The action of the epiglottis is automatically controlled by the brain, but sometimes it fails, and then liquids, or food particles go down the 'wrong way'. Unless a lump of food is so large that it sticks in a passage below the larynx, it will be coughed back up.

The vocal cords serve a function similar to that of the reed in a wind instrument such as a clarinet. When a musician blows air over the reed, the thin wood or plastic vibrates, producing the basic sound which is then modified by the pipes and holes of the instrument. Similarly, the vocal cords vibrate when someone vocalizes, and the sounds produced are modified by the throat, nose and mouth.

The vocal cords consist of two delicate ligaments, shaped like lips which open and close as air passes through them. One end is attached to a pair of

Position and structure of the larynx

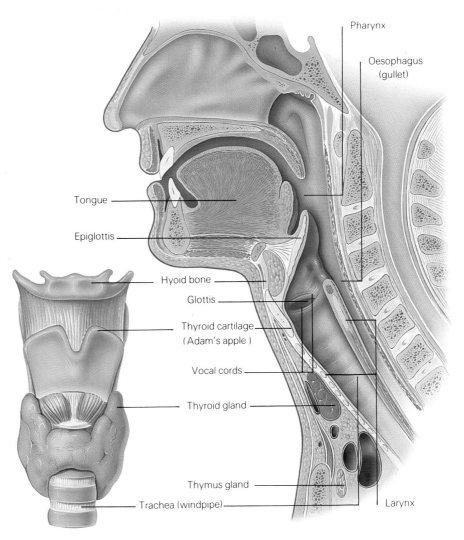

Front and side views of the larynx. Within the larynx are the vocal cords, mounted on specially shaped pieces of cartilage. Air breathed out over them makes them vibrate, which produces sound. The cartilages can tighten or relax the cords, producing high or low-pitched sounds.

movable cartilages called the arytenoids, while the other is firmly anchored to the thyroid cartilage which is part of the Adam's apple. The arytenoid cartilages alter position so that the space between the cords (the rima) varies in shape from a wide V during speech to a closed slit during swallowing. The vibration of the vocal cords during speech occurs when the rima narrows and air from the lungs is expelled over the cords and through the larynx. This is called phonation. The loudness of the voice is controlled by the force with which the air is expelled, and the pitch by the length and tension of the cords. The natural depth and timbre of the voice is due to the shape and size of the throat, nose and mouth: this is why men, who generally have large larynxes and long, slack vocal cords, tend to have deeper voices than women who generally have smaller larynxes than men.

The mouth is intimately involved in speech because it helps to shape sounds emanating from the voice box or larynx. Making the sounds of consonants such as K or T, for example, demands that the air coming from the larynx is cut off sharply by the tongue and palate, while vowel sounds such as A and E need no truncation but certain positions of the tongue and teeth. Each sound in any language is determined by a slightly different movement of the lips, tongue and

Messages from the motor cortex in the brain control, with nerve impulses, all the complicated actions involved in speech production. The sound produced by the vocal cords is turned into words by the lips, tongue, soft palate and shape of the mouth.

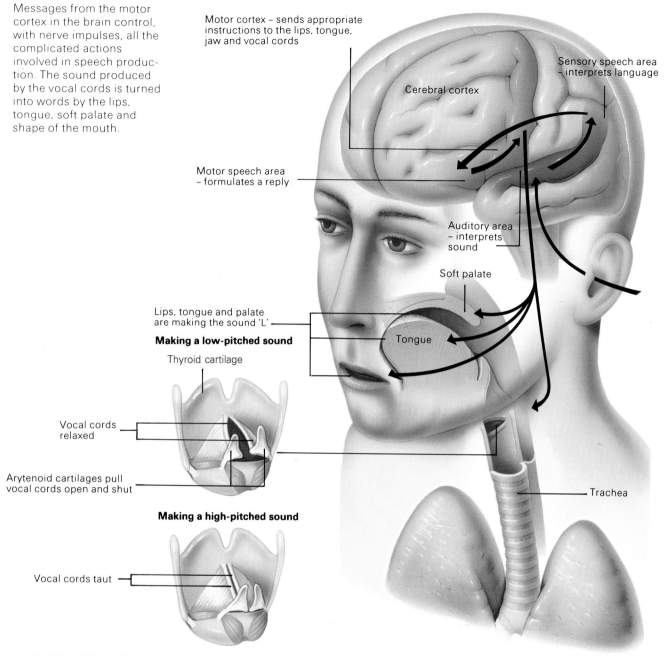

Motor cortex – sends appropriate instructions to the lips, tongue, jaw and vocal cords

Sensory speech area – interprets language

Cerebral cortex

Motor speech area – formulates a reply

Auditory area – interprets sound

Soft palate

Lips, tongue and palate are making the sound 'L'

Making a low-pitched sound

Tongue

Thyroid cartilage

Vocal cords relaxed

Arytenoid cartilages pull vocal cords open and shut

Trachea

Making a high-pitched sound

Vocal cords taut

teeth. The ability of deaf people to lip-read is proof of the role which the mouth plays in the production of speech.

Producing speech sounds

To turn the simple sounds produced by the vocal cords into intelligible words, the lips, the tongue, the soft palate and the chambers which give resonance to the voice all play a part. The resonating chambers include the whole mouth chamber, the nose, the pharynx (the part of the throat between the mouth and the oesophagus) and to a lesser degree the chest cavity.

The control of these structures is achieved by hundreds of tiny muscles which work very closely together and at incredible speed. Put simply, speech is made up of vowels and consonants – vowels are all phonated sounds.

The resonant qualities of the various chambers of the mouth and respiratory system provide us with the individuality of our voices. For instance, the so-called 'nasal sounds' like **m**, **n** and **ng** depend for their correct vocalisation on free resonance in the nose; try pinching your nose when you say something – the comic effect shows how the air space of the nose gives our speech roundness and clarity. Different people have different shapes of nose, chest and mouth, hence different people have different sounding voices.

The skull also resonates when we speak, and we hear part of what we say transmitted through the bones of the skull, as well as what is picked up by the ears. This not only provides us with vital 'feedback' about what we are saying, but also explains why our

voices sound so strange when played back through a tape recorder – the sounds we then hear being only those transmitted through air.

The role of the brain

Speech and its associated functions are usually concentrated in one hemisphere. In a right-handed person this is usually in the left hemisphere and in a left-handed person it is usually in the right hemisphere. This area of the brain is divided into the motor speech centre which controls the muscles of the mouth and throat, and the sensory speech centre which interprets the incoming sound signals coming along the nerves from the ears. Also nearby are the parts of the brain which co-ordinate hearing (by which we comprehend what others around us are say-

Muscles which move the lips

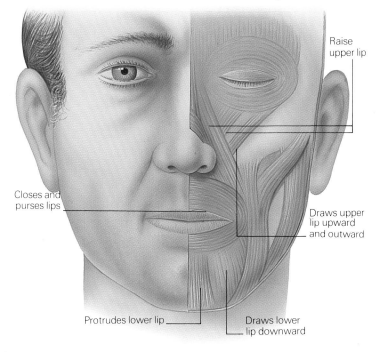

Raise upper lip

Closes and purses lips

Draws upper lip upward and outward

Protrudes lower lip

Draws lower lip downward

Left: The movement of the lips are orchestrated by the muscles shown above. The lips play a vital role in speech — for example, when we produce the sound **b** the lips are at first pressed together so that the outward flow of air is held up and then suddenly opened to give the noise.

Below: The position of the tongue and its surrounding musculature. As with the larynx, and lips, the tongue is all-important to human communication through the enunciation of speech. The difference between a crisp, clearly spoken **s** sound and the fuzzy tone of a lisped one is, for example, all to do with tongue action.

Position of the tongue

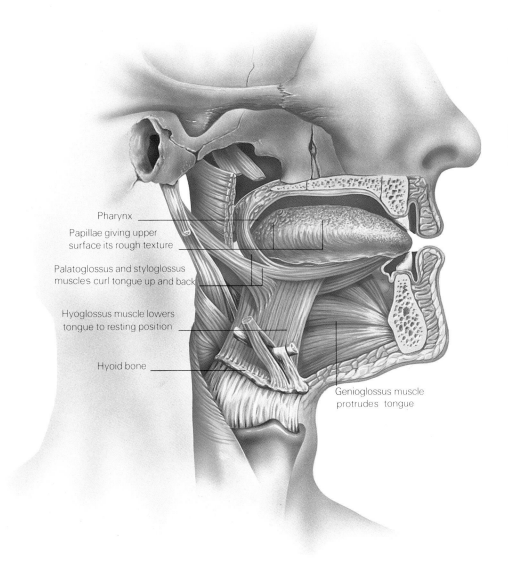

Pharynx

Papillae giving upper surface its rough texture

Palatoglossus and styloglossus muscles curl tongue up and back

Hyoglossus muscle lowers tongue to resting position

Hyoid bone

Genioglossus muscle protrudes tongue

ing), vision (by which we decipher the written word) and the complex hand movements used in writing, playing an instrument and so on.

Conversation is a very complicated procedure, and the first thing that happens when we hear a person speaking is that the hearing centres, in the cerebral cortex, recognize the jumble of incoming auditory signals from the ears. The sensory speech centre decodes the words so that the other parts of the brain involved in the process can then recognize the words and formulate an answer. Once a reply has been thought up, the motor speech centre and the brain stem come into operation. The brain stem controls both the intercostal muscles, between the ribs, which inflate the lungs, and the abdominal muscles which determine the pressure of the incoming and outgoing air. As air is expelled from the lungs, the motor speech areas signal the vocal cords simultaneously to move into the stream of air in the throat, causing the cords to vibrate and produce a simple sound.

The amount of pressure applied to the lungs during exhalation governs the speed with which the air passes over the vocal cords, and the faster the air, the louder the sound produced. During whispering, the vocal cords are set wide apart so that they do not actually vibrate as the air passes between them, they merely act as friction surfaces. But for the most part, the shaping of words is performed by movements of the lips, tongue and soft palate – controlled by the cortex.

Co-ordination

The supple movements of a champion gymnast or athlete reveal in their movements how delicately the human brain can control the hundreds of muscles in the torso and limbs. To achieve such intricate sequences of action, the human brain has evolved a complex system of control and guidance, which makes our sophisticated computers look primitive.

Babies are born with many reflexes. As an example of these reflexes in an adult, think how quickly you would withdraw your hand from a hot saucepan! On to this simple reflex action are superimposed the movements that are directed by the brain. For every action you perform, some muscles will contract, others relax and still more maintain their contraction to stabilize the rest of the body. The process by which all the individual muscle contractions are synchonized by the brain to produce a smooth order of activity, is called co-ordination.

How co-ordination works
To understand this, it is best to take an everyday action, such as leaning over a table to pick up a cup of coffee. How does the brain direct this apparently simple task? Before the cup of coffee can be picked up, a series of events must happen.

First, you must 'know' where the cup and your hand are, and the relationship between them. This means that your brain must be able to generate a 'map' of the outside space for the necessary movement to be planned. This is called spatial perception.

This map of the outside world must then be interpreted by the brain, so that the problem of getting the coffee cup from the table to your hand can be solved. This plan of action must then be translated into a detailed set of instructions which is given to the muscles, so that they will contract in the right order.

During the movement started by the planning parts of the brain, continuous streams of information are pouring in from all the sensors (nerves) in the muscles and joints as to their position and state of contraction. All this information has to be organized and relayed back to keep the map up to date and to make any adjustments which then become necessary.

In order to move your hand to pick up the cup of coffee, you also need to lean slightly towards it. This alters the centre of gravity in your body. All the reflex balance mechanisms must be controlled to ensure that the correct changes in muscle tone are made, allowing the movement across the table that your brain has ordered. This means that the background tone of many other muscles has to be monitored and co-ordinated.

First stages of co-ordination
All intentional movements need practice before they become co-ordinated. Even such ordinary actions as walk-

The high level of co-ordination achieved by athletes, such as this champion hurdler, uses most of the brain. Eye movements are co-ordinated with visual receptive centres of the brain, which are then co-ordinated with nerves and muscles that make possible the very finely controlled and precisely timed movements of the rest of the body.

How the brain enables us to pick up a cup of coffee

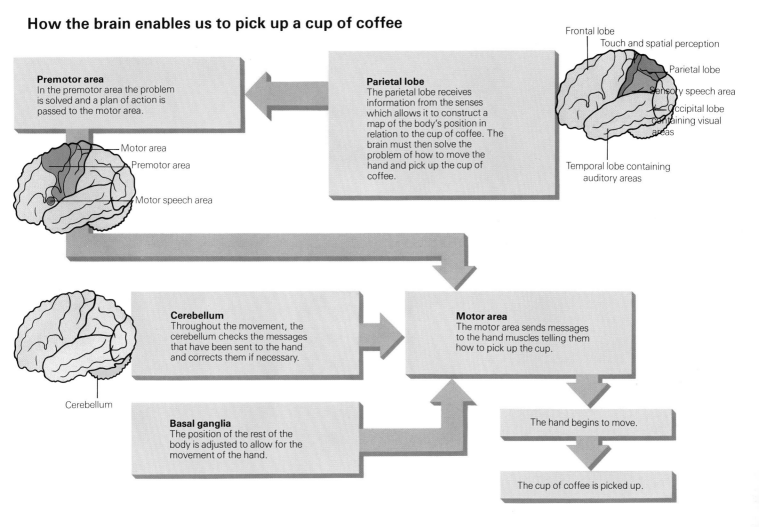

Premotor area
In the premotor area the problem is solved and a plan of action is passed to the motor area.

Motor area
Premotor area
Motor speech area

Parietal lobe
The parietal lobe receives information from the senses which allows it to construct a map of the body's position in relation to the cup of coffee. The brain must then solve the problem of how to move the hand and pick up the cup of coffee.

Frontal lobe
Touch and spatial perception
Parietal lobe
Sensory speech area
Occipital lobe containing visual areas
Temporal lobe containing auditory areas

Cerebellum
Throughout the movement, the cerebellum checks the messages that have been sent to the hand and corrects them if necessary.

Cerebellum

Motor area
The motor area sends messages to the hand muscles telling them how to pick up the cup.

The hand begins to move.

Basal ganglia
The position of the rest of the body is adjusted to allow for the movement of the hand.

The cup of coffee is picked up.

The diagram shows clearly how even simple, everyday actions that we carry out are actually comprised of numerous activities involving the brain, nerves and muscles — all of which may be carried out in a fraction of a second.

ing were once major motor problems for every developing child. As a baby's brain matures and its interconnections increase, the primitive reflexes with which it was born (such as the 'startle' reaction, causing the hands to be out-stretched) are overlaid with progress-ively more complicated ways of moving.

These arrive as a result of the child's increasing senses. A toy might attract its eye, because its bright colour causes a strong signal in the child's visual centres, but the baby finds that reaching out is not enough to arrive at this object, so it is impelled to move towards it. The first attempts to move are not co-ordinated; the limbs simply thrash about wildly. But these enable the necessary brain con-nections to develop for the set of

actions that make up a co-ordinated crawl. Once crawling has been achiev-ed, the messages sent from the brain to the muscles can be improved upon until nothing at ground level is safe from the child's grasp.

When the baby discovers that it can pull itself into an upright position, the cerebellum has to analyze a new set of information coming from the balance centres in the brain stem. Walking is another new skill to learn, requiring many attempts during which the cere-bellum co-operates with the motor cortex to develop efficient 'tunes' to play on the muscles.

The separate parts of each action learnt in this way are pre-programmed into the spinal cord, but they must form a coherent pattern to produce a co-ordinated movement, in the same way that an orchestra must have a conductor before it can produce a tuneful sound from the concerted action of all its instruments.

Once these relatively simple skills have been perfected, the brain has been so well programmed that no con-centration is necessary – the premotor cortex says 'walk' and the right set of instructions go into action to produce the very complicated mechanical

actions that are involved. The cere-bellum monitors the progress of the action, but this is less and less a con-scious event. If a problem is introduced into the system, such as the change in the posture of the foot that is caused by wearing high heels, some repro-gramming is necessary and concen-tration needed whilst the motor cortex is instructed in this new 'tune'.

Advanced co-ordination

This involves the co-ordination of the movement of the eyes with the visual receptive centres of the brain and then with the movement of the rest of the body.

It is evident that this type of co-ordination, using most of the brain, is the last to mature in childhood. It forms the basis for learning the com-plex movements that are needed in various sports or skills, such as play-ing a musical instrument.

Some people's brains seem better equipped from birth to develop in particular ways. However, to a large extent, the differences between people's abilities in complex types of co-ordination depends on the extent to which they can concentrate to build up these programmes.

CHAPTER 5

ENDOCRINE SYSTEM

Many of the body's functions are controlled by endocrine glands which help to keep the various parts of the body working harmoniously with each other. By secreting the chemicals called hormones into the bloodstream they are able to relay messages to organs and stimulate them to carry out specific processes which include such critical activities as growth and reproduction. Since all hormones are concerned with metabolism they tend to interact with one another to bring about the desired end.

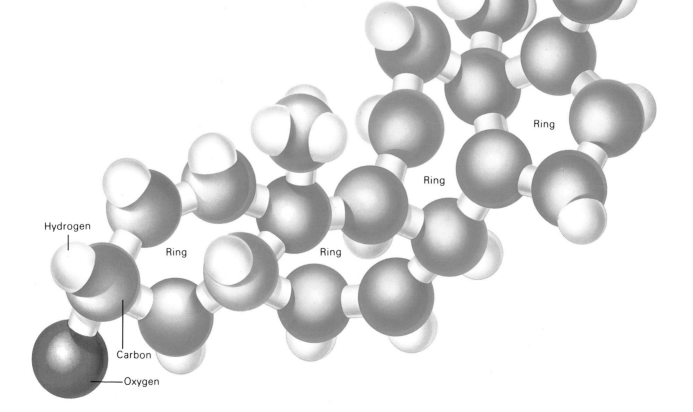

Branch

Ring

Ring

Ring

Hydrogen

Ring

Ring

Carbon

Oxygen

Hormones

Hormones are the body's chemical messengers. They are formed in special glands sited in various places in the body and are circulated in the blood to other body cells – known as targets – where their effects are brought about. The glands largely responsible for making and releasing most of the body's hormones are the collection of ductless or endocrine glands so-called because they discharge their products directly into the blood and not via a tube or duct as exocrine glands do.

How hormones work

Compared with nerves, hormones tend to act more slowly and also to spin out their activity over a much longer time. Not all hormones act so slowly, but many of those that do are involved in fundamental whole life activities, such as growth and reproduction. In general, hormones tend to be concerned with controlling or influencing the chemistry of the target cells, for example, by determining the rate at which they use up food substances and release energy, or whether or not these cells should produce milk, hair or some other product of the body's metabolic processes.

Because they have the most widespread effects, the hormones made by the major endocrine glands are known as general hormones; these include insulin and the sex hormones. The body makes many other hormones

Left: Model of a steroid molecule. Hormones are either proteins or protein derivatives, or steroids. The latter include the sex hormones and those secreted by the adrenal cortex. All steroids have the same molecular structure and pattern. The molecule is composed of oxygen, hydrogen and carbon atoms, and these are set in a pattern of 17 carbon atoms arranged in four linked rings. The chemical composition of different steroids only shows changes in the branches off the ring.

Right: Adrenalin, secreted by the adrenal medulla, is known as the fight or flight hormone. Once released from the adrenal gland its effects on the body are instantaneous. These hormones affect part of the autonomic nervous system so that in an emergency the body prepares to stand and fight or to flee. Adrenalin is not only produced in the face of physical danger but also in times of psychological stress. When its production is sustained over a long period it can have adverse effects on the body.

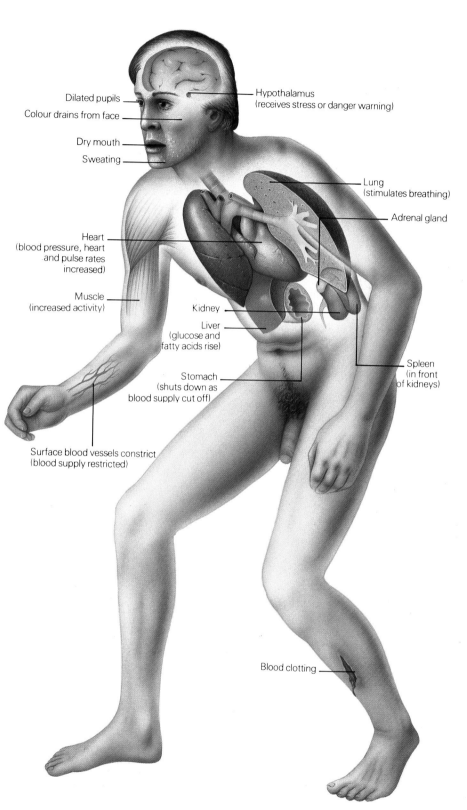

Dilated pupils
Colour drains from face
Dry mouth
Sweating
Hypothalamus (receives stress or danger warning)
Lung (stimulates breathing)
Adrenal gland
Heart (blood pressure, heart and pulse rates increased)
Muscle (increased activity)
Kidney
Liver (glucose and fatty acids rise)
Spleen (in front of kidneys)
Stomach (shuts down as blood supply cut off)
Surface blood vessels constrict (blood supply restricted)
Blood clotting

which act much nearer to their point of production.

One example of such a local hormone is secretin, which is made in the duodenum in response to the presence of food. The hormone then travels a short distance in the blood to the nearby pancreas and stimulates it to release a flood of watery juice containing enzymes (chemical transformers) essential to digestion.

Other examples of local hormones, or transmitters, include the substance acetyl choline, which is made every time a nerve passes a message to a muscle cell, telling it to contract.

Proteins and steroids

All hormones are active in very small amounts. In some cases, less than a millionth of a gram is enough for a task to be carried out.

Chemically, hormones fall into two basic categories: those that are proteins or protein derivatives and those that have a ring, or steroid structure. The sex hormones and the hormones made by the outer part or cortex of the adrenal gland are all steroid hormones.

Insulin is a protein and the thyroid hormones are manufactured from a protein base and are protein derivatives.

When each hormone reaches its target, it can only go to work if it finds itself in a correctly-shaped site on the target cell membrane. Once it has become locked into this receptor site, the hormone does its work by stimulating the formation of a substance called cyclic AMP (adenosine monophosphate). The cyclic AMP is thought to work by activating a series of enzyme systems within the cell, so that particular reactions are stimulated and the required products are made.

The reaction of each target cell depends on its own chemistry. Thus, cyclic AMP produced by the presence of the hormone insulin, triggers cells to take up and use glucose, while the hormone glucagon, also made by the pancreas, causes glucose to be released by cells and built up in the blood to be 'burned off' as energy-giving fuel for physical activity.

After they have done their work, the hormones are rendered inactive by the target cells themselves, or are carried to the liver for deactivation, then broken down and either excreted or used to make new hormone molecules.

The role of the hypothalamus

The hypothalamus is the link between the nervous system and the endocrine glands. One of its major functions is to relay impulses and stimuli between the brain and organs such as the kidneys. It does this by receiving certain of the chemical transmitter substances released by the nerve cells of the brain, and in response to the trigger, releases hormones.

Two hormones made in the posterior pituitary gland, antidiuretic hormone, ADH, and oxytocin, are released from the pituitary under the direct control of nerve impulses generated in the hypothalamus. There is also a link between the nerve cells of the hypothalamus and the secretions of the anterior, or front, part of the pituitary gland. Again, special nerve cells in the hypothalamus make releasing factors which must act on the cells of the

Major hormones secreted by the endocrine system

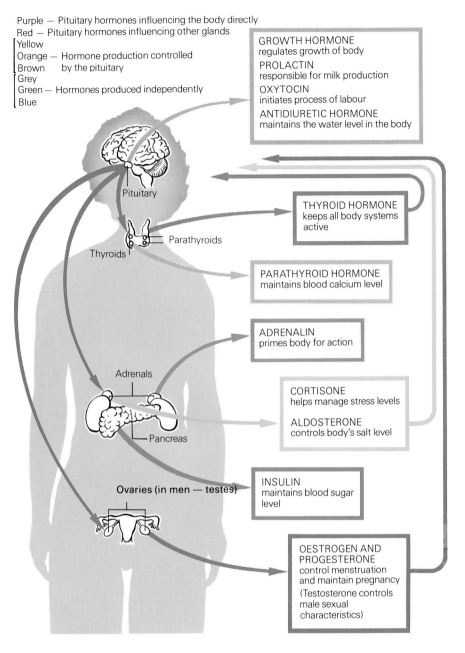

Purple — Pituitary hormones influencing the body directly
Red — Pituitary hormones influencing other glands
Yellow
Orange — Hormone production controlled
Brown   by the pituitary
Grey
Green — Hormones produced independently
Blue

GROWTH HORMONE
regulates growth of body
PROLACTIN
responsible for milk production
OXYTOCIN
initiates process of labour
ANTIDIURETIC HORMONE
maintains the water level in the body

THYROID HORMONE
keeps all body systems active

PARATHYROID HORMONE
maintains blood calcium level

ADRENALIN
primes body for action

CORTISONE
helps manage stress levels
ALDOSTERONE
controls body's salt level

INSULIN
maintains blood sugar level

OESTROGEN AND PROGESTERONE
control menstruation and maintain pregnancy
(Testosterone controls male sexual characteristics)

Pituitary

Parathyroids

Thyroids

Adrenals

Pancreas

Ovaries (in men — testes)

anterior pituitary before they can send out their hormones.

Effects on emotions

The strong link between the brain and the pituitary goes a long way towards explaining why there is such a definite connection between the hormones and the emotions. Many women find, for example, that if they are anxious or upset, the timing of their periods may be altered. And the levels of the same hormones – oestrogen and progesterone – that control the periods can also have profound effects on a woman's moods.

The sudden fall of hormone levels that happens just before menstruation is thought to play an important part

As well as producing its own hormones, the pituitary has an enormous influence on many of the other endorine glands. Pituitary hormones affect the activity of the adrenal, thyroid and reproductive glands. The pituitary also controls the production of parathyroid hormone.

in creating the symptoms of what has become known as premenstrual tension, while the high hormone levels in mid-cycle are thought to give many women a sense of well-being. And it may not be an accident, that this is the time at which women are both most fertile and most responsive sexually. But hormone levels can also be altered by emotional factors.

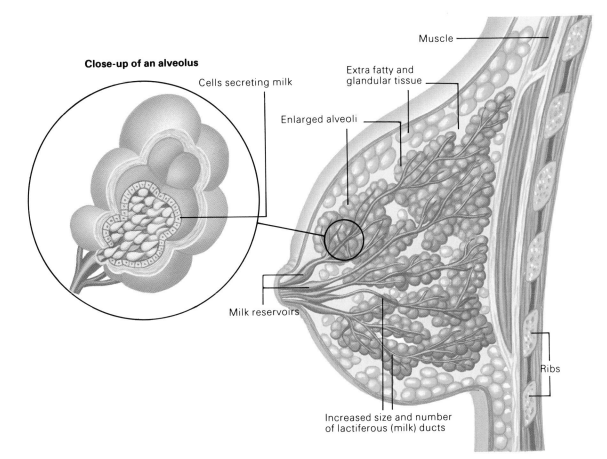

Close-up of an alveolus

Cells secreting milk

Muscle

Extra fatty and glandular tissue

Enlarged alveoli

Milk reservoirs

Ribs

Increased size and number of lactiferous (milk) ducts

Right: Two pituitary hormones are responsible for the production of breast milk: prolactin stimulates the breast to produce milk and oxytocin starts milk flow. Breast milk is secreted by the lining of the alveoli (above). As the baby feeds the milk is drawn down the ducts, from where it is sucked out of the nipple.

During sexual foreplay, for example, it is thought that levels of oestrogen and progesterone rise, as a direct result of pleasurable impulses on the brain, while the very thought of having sexual intercourse with someone who is physically repulsive is, quite literally, a 'turn off', because it inhibits hormone production.

At the end of her reproductive life, i.e. the time of the menopause, a woman may experience great emotional ups and downs. This is partly because her ovaries stop responding to follicle-stimulating hormone, and so stop making oestrogen and progesterone. These changes of mood may also be due to psychological factors. But it is interesting to note that the sudden withdrawal of hormones from the system after a woman has given birth may have emotional effects similar to those of the menopause.

Endocrine Glands

The pituitary gland is the master-gland of the body. It not only produces its own hormones, but it also influences the hormonal production of the other glands. The pituitary gland is found in the base of the brain. It is connected to the hypothalamus by a stalk of nervous tissue and works closely with this area of the brain. Together the pituitary and the hypothalamus control many aspects of the body's metabolism – that is, the various chemical processes whose function is to keep every part of the human body functioning.

Structure and function

The pituitary sits inside a protective bony 'saddle' called the sella turcica (a Latin word meaning 'turkish saddle'). The sella turcica – or sella, as doctors refer to it – can be seen clearly on an X-ray of the skull; enlargement of the sella is a good indication that some-thing is wrong with the pituitary gland and tests must be done.

The gland is divided into two halves, each of which is quite separate from the other in the way that it acts. The back half, or posterior pituitary, is connected to the hypothalamus through the pituitary stalk. It is concerned with the production of only two main hormones, which are actually produced in the hypothalamus. From there they travel along specialized nerve cells to the posterior pituitary and are released when the hypothalamus receives appropriate messages about the state of the body. The posterior pituitary and the hypothalamus are therefore very much a self-contained unit.

The anterior pituitary produces the hormones that activate other important glands in the body as well as producing one or two important hormones that act directly on the tissues. Although it is not linked directly with the hypothalamus it is still very closely bound up with it in the way that it works.

Since the anterior pituitary has no direct nerve paths to link it with the hypothalamus, it has to depend on a series of special releasing and inhibiting factors to control hormone release. Some of these factors are themselves specialized hormones that are released by the hypothalamus and act on the pituitary gland a few millimetres away. They are carried in a special set of blood vessels called the pituitary portal system. This system runs between the hypothalamus and the pituitary gland.

Although many of the instructions to release hormones come from the hypothalamus, the anterior pituitary itself also has a good deal of independent control over their release. The release of some of the secretions is inhibited by substances that are circulating in the bloodstream. An example of this is the hormone TSH (thyroid stimulating hormone) which stimulates the thyroid gland in the neck to produce its hormones. The release of TSH by the pituitary is inhibited when high levels of thyroid hormone are in the blood. This is an important principle in the control of many of the pituitary hormones and is called 'negative feedback'. It means that the levels of the final hormone produced in glands remote from the pituitary (but dependent on it) can never rise too high, since negative feedback on the pituitary will turn off the production of stimulating hormones.

The pituitary hangs from the underside of the brain, protected by a bony saddle known as the sella turcica.

Location and structure of pituitary gland

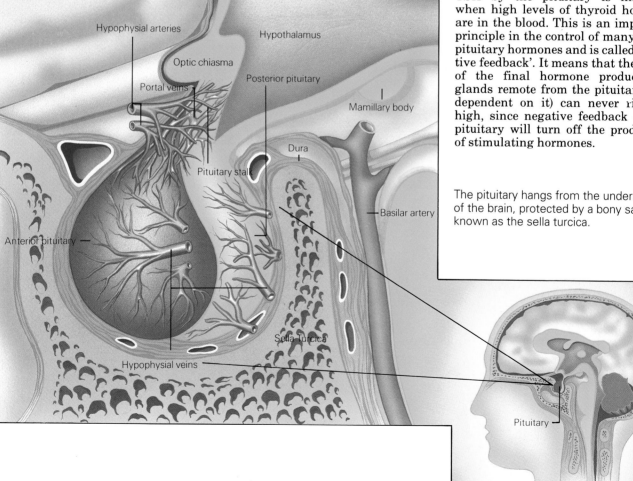

Labels: Hypophysial arteries · Hypothalamus · Optic chiasma · Posterior pituitary · Portal veins · Mamillary body · Dura · Pituitary stalk · Basilar artery · Anterior pituitary · Sella Turcica · Hypophysial veins · Pituitary

Hormonal activity of the pituitary

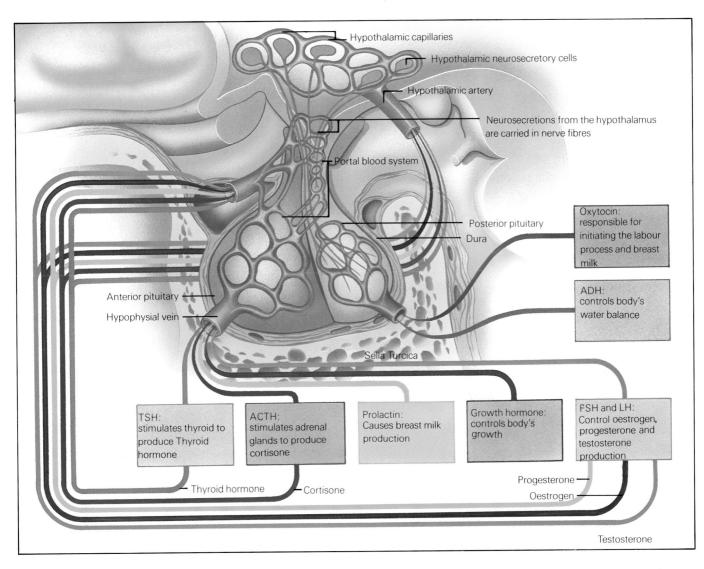

Hypothalamic capillaries

Hypothalamic neurosecretory cells

Hypothalamic artery

Neurosecretions from the hypothalamus are carried in nerve fibres

Portal blood system

Posterior pituitary

Dura

Oxytocin: responsible for initiating the labour process and breast milk

ADH: controls body's water balance

Anterior pituitary

Hypophysial vein

Sella Turcica

TSH: stimulates thyroid to produce Thyroid hormone

ACTH: stimulates adrenal glands to produce cortisone

Prolactin: Causes breast milk production

Growth hormone: controls body's growth

FSH and LH: Control oestrogen, progesterone and testosterone production

Thyroid hormone

Cortisone

Progesterone

Oestrogen

Testosterone

Hormones of the pituitary

The posterior pituitary produces two hormones called antidiurectic hormone, or ADH, and oxytocin. It also produces a number of substances called neurophysins, whose function and importance are not quite certain. However, there is no evidence that they act as true hormones.

ADH is concerned with the control of water in the body. It acts on the tubules of the kidney, affecting their ability to retain or release water. That is, the kidney tissue is able to suck more or less water, as necessary, out of the urine as it leaves the tubule. When ADH is secreted into the blood the kidneys tend to conserve water. When the hormone is not secreted, more water is lost from the body in the urine.

The role of oxytocin is less clear. It is concerned with starting off labour and causing the uterus to contract. It also plays an important part in starting the secretion of milk from the

breasts during lactation. In males, it is thought that oxytocin may be concerned with generating an orgasm.

The anterior pituitary produces six main hormones. Four of these are concerned with the control of other important glands in the body: the thyroid, the adrenal glands and the gonads (the testes in the male, the ovaries in the female).

The activity of the thyroid gland is triggered off by TSH while the cortex (outer part) of the adrenal gland is affected by the hormone ACTH (adreno-cortico trophic hormone). The overall levels of thyroid hormone and cortisone from the adrenal glands are maintained by a combination of negative feedback acting on the pituitary and extra signals that come from the hypothalamus – for example, in times of stress.

The anterior pituitary also releases the hormones FSH (follicle stimulating hormone) and LH (luteinizing hormone). These are known as gonadotro-

Four of the pituitary hormones activate an organ to produce another related hormone. Some of this hormone in the blood will feed back into the pituitary, thus regulating its production; some of it will pass through the hypothalamus, stimulating neurosecretions that travel to the portal blood vessels back into the pituitary to control the release of various hormones.

phins hormones that affect the sex glands. They stimulate the production of two major sex hormones, oestrogen and progesterone, which in the female control the menstrual cycle. In the male, FSH and LH stimulate the production of male hormones and sperm.

The hormone prolactin is one of two hormones of the anterior pituitary that seem to act directly on the tissues without stimulating some other gland. Like the gonadotrophins prolactin is very much concerned with controlling the means of reproduction. Similarly, prolactin has a much more complicated role in the female than in the male. In fact its role in the male is not clear, although when present in excess it can have ill effects.

In the female, prolactin stimulates the breast to produce milk. When it is present in large amounts it also inhibits ovulation and the menstrual cycle. This explains the fact that women who are breast feeding are unlikely to conceive (although breast feeding is not a foolproof means of contraception).

The other hormone that the anterior pituitary produces is called the growth hormone; its role, as its name suggests, is to promote normal growth. While this is of most importance during childhood and adolescence, the hormone continues to have some importance in later life, as it determines the way that body tissues handle carbohydrates.

Below: The anatomical drawing shows the position of the thyroid gland in relation to the surrounding structures in the throat, which include the Adam's apple and the trachea. The inset is a section of the thyroid, which shows clearly the cells that produce and store the essential hormone thyroxine.

Thyroid gland

The thyroid gland is found in the neck, just below the level of the larynx. There are two lobes to the gland, and these lie just in front and at either side of the trachea as it passes down the front of the neck. The two lobes are connected by a small bridge of tissue, and there may be a smaller central lobe called the pyramidal lobe. In an adult, the gland will weigh about 20 gm (2/3 oz).

The function of the gland is to make the thyroid hormone, thyroxine. When the gland is looked at under a microscope, many small 'follicles' can be seen; these are islands of tissue containing collections of colloid, a protein substance to which thyroid hormone is bound and from which it can be released by enzymes.

It is not possible to tie the activity of thyroxine down to one specific thing. It is released from the gland and is then probably taken up from the blood into all the cells of the body. There appears to be a receptor on the surface of the cell nucleus that responds to the hormone. The overall effect of the hormone is to increase the amount of energy that the cell uses; it also increases the amount of protein that the cell manufactures.

Although the exact role of the hormone in the cell is not known, it is essential for life.

The thyroid gland contains iodine that is vital for its activity. This is the only part of the body that requires iodine and the thyroid is very efficient at trapping all the available iodine from the blood. An absence of iodine in the diet results in malfunction of the thyroid and the growth of the gland, a condition called endemic goitre.

Like so many of the endocrine glands, the thyroid is under the control of the pituitary. When the pituitary produces TSH, it increases the amount of thyroid hormone that is released from the gland. The amount of TSH that the pituitary produces increases if the amount of thyroxine circulating in the system falls, and decreases if it rises, which will result in a relatively constant level of thyroid hormone in the blood.

The pituitary is itself under the influence of the hypothalamus and the amount of TSH that is produced will be increased if there is a release of a substance called TRH (TSH releasing hormone) from the hypothalamus.

This situation is further complicated by the fact that thyroid hormone

The thyroid gland

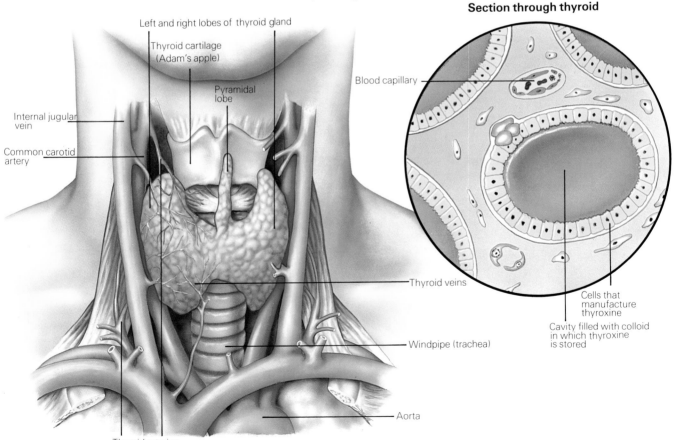

Left and right lobes of thyroid gland

Thyroid cartilage (Adam's apple)

Pyramidal lobe

Internal jugular vein

Common carotid artery

Thyroid veins

Windpipe (trachea)

Thyroid arteries

Aorta

Section through thyroid

Blood capillary

Cells that manufacture thyroxine

Cavity filled with colloid in which thyroxine is stored

The parathyroids help to control the level of calcium in the body. The upper two – the superior parathyroids – are found behind the thyroid. Curiously, the lower two – the inferior parathyroids – can be situated inside the thyroid (as in the illustration), or right down inside the throat.

The parathyroids

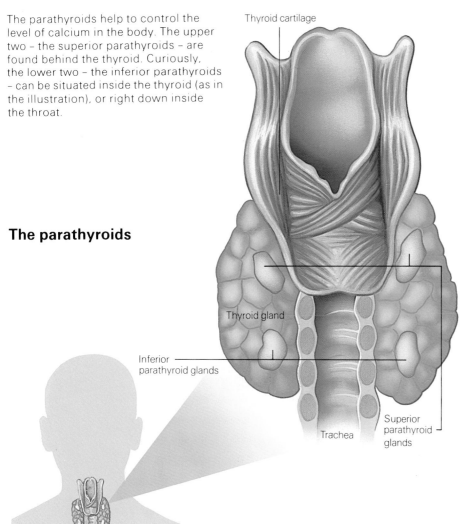

Thyroid cartilage

Thyroid gland

Inferior parathyroid glands

Trachea

Superior parathyroid glands

Parathyroid glands

The parathyroids are four tiny glands situated behind the thyroid glands. They play a major part in controlling the levels of calcium in the body. Calcium is a vital mineral, not only because it is the major structural element in the formation of bones and teeth, but also because it plays a central role in the workings of the muscles and nerve cells. The body's calcium levels have to be kept within fairly constant boundaries, otherwise the muscles stop working and fits may occur. This is where the parathyroid glands come in: they keep the calcium levels in balance.

The absorption of calcium into the bloodstream is controlled by vitamin D, which we get from sunlight and some foods, and an important hormone produced by the parathyroids called parathyroid hormone or PTH. If the level of calcium is too low, the parathyroids secrete an increased quantity of the hormone, which actually releases calcium from the bones to raise the level in the bloodstream. Conversely, if there is too much calcium, the parathyroids reduce or halt the production of PTH, thus bringing the level down.

The parathyroids are so small that they can be difficult to find. The upper two are situated behind the thyroid gland; the lower two, however, may actually be inside the thyroid or occasionally right down inside the throat.

comes in two versions, according to the number of iodine atoms that it contains. Most of the hormone released from the gland is in the form of tetraiodothyronine, which contains four iodine atoms and is known as T4. However, the active hormone at the cell level is triiodothyronine, which contains three atoms and is known as T3. Although the gland releases some T3 into the blood, most of its output is T4, and this is converted into T3 in the tissues. Sometimes the tissues switch the way that they convert T4 to produce an ineffective compound called reverse T3. This means that there will be less thyroid hormone activity in the tissues even though the hormone level in the blood is adequate.

When the level of thyroid hormone is low (left), the pituitary gland secretes TSH (thyroid-stimulating hormone), which sets off its production. When there is enough thyroid hormone (right), the pituitary stops producing TSH.

Interaction between the pituitary and thyroid

Thyroid–stimulating hormone (TSH)

Thyroid

Thyroid hormone

Pituitary

Low thyroid hormone

Thyroid hormone level restored

The pancreas

The pancreas, one of the largest glands in the body, is really two glands in one. Almost all of its cells are concerned with secretion. It is an endocrine gland secreting hormones, of which insulin is the most important. It is also an exocrine gland – one which secretes into the gut (or another body cavity), rather than the blood.

The pancreas lies across the upper part of the abdomen, in front of the spine and on top of the aorta and the vena cava (the body's main artery and vein). The duodenum is wrapped round the head of the pancreas. The rest of the duodenum consists of the body and tail, which stretches out over the spinal column to the left.

The basic structures in the pancreas are the acini, collections of secreting cells around the blind end of a small duct. Each duct joins up with ducts from other acini until all of them eventually connect with the main duct running down the centre of the pancreas. Among the acini are small groups of cells called the Islets of Langerhans: these constitute the whole 'other life' of the pancreas as an endocrine organ secreting the insulin which is needed by the body for the constant control of its sugar level.

The Islets also produce a hormone called glucagon which has the effect of raising rather than lowering the level of sugar in the blood. Exactly where glucagon fits into the scheme of things in everyday life is not clear.

The purpose of insulin is to keep the level of sugar in the blood down to normal levels. A lack of this hormone causes diabetes, a condition which can be treated with injections of insulin from animals, or manufactured insulin.

If the level of sugar in the blood begins to rise above certain limits, the Islets of Langerhans respond by releasing insulin into the bloodstream. The insulin then acts to oppose the effects of hormones such as cortisone and adrenalin – which raise the level of sugar in the blood.

The insulin exerts its effect by allowing sugar to pass from the bloodstream into the body's cells to be used as fuel. But if insulin is absent from the system the mechanism for balancing the blood sugar level is removed, because the sugar in the blood cannot be converted into fuel for the cells, then diabetes results.

There are two types of diabetes. The first type, diabetes mellitus (mellitus means 'like honey'), is the disease we know as plain diabetes. The second type, called diabetes insipidus, is extremely rare and results from a failure of the pituitary gland in the skull. In most diatebes sufferers, the lack of insulin is due to a failure of the pancreas and is caused by the destruction of its insulin-producing cells. No one knows exactly how the destruction occurs, but it is the subject of much research. It seems that some people are more likely to develop diabetes and that some event – possibly an infection – may trigger the onset.

The type of diabetes which develops suddenly due to a complete or serious failure of insulin tends to afflict young people and children, and is often called juvenile diabetes. Fortunately, it can be treated with injections of insulin made from the pancreases of cattle or pigs.

The majority of diabetics, however, suffer from what is called maturity onset, or senile, diabetes. In this case, the pancreas does produce insulin, often in normal amounts, but the tissues of the body are sensitive to its action and it is this which produces the high blood sugar level.

Position of the pancreas

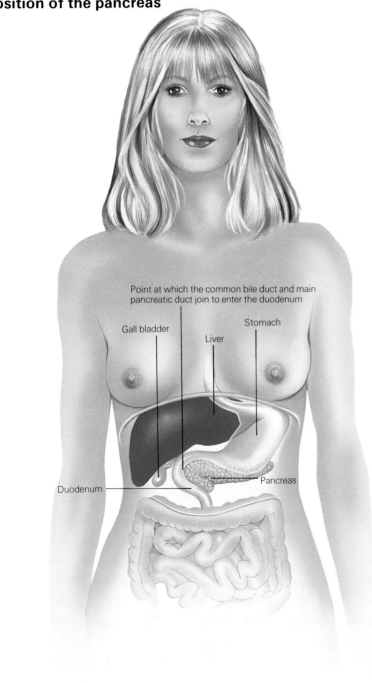

Point at which the common bile duct and main pancreatic duct join to enter the duodenum

Gall bladder

Stomach

Liver

Duodenum

Pancreas

The pancreas has a dual role: it produces the pancreatic hormones insulin and glucagon which help to balance the body's sugar level. It also has an important function in digestion as it secretes digestive enzymes into the small intestine.

How insulin is made in the body

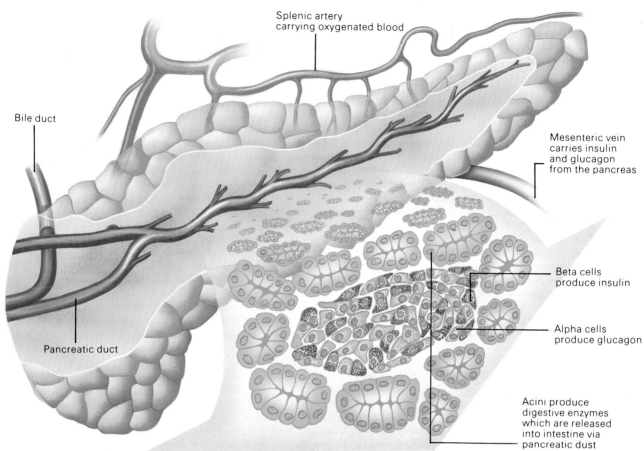

Splenic artery
carrying oxygenated blood

Bile duct

Mesenteric vein
carries insulin
and glucagon
from the pancreas

Beta cells
produce insulin

Alpha cells
produce glucagon

Pancreatic duct

Acini produce
digestive enzymes
which are released
into intestine via
pancreatic dust

The role the insulin plays

- ● Insulin
- ● Glucose

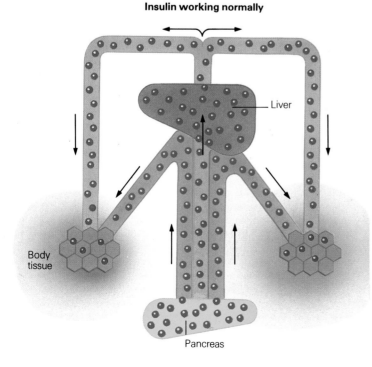

Insulin working normally

Liver

Body
tissue

Pancreas

Above: The hormones insulin and glucagon are produced in the Islets of Langerhans. They enter the bloodstream via the mesenteric vein and balance the body's sugar level. An insulin deficiency causes diabetes; treatment replaces the insulin.

Left: When insulin is being made by the pancreas, it enables glucose – which the body cells need to burn to produce energy – to be stored in the liver. When the body cells need more energy, and therefore more glucose, the glucose will be released and insulin enables it to be used by the cells.

The condition often goes hand in hand with being overweight, and the problem is treated by dieting so that the load of sugar is reduced. Usually there is a back-up to the diet in the form of tablets which stimulate the pancreas so that it produces more insulin.

Unfortunately, this picture of two separate sorts of diabetes is too simple. In reality, the two types tend to merge into each other.

Some people and even children seem to have the maturity onset type, while some elderly patients may require insulin to keep their blood sugar level down.

Adrenal hormones and their uses

Source	Hormone	Functions
Adrenal medulla	Adrenalin	Prepares body for physical action
	Noradrenalin	Maintains even blood pressure
Adrenal cortex	Aldosterone	Regulates excretion of salt by kidney Keeps balance of salt (sodium) and potassium Plays a part in the body's use of carbohydrates
	Cortisone	Stimulates manufacture and storage of energy-giving glucose Reduces formation of fat in the body
	Sex hormones	Supplement sex hormones secreted by gonads

Cortex Medulla

Kidney

Adrenal gland

Adrenal glands

The adrenal glands – known as the adrenals – are located immediately above the kidneys where they sit, like caps, one on top of each kidney. Each gland consists of two distinct parts: the inner medulla and the outer covering, called the cortex. These parts secrete different hormones, each of which has a separate function.

The medulla, or core, of the adrenals is the part of the gland which secretes adrenalin and its close relation, noradrenalin. Together these are known as the 'fight or flight' hormones because they prepare the body for the extra effort required to meet danger, cope with stress or carry out a difficult task.

The adrenal medulla is closely connected to the nervous system. This is exactly as you would expect of the gland responsible for priming the body to be ready for instant action.

Today, the dangers and stresses we face are as likely to be psychological as physical, but either way, the body has the same physical reaction. There is a surge in the production of adrenalin which makes the heart beat faster and more strongly. This raises the blood pressure, while at the same time constricting the blood vessels near the surface of the body and in the gut, redirecting the flow of blood toward the heart – the reason we go 'white with fear'. It also turns glycogen stored in the liver and muscles into glucose required for extra energy.

When the danger is over or the stress removed, adrenalin production is reduced and the body returns to normal. However, if the danger or stress is constant, or if we are continually over-excited or under pressure, the body remains primed for action – and in time this can lead to stress-related conditions such as high blood pressure.

The adrenal cortex

Wrapped around the adrenal core, the adrenal cortex secretes a series of hormones known as steroids, the most important of which are aldosterone and cortisone.

Aldosterone: There are three types of steroids, each one performing a quite different function. The first, known as the salt and water hormones, increase the water retention in the body. The principal hormone in this category is aldosterone, which acts as a chemical messenger and tells the kidneys to reduce the amount of salt being lost in the urine.

Salt determines the volume of blood in circulation, which in turn affects the heart's efficiency as a pump. Every molecule of salt in the body is accompanied by a large number of water

How salt levels are controlled

Sodium chloride, or salt, is a vital part of the fluid that bathes the cells and it also determines the amount of blood circulating in the body. The kidneys maintain a balance between the amount of salt in the excreted urine and sweat, and that retained in the body. This activity is controlled by the adrenal hormone aldosterone which tells the kidneys to reduce the amount of salt that is excreted if salt levels fall too low. Most of the sodium in salt is found outside the cells in extracellular fluid. It is kept there by the mechanism called the sodium pump. This pumps sodium out of the cell and keeps its complementary element potassium inside, a circumstance necessary for the transmission of impulses across the cell membrane.

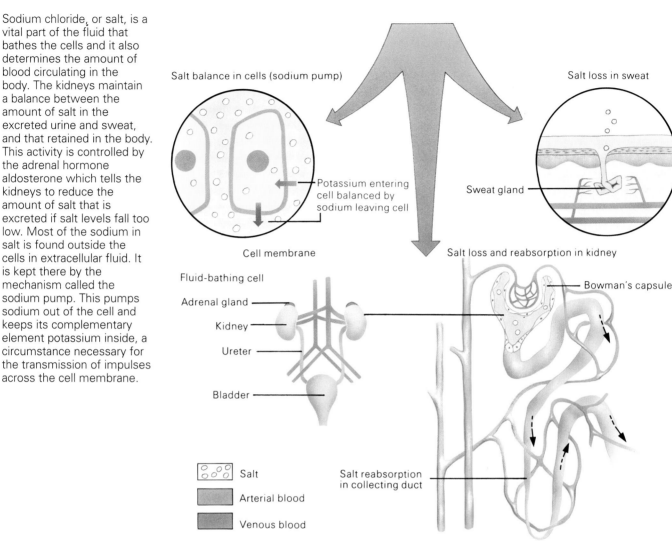

Salt balance in cells (sodium pump)

Potassium entering cell balanced by sodium leaving cell

Cell membrane

Fluid-bathing cell

Adrenal gland

Kidney

Ureter

Bladder

Salt loss in sweat

Sweat gland

Salt loss and reabsorption in kidney

Bowman's capsule

Salt reabsorption in collecting duct

Salt

Arterial blood

Venous blood

---

molecules. This means that in losing a lot of salt, the body loses even more water, and this reduces the volume and pressure of the circulating blood. As a result, the heart has difficulty in pumping enough blood around the body.

The secretion of aldosterone is controlled by the hormone renin which is produced by the kidneys. The system works rather like a see-saw: when aldosterone is low, the kidneys produce renin and the hormone level rises; when it is too high, the kidneys reduce their level of activity and the amount of hormone present in the blood returns to a normal level.

Cortisone: The sugar hormones, of which the most important is cortisone, are responsible for raising the level of glucose in the blood. Glucose is the body's principal fuel, and when extra amounts are needed, as in times of stress, cortisone triggers the convesion of protein into glucose.

Many hormones act to push up the level of sugar in the blood, but corti-

sone is the most important. By contrast, there is only one hormone that keeps the level down, insulin. Because of this imbalance, there is more likely to be a deficiency, a condition which is known as diabetes and which is treated with insulin in the form of tablets or injections.

As well as playing a key part in metabolism (the life-maintaining processes of the body), cortisone is also vital to the functioning of the immune system, which is the body's defence against illness and injury. But if the normal level of cortisone is raised through medical treatment (for example, to prevent rejection after transplant surgery), the resistance to infection is reduced. However, the body does not produce excessive cortisone naturally.

Sex hormones: The final group of hormones produced by the adrenals are those known as the adrenal sex hormones. These are secreted by the adrenal medulla and they complement the six hormones produced in even

larger quantities by the gonads – the male and female sex glands.

The principal male sex hormone – also present in women to a lesser degree – is testosterone, which is responsible for increasing the size of muscles. Anabolic steriods are synthetic derivatives of male sex hormones, among other things.

Control of cortisone

Cortisone is so crucial to body function that its secretion needs to be under strict control. The mechanism which regulates its production – and that of steroids – is the pituitary.

The pituitary secretes the hormone ACTH, which stimulates cortisone production and, as with the hormones renin and aldosterone, the two substances work in the see-saw action known as a feedback mechanism. When the cortisone is too low, the pituitary secretes ACTH and the level rises; when it is too high, the gland slows production and the level of cortisone falls.

CHAPTER 6

RESPIRATORY SYSTEM

Oxygen is the single most important substance on which our lives depend — it is essential to every cell and tissue in the body which use it to produce energy necessary to support life. Oxygen is brought into the body when we inhale and its by-products are given off when we exhale. This process, respiration, involves the lungs and diaphragm and the upper respiratory tract — the nose, mouth, larynx, pharynx and trachea.

Nasal cavities

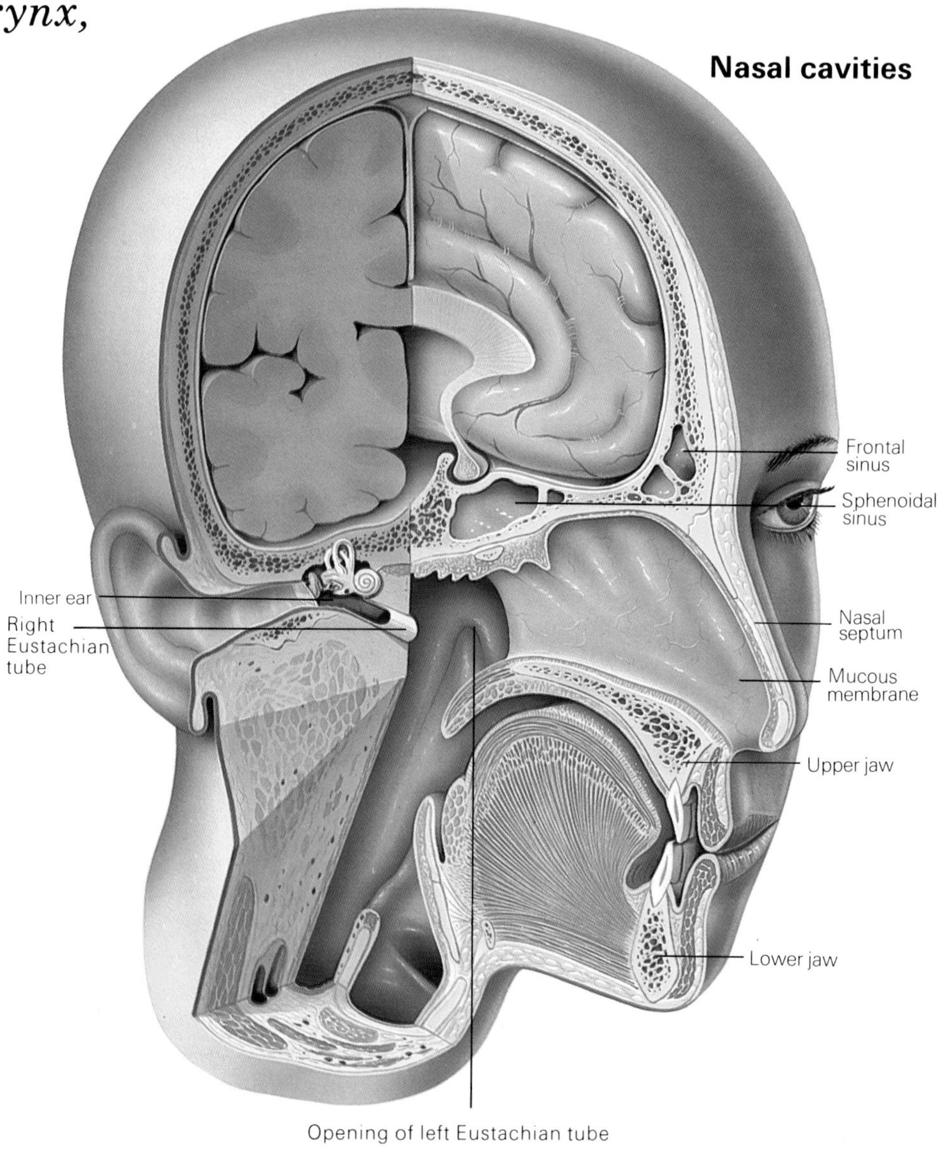

Frontal sinus

Sphenoidal sinus

Inner ear

Right Eustachian tube

Nasal septum

Mucous membrane

Upper jaw

Lower jaw

Right: The two cavities of the nose which open out at the bottom into the nostrils are called the nasal fossae. They are divided down the middle by the septum. A third cavity at the back of the throat is divided into three parts – the meatuses. The diagram shows the position of the Eustachian tubes in relation to the nasal cavities.

Opening of left Eustachian tube

The Nose

Apart from being the organ of smell, the nose is the natural pathway by which air enters the body in the normal course of breathing. In addition, it acts as a protective device against irritants such as dust, which are usually expelled by sneezing and therefore do not have a chance to damage the lungs.

The external nose consists partly of bone and partly of cartilage. The two nasal bones, one on each side, project downward and also form the bridge between the eyes. Below them, the nasal cartilages and the cartilages of the nostrils give the nose firmness, shape and pliability.

Inside, the nose is divided into two narrow cavities by a partition running from front to back. This partition, the septum, is made of bone and cartilage. It is covered with a soft, delicate membrane called a mucous membrane, which is continuous with the lining of the nostril. The nostrils themselves are lined with stiff hairs that grow downwards and protect the entrance. They are quite noticeable in some people, especially men.

The two cavities created by the septum are called nasal fossae. They are very narrow, less than 6 mm (¼ in) wide. At the top of the fossae are thin plates of bone with numerous small receptors from the olfactory nerve. When we have a cold, these receptors get covered in thick mucus, which reduces our sense of smell as well as our sense of taste.

Meatuses

The cavity at the back of the nose is divided into sections by three ridges of bone called the nasal conchae. They are long and thin and run lengthwise, sloping downwards at the back. The passage between each concha is called a meatus. It is lined with mucous membrane having a very rich blood supply, and it is this which moistens and warms the air that is inhaled.

This membrane secretes 0.5 litres (just under a pint) of mucus every day and is covered with thousands of tiny hairs called cilia. The mucus and cilia trap dust particles, which are moved on by the cilia and usually swallowed.

The sinuses – spaces in the front of the skull – are connected with the inside of the nose. They are located behind the eyebrows and behind the cheeks, in the triangle between the eyes and the nose. Sinuses will help cushion the impact of any blows to the face.

Two other passages lead off the meatuses. Tear ducts carry away tears from the eyes (which is why we have to blow our nose when we cry). The other, the auditory tube, is at the back of the nose near the throat junction.

Sections of the nose

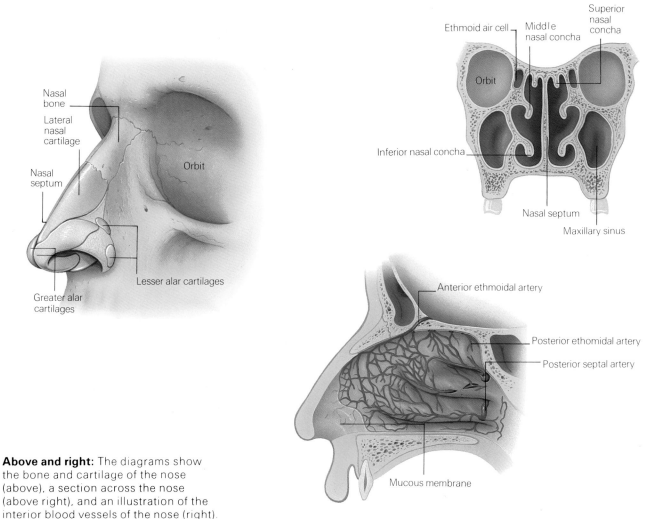

Nasal bone
Lateral nasal cartilage
Nasal septum
Orbit
Lesser alar cartilages
Greater alar cartilages

Ethmoid air cell
Middle nasal concha
Superior nasal concha
Orbit
Inferior nasal concha
Nasal septum
Maxillary sinus

Anterior ethmoidal artery
Posterior ethomidal artery
Posterior septal artery
Mucous membrane

Above and right: The diagrams show the bone and cartilage of the nose (above), a section across the nose (above right), and an illustration of the interior blood vessels of the nose (right).

The Throat

Throat is a term popularly used to describe the area that leads into the respiratory and digestive tracts. It is usually considered to extend from the oral and nasal cavities to the oesophagus and trachea. Anatomically, this area is described as two separate parts, the pharynx and the larynx. Here it will be considered as the larynx, pharynx and trachea, which, together with the nose and mouth, form the upper respiratory tracts.

Because the throat is an assembly of different components, it has a variety of functions. The most obvious of these is to channel food and liquid into the digestive tract and air into the lungs; this task is carried out by the pharynx. The role of the larynx in breathing is centred mainly on the vocal cords, which can be brought together by muscular action to momentarily close the airway, for example when coughing. (For details of the structure of the larynx and its role in speech production, see page 61. The parts of the throat involved in digestion are discussed in Chapter 9.)

Section of throat through cervical vertebra

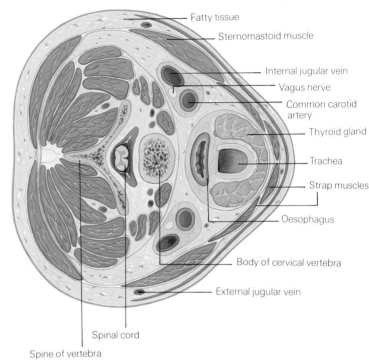

- Fatty tissue
- Sternomastoid muscle
- Internal jugular vein
- Vagus nerve
- Common carotid artery
- Thyroid gland
- Trachea
- Strap muscles
- Oesophagus
- Body of cervical vertebra
- External jugular vein
- Spinal cord
- Spine of vertebra

Structure of the pharynx

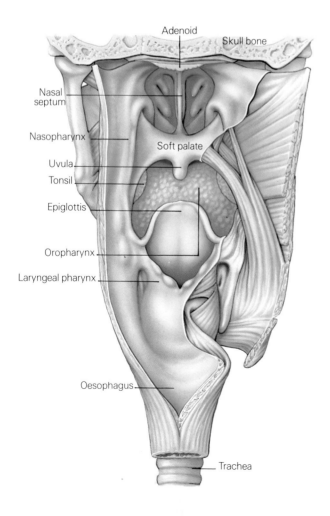

- Adenoid
- Skull bone
- Nasal septum
- Nasopharynx
- Soft palate
- Uvula
- Tonsil
- Epiglottis
- Oropharynx
- Laryngeal pharynx
- Oesophagus
- Trachea

The pharynx

The pharynx is the area at the back of the mouth, extending a little way down inside the neck. Deeply lined with muscles, it is shaped, very roughly, like an inverted cone, extending for about 12 cm (5 in) behind the arch at the back of the mouth to where it joins up with the gullet or oesophagus.

The upper and wider part of the pharynx is given rigidity by the bones of the skull, while at the lower and narrow end its muscles are joined to the elastic cartilages of the voice box or larynx. The outermost tissue layer of the pharynx, continuous with the lining of the mouth, contains many mucus-producing glands which help to keep the mouth and throat well lubricated during eating and speaking.

Anatomically, the pharynx is divided into three sections according to their positions and the jobs each is designed to perform. The uppermost part, the nasopharynx, gets its name from the fact that it lies above the level of the soft palate and forms the back of the nose. Below, the nasopharynx is bordered by the soft palate itself; upward movement of this palate closes off the nasopharynx when you swallow to prevent food being forced up and out of the nose. The uncomfortable outcome of a failure in co-ordination of this mechanism can sometimes be experienced when you sneeze.

In the roof of the nasopharynx are

Left: Cross-section through the throat.

Below left: The main component of the throat is the pharynx, a muscular tube stretching from the base of the skull into the oesophagus. It is the passage through which everything we eat, drink and breathe has to pass, the junction point of all nasal and oral passages.

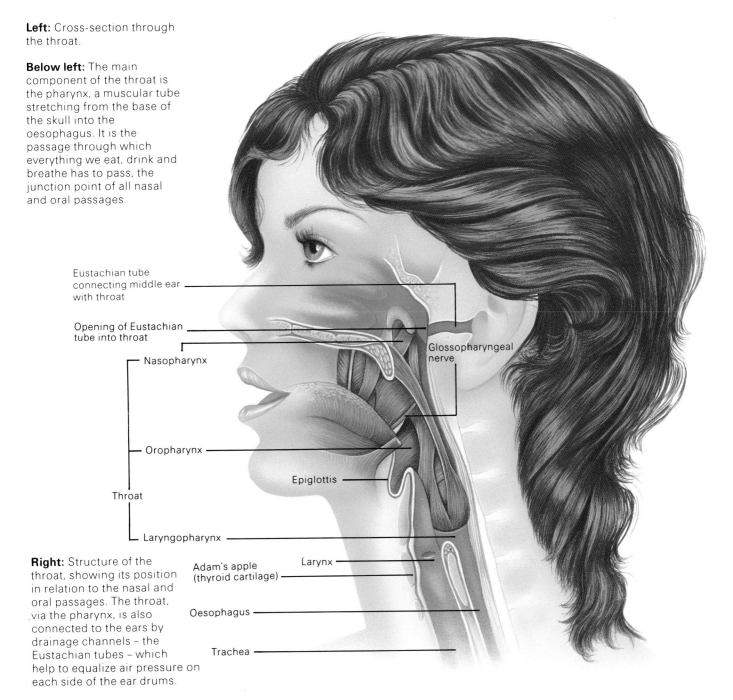

Eustachian tube connecting middle ear with throat

Opening of Eustachian tube into throat

Nasopharynx

Glossopharyngeal nerve

Oropharynx

Epiglottis

Throat

Laryngopharynx

Right: Structure of the throat, showing its position in relation to the nasal and oral passages. The throat, via the pharynx, is also connected to the ears by drainage channels – the Eustachian tubes – which help to equalize air pressure on each side of the ear drums.

Adam's apple (thyroid cartilage)

Larynx

Oesophagus

Trachea

two clumps of tissue particularly prominent in children, known as the adenoids. The nasopharynx also contains, either side of the head, an entrance to the Eustachian tube, the passage between the middle ear and the throat. This can create problems as disease-causing micro-organisms of the mouth, nose and throat have easy access to the ears and commonly cause middle ear infections.

The part of the pharynx at the back of the mouth, the oropharynx, is part of the airway between mouth and lungs. Much more mobile than the nasopharynx, the squeezing actions of the muscles of the oropharynx help shape the sounds of speech as they come from the larynx. With the aid of the tongue, these muscles also help to push food down towards the entrance to the oesophagus. The most important organs of the oropharynx are the notorious tonsils, two mounds of tissue which are often implicated in the sore throats common in childhood.

The lowermost or laryngeal section of the pharynx is involved entirely with swallowing.

The movements of the pharynx must be co-ordinated to ensure that the respiratory gasses end up in the lungs and food ends up in the oesophagus. This co-ordination is achieved by a plexus, or network, of nerves – the pharyngeal plexus. Its activity is controlled in the lower brain stem which brings together information from both the respiratory and swallowing centres higher in the brain.

The trachea

The upper part of the trachea is at the front of the throat and consists of hoops of cartilage that hold open elastic tissue. You can feel this part of the trachea quite easily with your fingers through the skin at the base of the neck. At the upper part of the neck, the trachea is covered by the thyroid cartilage, or Adam's apple. From here it extends to the bronchi. The trachea, like the nose, is lined with a mucous membrane that contains cells with cilia, which waft invading germs and dust back up into the throat to be swallowed.

The Lungs

The two lungs fill most of the thorax. Of the two, the right is larger than the left as the heart takes up more room on the left side of the thorax. Each lung is divided into lobes; the right lung has three lobes, upper, middle and lower, and the left lung has two, upper and lower. The lobes are separate from one another and marked by grooves on the surface – fissures.

The lungs themselves form little more than a dense latticework of tubes. The largest of these are the bronchi, which, at the top of the lungs, divide off from the trachea to the left and right, each entering its respective lung. Inside the lung the bronchi branch out into secondary and tertiary (third) bronchi, and these branch further into smaller tubes called bronchioles. The bronchioles terminate in air sacs called alveoli.

A second system of tubes is formed by the pulmonary arteries which enter the lungs alongside the right and left bronchi. They also branch into smaller tubes, or blood vessels, which run alongside the bronchioles. At the alveoli they form small capillaries.

How the lungs work

If the lungs were removed from the chest they would shrink like deflated balloons. They are held open by surface tension which is created by fluid produced by a thin lining around the lungs and the chest wall, the pleural membrane. To picture this, think of two sheets of glass. If dry and laid on top of one another, they can be easily separated, but if wet the surface tension of the water sticks the glass sheets together. The only way in which they can be separated is by sliding them apart. In the same way, as long as a thin layer of fluid separates the lungs from the chest wall, the lungs are held open. When the chest expands the lungs are pulled out and the air is taken into the alveoli.

When we exhale, the rib muscles relax gradually. If we were to relax completely the lungs would spring back rapidly, unless we purposely held them empty. If air gets between the lungs and chest wall, surface tension is broken and the lungs collapse.

The pleura

There are two types of pleural membrane in the lungs; the inner, or visceral pleura, and the outer, or parietal pleura. The visceral pleura lines the whole of the outside of the lung, including the fissures. The parietal pleura lines the inside of the thorax. These two layers meet only at the

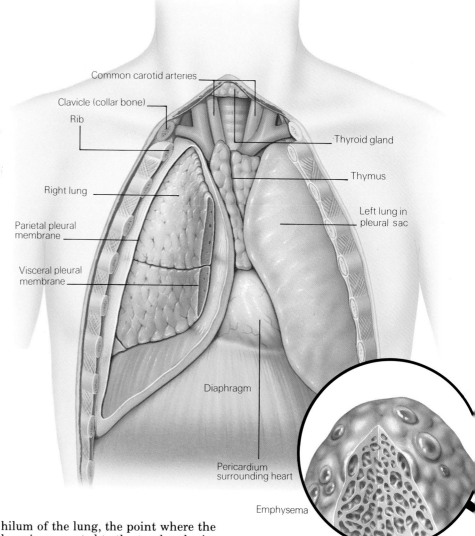

Common carotid arteries

Clavicle (collar bone)

Rib

Thyroid gland

Thymus

Right lung

Left lung in pleural sac

Parietal pleural membrane

Visceral pleural membrane

Diaphragm

Pericardium surrounding heart

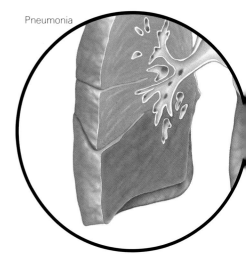

Emphysema

Pneumonia

hilum of the lung, the point where the lung is connected to the trachea by its bronchus and to the heart by its pulmonary blood vessels. In all other areas they are quite separate.

In healthy people the visceral and parietal layers of pleura are always in contact with each other, and they slide over each other as the lung moves in the act of breathing. Of course, there is some space between the two layers. In healthy people this 'potential' space is minimal: just enough to accommodate tiny amounts of fluid that help to lubricate the two layers as they glide over each other. In one aspect of pleurisy, however, the space can fill up with large amounts of fluid: this is called a pleural effusion.

Unlike the lung, the pleura is equipped to feel pain, and it is this pain that is characteristic of pleurisy. Any sort of inflammation will make the surface of the pleura raw, and the pain will arise as the visceral and parietal pleura slide past each other in the process of breathing.

Lung-structure and disorders

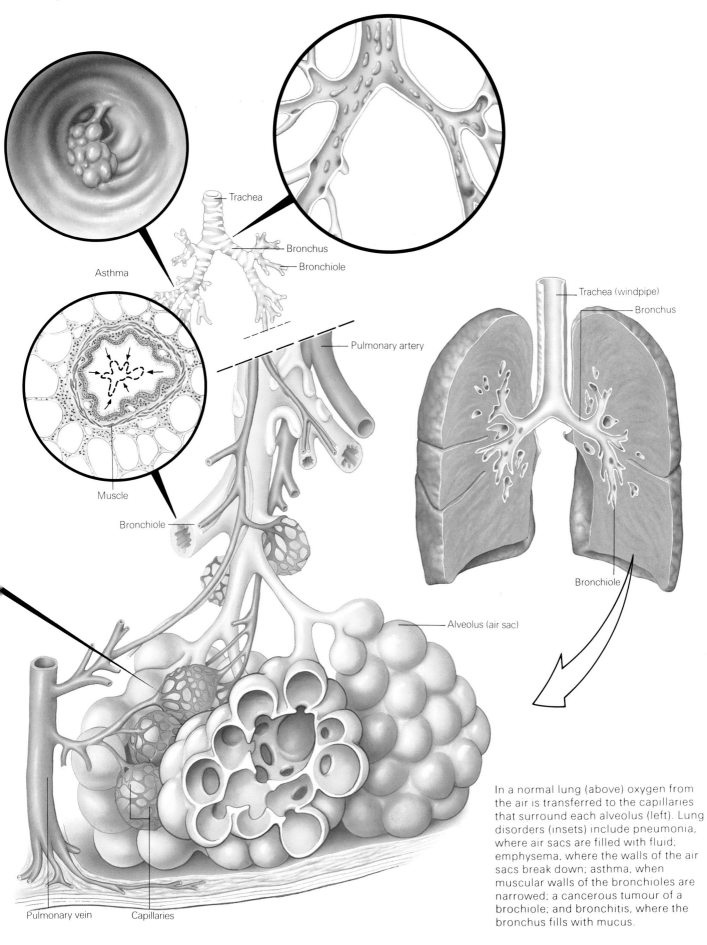

Asthma

Trachea

Bronchus

Bronchiole

Muscle

Bronchiole

Pulmonary artery

Trachea (windpipe)

Bronchus

Bronchiole

Alveolus (air sac)

Pulmonary vein

Capillaries

In a normal lung (above) oxygen from the air is transferred to the capillaries that surround each alveolus (left). Lung disorders (insets) include pneumonia, where air sacs are filled with fluid; emphysema, where the walls of the air sacs break down; asthma, when muscular walls of the bronchioles are narrowed; a cancerous tumour of a brochiole; and bronchitis, where the bronchus fills with mucus.

Breathing

Awake or asleep we breathe an average of 12 times a minute, and in 24 hours we breathe in and breathe out more than 8000 litres (282 cu ft) of air. During heavy physical exercise, the breathing rate will increase considerably: up to 80 times a minute.

The purpose of moving so much air in and out of the body is to enable the lungs to do two things: to extract the oxygen needed to sustain life and to rid the body of the carbon dioxide, the waste product of internal chemical processes.

Oxygen makes up about a fifth of the air that we breathe, and the work of the lungs, the heart and the blood vessels is primarily concerned with carrying oxygen from the air to the body's tissues, where it is needed to produce the energy that the body requires in order to stay alive.

Just as a car burns petrol with oxygen, and a coal fire uses both coal and the oxygen in a room to produce heat, so the body's cells use oxygen in exactly the same way: they burn up their fuel – which usually comes in the form of sugar – with oxygen to produce energy. The waste products of this chemical reaction are the same in both the body's cells and the car – namely carbon dioxide and water.

Although some of the body's cells are able to function for a while without oxygen, the brain cannot.

As we breathe, most of the work is done by the diaphragm, a sheet of muscle and fibrous tissue that forms a complete wall between the chest and the abdomen. The ribs provide the upper part of the cage that encloses the heart and lungs and the diaphragm forms the bottom.

If you were to look at the diaphragm from above, you would see a large central fibrous portion, connected by muscle fibres to the inside of the lower six ribs. This looks rather like the sun, with rays spreading out towards the rib cage to anchor it. From the front, the diaphragm appears as a dome, attached by muscular strings to the inside of the ribs.

The muscular fibres of the diaphragm contract when we breathe in, and flatten the 'dome' of the diaphragm, drawing the highest central part down into the abdomen. This increases the volume of the lungs and draws air into them through the trachea, nose and mouth. Once in the lungs, the air travels to the alveoli, where the exchange of oxygen and carbon dioxide takes place. Oxygen is taken up by the haemoglobin in the

blood and the red blood cells discharge their load of carbon dioxide back into the alveoli to be exhaled by the lungs. Breathing out happens by simple relaxation of the muscles, with the air being driven out in much the same way as when you let go of a balloon.

Like any other muscle, the diaphragm receives instructions to contract or relax from the nervous system. The nerves which supply the diaphragm are called the left and right phrenic nerves. Oddly enough, these nerves arise from high in the spinal cord, and because of this have to make a fairly long journey from the neck down to the bottom of the chest. The phrenic nerves can be damaged by injury or disease.

Breathing rates

The rate of breathing is controlled by the respiratory centre of the brain, the medulla oblongata, and is regulated according to the levels of carbon dioxide in the blood, rather than the amount of oxygen present. The brain will respond to an increased production of carbon dioxide, such as when the body undergoes physical exercise, and adjust the breathing rate accordingly. Breathing will become deeper and faster so that more oxygen is inhaled, stimulating the heartbeat, blood flow will increase and the carbon dioxide will be burned off. Once the exercise ceases, the carbon dioxide level falls and breathing will return to normal.

Voluntary alterations in breathing rates occur during talking, singing and eating. Yawning, sighing, coughing and hiccuping involve still other kinds of respiration. Laughing and crying, both long breaths followed by short bursts of exhalation, are respiratory changes due to emotional stimuli.

Holding your breath, either deliberately (when swimming under water), or unwittingly (as a result of an attack of nerves) also alters the breathing pattern. The carbon dioxide level falls after the first few deep breaths, which are then held, and the brain ceases to be stimulated. This can lead to a blackout and, when swimming underwater, death by drowning if the person cannot return to the surface.

The diaphragm

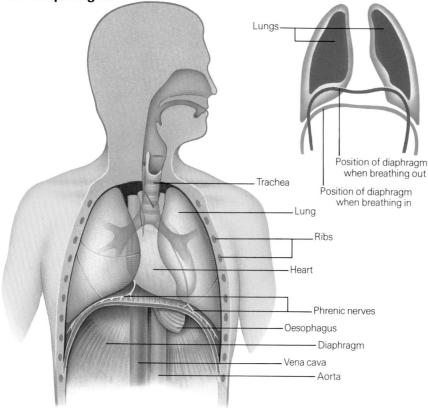

Lungs

Position of diaphragm when breathing out

Position of diaphragm when breathing in

Trachea

Lung

Ribs

Heart

Phrenic nerves

Oesophagus

Diaphragm

Vena cava

Aorta

The diaphragm separates the chest from the abdomen and controls the volume of the lungs as air is inhaled and exhaled.

How oxygen is carried around the body

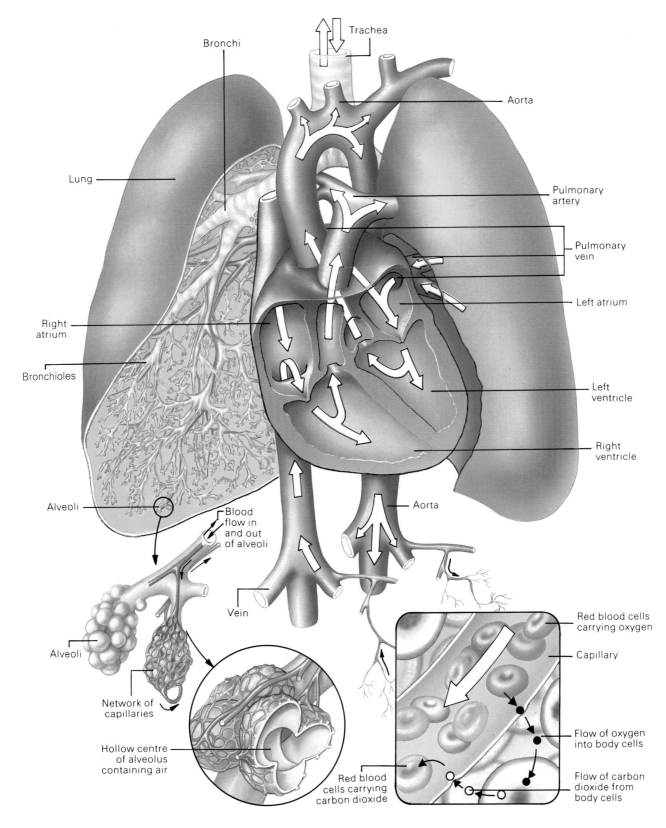

Bronchi

Trachea

Aorta

Lung

Pulmonary artery

Pulmonary vein

Left atrium

Right atrium

Bronchioles

Left ventricle

Right ventricle

Alveoli

Blood flow in and out of alveoli

Aorta

Vein

Alveoli

Red blood cells carrying oxygen

Capillary

Network of capillaries

Flow of oxygen into body cells

Hollow centre of alveolus containing air

Red blood cells carrying carbon dioxide

Flow of carbon dioxide from body cells

Above: Air inhaled via the trachea, bronchi and bronchioles reaches the alveoli where oxygen from the air is transferred to the capillaries surrounding each alveolus. The oxygenated blood is carried to the pulmonary vein and into the left side of the heart and pushed into the aorta. Blood then proceeds around the body, through arteries to the capillaries. The oxygen carried by the red blood cells is given to the tissue cells which transfer their waste product, carbon dioxide, to the red cells. This is carried back through the veins into the right side of the heart and finally the blood flows out through the pulmonary artery and into the lung. At the site of the alveoli the circulating blood gives up its carbon dioxide which is exhaled, and takes in oxygen again.

CHAPTER 7

CARDIO-VASCULAR SYSTEM

The cardio-vascular system consists of the heart and the network of blood vessels. Composed almost entirely of muscle, the heart is responsible for pumping blood around the body. Blood not only transports nutrients and gases from one part of the body to another, it also acts as a means of communication by conveying chemical messages in hormones from the endocrine glands to organs and tissues.

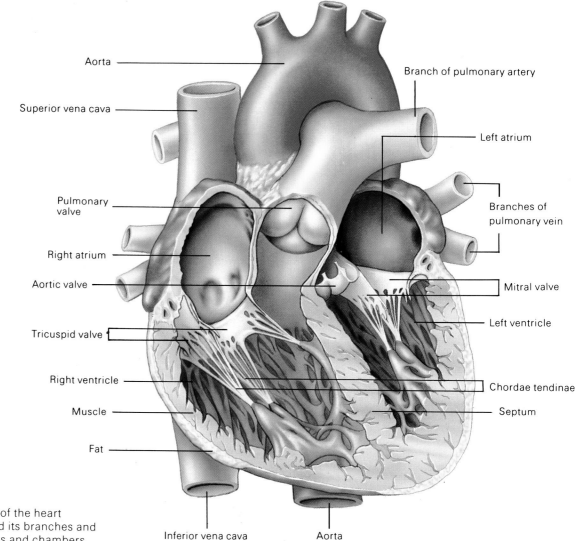

Aorta

Superior vena cava

Pulmonary valve

Right atrium

Aortic valve

Tricuspid valve

Right ventricle

Muscle

Fat

Branch of pulmonary artery

Left atrium

Branches of pulmonary vein

Mitral valve

Left ventricle

Chordae tendinae

Septum

Inferior vena cava

Aorta

Right: Cross-section of the heart showing the aorta and its branches and the major valves, veins and chambers.

Blood

Blood is essential to body function. It is pumped by the heart round the interior network of arteries and veins, from before birth until death, delivering oxygen, food and other essential substances to the tissues and, in return, extracting carbon dioxide and other waste products that might otherwise poison the system. Blood also helps to destroy disease-producing micro-organisms, and through its ability to clot, it acts as an important part of the body's natural defence mechanism.

Blood is not simply a fluid. Its proverbial thickness is due to the presence of millions of cells whose activities make it as much a body tissue as bone or muscle. It consists of a colourless liquid called plasma in which float red cells (also known as erythrocytes), white cells, or leucocytes, and very small cells called platelets.

Like so much of the body, plasma consists mainly of water. Since it is a liquid it can diffuse through the walls of small blood vessels such as the capillaries. It is therefore directly connected with the extra-cellular fluid – the fluid that actually bathes the surface of all the body's cells. This means that minerals and other substances can be carried from cell to cell throughout the body via the plasma.

Plasma

The plasma is a vehicle for the transport of the body's important fuels such as glucose and basic fats. Other substances that are carried in the plasma include iron, which is essential for the formation of the oxygen-carrying pigment haemoglobin, and a number of important hormones such as thyroid hormone. Plasma therefore consists of a water solution of minerals, foods and small amounts of essential compounds such as hormones plus one other essential component – the protein that makes up a major part of it.

Each litre of plasma contains about 75 gm (2½ oz) of protein. This is divided into two main types: albumin and globulin. Albumin is manufactured in the liver. As well as being a source of food for the tissues, it provides the osmotic pressure that keeps the fluid part of the blood inside the blood vessels and stops it flooding out into the tissues and then into the cells. Albumin can be thought of as a sort of circulating liquid sponge that keeps necessary water in the bloodstream and stops the body degenerating into a soggy, jelly-like mass.

Possibly the most important of the globulins are those that act as antibodies against infection. In addition, some protein globulins are active in the formation of blood clots, together with the cells.

Platelets

Platelets are the tiniest cells in the body. One millilitre of blood contains about 250 million platelets, and each platelet cell is about three microns across (a micron is about one-thousandth of a millimetre).

Platelets have one basic function: to make the blood clot when bleeding has to be stopped. Recently doctors have become intrigued by the way platelets work, because evidence is accumulating that they may be very important in arteriosclerosis – harden-

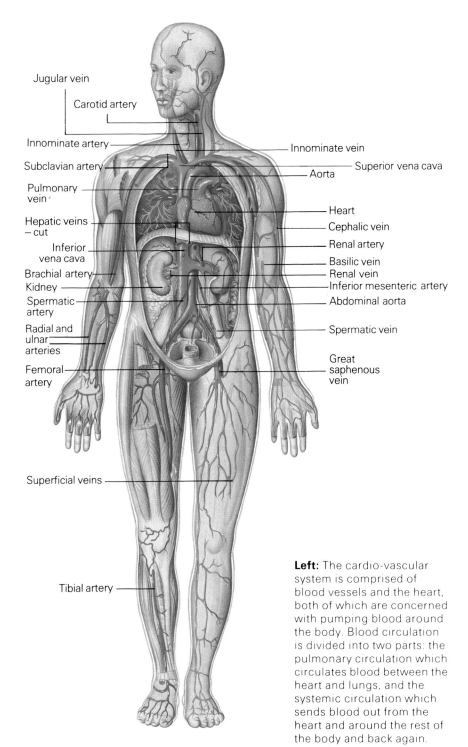

Jugular vein
Carotid artery
Innominate artery
Subclavian artery
Pulmonary vein
Hepatic veins – cut
Inferior vena cava
Brachial artery
Kidney
Spermatic artery
Radial and ulnar arteries
Femoral artery
Superficial veins
Tibial artery

Innominate vein
Superior vena cava
Aorta
Heart
Cephalic vein
Renal artery
Basilic vein
Renal vein
Inferior mesenteric artery
Abdominal aorta
Spermatic vein
Great saphenous vein

Left: The cardio-vascular system is comprised of blood vessels and the heart, both of which are concerned with pumping blood around the body. Blood circulation is divided into two parts: the pulmonary circulation which circulates blood between the heart and lungs, and the systemic circulation which sends blood out from the heart and around the rest of the body and back again.

ing of the arteries - a disease that is endemic in the western world.

Since there are so many platelets in the blood, there are always going to be a large number near the site of any bleeding that may occur.

The walls of a blood vessel are normally lined with a smooth pavement of cells called the epithelial cells. Once this pavement is broken - that is, bleeding occurs - the constituents of the blood come into contact with other parts of the blood vessel wall. This contact stimulates the platelets to stick to the wall, and to each other, so that a plug is formed which stops the bleeding. After this, other constituents of the blood interact to form fibrin, which effects a more permanent repair of the injury.

The ability of the blood to clot, or coagulate, and so prevent bleeding to death if a blood vessel is severed, comes from the combined action of the platelets and a dozen biochemical substances, called clotting factors, among which is the important substance called prothrombin. These factors are found in the fluid part of the blood - the plasma. Defects of the clotting process are of two kinds - failure of clots to form, and thrombosis, in which blood clots form in the vessels.

Red blood cells
The red blood cells act as transporters, taking oxygen from the lungs to the tissues. Having done this, they do not return empty but pick up carbon dioxide, a waste product of cell function, and take it back to the lungs, from where it is breathed out. They are able to do this because they contain millions of molecules of a substance called haemoglobin.

In the lungs, oxygen combines very quickly with the haemoglobin to give the red cells the bright red colour from which their name is derived. Carried in the arteries, this 'oxygenated' blood arrives at the tissues. With the help of enzymes in the red cells, carbon dioxide and water, which is another waste product of cell activity, are locked on to the red cells and taken back to the lungs in the veins.

The production of red blood cells begins in the first few weeks after conception and for the first three months, manufacture takes place in the liver. Only after six months of foetal development is production transferred to the bone marrow, where it continues for the rest of life. Until adolescence, the marrow in all the bones makes red blood cells, but after the age of about 20, red cell production is confined to the bone marrow in spine, ribs and breastbone.

Red blood cells begin their life as irregular, roundish cells known as haemocytoblasts, with huge nuclei. These cells then go through a rapid series of divisions during which the nucleus becomes progressively smaller and then is lost altogether. For red cell manufacture, the body needs iron - the major constituent of the substance - haemoglobin, vitamin B_{12}, folic acid and proteins.

In their travels round the bloodstream the red cells are subjected to enormous wear and tear and so need constant renewal. Each red cell has an average life of 120 days. After this, cells made in the bone marrow and spleen attack those blood cells that are worn out. Some of the chemical remains are immediately returned to the plasma for re-use, while others, including haemoglobin, are sent to the liver for further destruction.

The body has a remarkable ability

Below: In the case of a wound, injured blood vessels bleed and platelets (small sticky cells in blood) rush to the site to help seal it (A). Tissue-clotting factors are released and plasma factors enter the area (B). The reaction of the platelets, both types of factors and other clotting agents convert fibrinogen (a protein) into strands of fibrin. This becomes a jelly-like mesh across the break (C). Platelets and blood cells trapped in this mesh ooze out serum (blood without clotting factors) which helps form a scab (D). This prevents bacteria entering and causing an infection.

to control the number of red cells in circulation, according to its needs. If a lot of blood is lost, if parts of the bone marrow are destroyed or if the amount of oxygen reaching the tissues is decreased through heart failure or because a person is at a high altitude, the bone marrow immediately begins to increase red blood cell production. And even strenuous daily exercise stimulates extra red cell output because the body has a regular need for more oxygen. Counts of blood cells show that athletes can have twice as many red blood corpuscles as people living sedentary lives.

White blood cells
The white cells in the blood, leucocytes, are bigger than, and very different from, their red counterparts. Unlike red cells, white cells do not all look alike and are capable of moving with a creeping motion. Involved in the body's defence against disease, white cells are classified into three main groups known technically as polymorphs, lymphocytes and monocytes.

The polymorphs, which make up 50 to 75 per cent of the white cells, are also subdivided into three kinds. Most numerous are those called neutrophils.

When the body is invaded by disease-causing bacteria, these go to work. Attracted by chemicals released by the bacteria, they 'swim' to the site of infection and start to engulf the bacteria. As they do this the granules

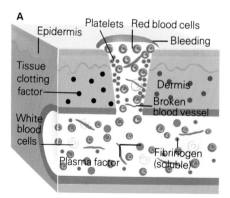

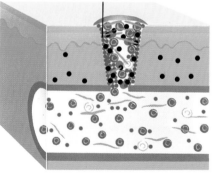

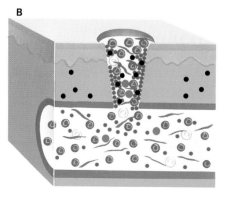

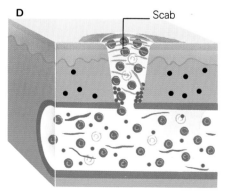

inside the neutrophils begin to make chemicals which destroy the trapped bacteria. The familiar pus that collects at the site of an infection is the result of the work of the polymorphs and is largely made up of dead white cells.

The second kind of polymorphs are known as eosinophils because their granules become stained pink when blood is mixed with the dye eosin. Composing only one to four per cent of the white cells, eosinophils combat bacterial attack but also have another vital role. When any foreign proteins or antigens get into the blood, substances called antibodies are made to combine with the antigens and neutralize their effects. While this is going on, the chemical histamine is released. The eosinophils damp down the effects of histamine, for if too much is made, the result can be an allergic reaction. And once the antibodies and antigens have combined, the eosinophils remove the chemical remains.

The third type of polymorphs are the basophils. They make up less than one per cent of all the white cells, but are essential to life because their granules make and release heparin which works to stop the blood from clotting inside the vessels.

Lymphocytes

Making up about 25 per cent of the blood's white cells are the lymphocytes, which all have dense, spherical nuclei or centres. Lymphocytes play a vital role, giving the body its natural immunity to disease. They do this by making antitoxins to counteract the potentially damaging effects of the powerful toxins (poisons) or chemicals produced by some bacteria. The other essential task of the lymphocytes is to make antibodies and the chemicals which help prevent body cells from succumbing to bacterial invasion. Last of the white cells are the monocytes, which form up to eight per cent of the white cells. The largest monocytes contain large nuclei which engulf bacteria and remove the cell debris resulting from bacterial attack.

The activity of polymorphs and monocytes in dealing with disease-carrying bacteria is called an inflammatory response – inflammation being the body's response to injury at a local level. The activity of lymphocytes in dealing with invading microorganisms and other substances is known as the immune response. (This is discussed in more detail in Chapter 8.) Both responses may be activated at the same time.

Where white cells are made

The bone marrow is also the site of some white blood cell manufacture. All three types of polymorphs are made here, from cells called myelocytes, again by a series of divisions. The average polymorph lives only 12 hours and only two or three hours when the cells are involved in fighting bacterial invasion. In such circumstances, the output of all white cells is increased to meet the body's demands. The lymphocytes, which live on average 200 days, are formed in the spleen and in areas such as the tonsils and the lymph glands scattered throughout the body. Both monocytes and platelets are made in the bone marrow. The length of monocyte life is still a mystery, for they seem to spend part of their time in the tissues, and part in the plasma, but in a never-failing production line the body manages to replace all its millions of platelets on average about once every four days.

Although bleeding, whether internal or external, is always a situation that should be taken seriously, the body's in-built survival mechanisms ensure that a person can lose as much as a quarter of all his or her blood without suffering any long-term ill effects, even if a blood transfusion is not given. And because blood is the supply line to and from the tissues, it is not surprising that body disorders and diseases show up via alterations in the blood. Apart from being a reflection of the body's state of health, the blood itself can be the site of a whole range of disorders affecting the red cells, white cells, platelets and plasma, each of which requires identification and treatment.

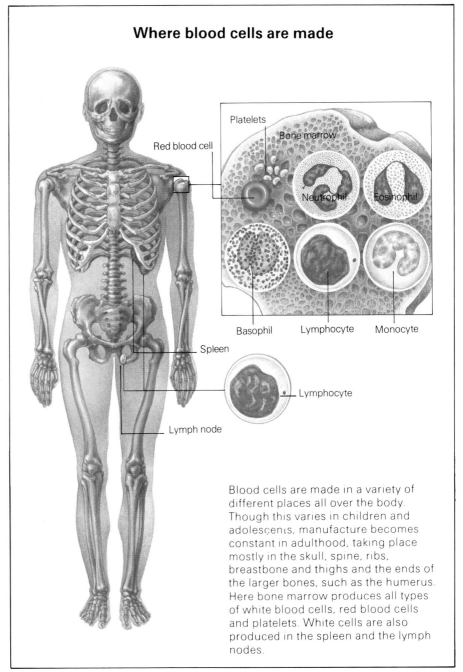

Where blood cells are made

Platelets

Bone marrow

Red blood cell

Neutrophil

Eosinophil

Basophil   Lymphocyte   Monocyte

Spleen

Lymphocyte

Lymph node

Blood cells are made in a variety of different places all over the body. Though this varies in children and adolescents, manufacture becomes constant in adulthood, taking place mostly in the skull, spine, ribs, breastbone and thighs and the ends of the larger bones, such as the humerus. Here bone marrow produces all types of white blood cells, red blood cells and platelets. White cells are also produced in the spleen and the lymph nodes.

The Heart

The heart is a large muscular organ in the middle of the chest. Although it is often thought of as being in the left-hand side of the body it actually straddles the mid-line with more of it on the left than the right. It weighs about 12 oz (340 gm) in men and a little less in women.

The right-hand border of the heart lies more or less behind the right-hand border of the breastbone. On the left side of the breastbone the heart projects out as a sort of rounded triangle with its point lying just below the left nipple. This point can be felt pulsating with each heartbeat. It is called the apex beat.

The job of the heart is to pump blood around two separate circulations. First it pumps blood out into the arteries via the aorta, the central artery of the body.

This blood circulates through the organs and tissues delivering food and oxygen to them. The blood then returns to the heart in the veins, having had all the oxygen absorbed from it.

The heart then pumps the blood on its second circuit, this time to the lungs to replace the oxygen. It is then returned to the heart with its oxygen renewed.

There are four main chambers in the heart operating the pumping arrangement. Each chamber is a muscular bag with walls which contract to push blood onward. The thickness of the musclar wall depends on the amount of work the chamber has to do. The left ventricle has the thickest walls as it does the largest share of the pumping.

The chambers are arranged in pairs, each having a thin-walled atrium which receives blood from the veins. Each atrium pumps the blood through a valve into a thicker-walled ventricle which pumps the blood into a main artery.

The two atria lie behind and above the two ventricles. Both the atria and both the ventricles lie side by side. The portions of their walls which separate them are called the interatrial and interventricular septums.

How it works

Blood returns to the heart from the lungs in the pulmonary veins with its oxygen store renewed. It goes into the left atrium which contracts and pushes the blood through a valve called the mitral valve into the left ventricle.

The left ventricle then contracts and as it does so the mitral valve shuts so the blood can only go out through the open aortic valve into the aorta. It then goes on into the tissues where it gives up its oxygen.

The blood returns to the heart from the body in a large vein, the inferior vena cava, and from the head in the superior vena cava. It goes into the right atrium. This contracts and the blood passes through the tricuspid valve into the right ventricle.

A right ventricular contraction sends it out into the pulmonary artery, through the pulmonary valve, and through the lungs, where it has its oxygen renewed. It then returns to the heart in the pulmonary veins ready to start all over again. This process is repeated 50-60 times every minute.

The valves

Like so many pumps, the heart depends on a series of valves to work properly. On the right-hand side are the pulmonary and tricuspid valves; on the left-hand side are the aortic and mitral valves. The four valves open and close automatically to receive and discharge blood from and to the chambers, so that it can flow in only one direction.

The pulmonary and aortic valves are similar in structure. They have three leaf-like cusps, or leaflets, and are made of tough but thin fibrous tissue. The mitral and tricuspid valves are more complicated, though they are similar in structure. The mitral valve has two leaflets; the tricuspid valve three.

Each of these valves sits in a ring between the atrium and the ventricle. The bases of the leaflets are attached to the ring, while the free edges touch each other and close the passage between the ventricle and atrium when the valve is closed. These free edges are also attached to a series of fine strings – called the chordae tendineae

The heart's pumping action

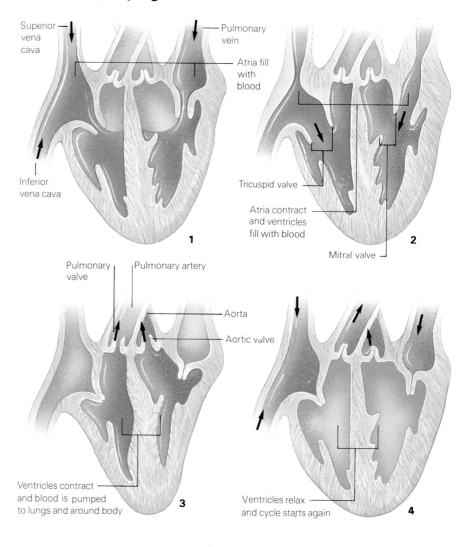

Superior vena cava

Pulmonary vein

Atria fill with blood

Inferior vena cava

1

Tricuspid valve

Atria contract and ventricles fill with blood

Mitral valve

2

Pulmonary valve

Pulmonary artery

Aorta

Aortic valve

Ventricles contract and blood is pumped to lungs and around body

3

Ventricles relax and cycle starts again

4

- which pass down into the ventricle and stop the valve from springing back into the atrium when under pressure.

Timing system

With each heartbeat the two atria contract together and charge up the ventricles with blood. Then the ventricles both contract.

This ordered series of contractions depends upon a sophisticated electrical timing system.

The basic control comes from the sinuatrial node which is in the right atrium. Impulses pass from it through both atria and make them contract. There is another node, the atrioventricular, at the junction of the atria and ventricles.

This delays the impulse to contract and then passes it down through a bundle of conducting fibres in the intraventricular septum called the Bundle of His. After passing though the bundle, the impulse spreads out into the ventricles causing them to contract after the two atria.

Valves-viewed from above

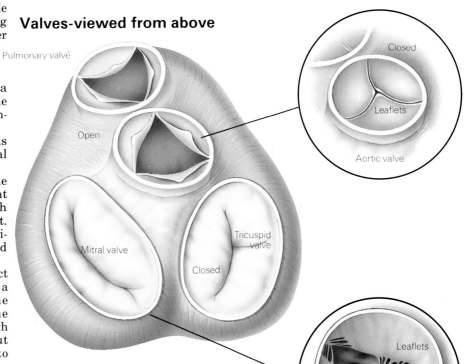

Position of valves viewed from the front

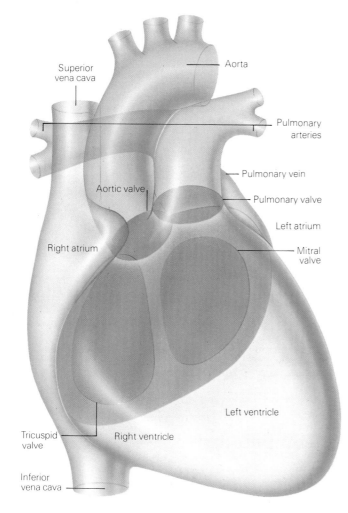

The valves ensure that blood travels in only one direction through the heart by preventing backflow. They consist of two or three 'leaflets' which close off when blood has passed through. The mitral and aortic valves govern the flow of oxygenated blood on the left side of the heart; the tricuspid and pulmonary valves control the passage of deoxygenated blood on the right.

Blood Vessels

The arteries and veins are the two sorts of large blood vessels in the body. The arteries are like pipes, carrying blood outwards from the heart to the tissues while the veins carry the blood on the return journey.

The main pumping chamber on the left side of the heart, the left ventricle, ejects blood into the main artery of the body – the aorta. The first of the aorta's branches arise from it as soon as it leaves the heart. These are the coronary arteries which supply blood to the heart itself.

Almost as soon as it branches off the aorta, the left coronary artery splits into two big branches. So there are, in effect, three coronary arteries: the right and the two branches of the left. They go on to completely encircle and penetrate the heart, supplying blood to every part of it. The rest of the body's arteries carry blood to all the other parts of the body, dividing first into branches called arterioles, and finally into capillaries.

The left ventricle generates a considerable pressure to force the blood through the arterial network. The tightness which the inflatable cuff, used in taking blood-pressure, around your arm reaches is the same as the maximum squeeze in the left ventricle with each heartbeat.

The structure of arteries

Since the arteries are subjected to this force with each heartbeat, they have to be thick-walled to cope with the pressure. The outer wall of an artery is a loose, fibrous tissue sheath. Inside this there is a thick elastic and muscular sheath which gives the artery its strength. There are also rings of muscle fibres encircling the artery in among the elastic tissue (the endothelium). The inner layer of the artery is made of a smooth layer of cells which allows the blood to flow freely.

The thick elastic walls are most important to the way in which the system works. Much of the force of each heartbeat is taken up in the elastic walls of the large arteries. They continue to push the blood forward in the pause between each heartbeat.

The body's pulses

When a doctor feels the pulse, he is feeling the action of the heart pumping blood with each beat around the body by means of the arteries.

The force of each heartbeat is transmitted along the arterial walls just as a wave travels across the surface of a lake. The walls of the arteries are

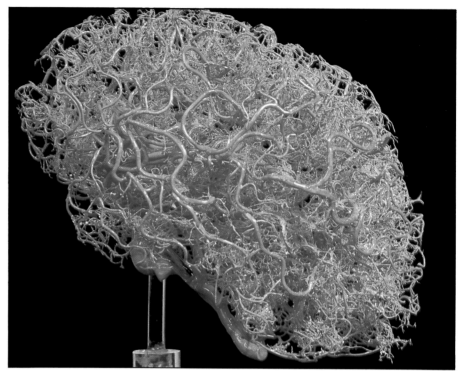

elastic and expand to take the initial force of a heartbeat. Later in the course of the beat they contract and in this way push blood smoothly along the system.

The pulse can be felt in a number of the arteries that lie near the surface of the body. The most common is the radial artery in the wrist which can be felt on the inner surface of the wrist just below the thumb. It is customary to feel this pulse with one or two fingers rather than the thumb, which has its own pulse and can therefore cause some confusion.

The brachial artery in the arm has a pulse which can likewise be easily felt on the inside of the elbow joint almost in line with the little finger.

A doctor may also examine the pulse in the neck created by the carotid artery. This pulse is located about 2.5 cm (1 in) below the angle of the jaw. He may listen to a major artery like the carotid with a stethoscope which can reveal a 'bruit' – a regular whooshing noise with each heartbeat. This may indicate a partial blockage of the artery even though the pulse feels quite normal.

There are also pulses in the groin, behind the knees, on the inside of the ankle and on top of the foot.

Capillaries

Measuring only about eight thousandths of a millimetre, the capillaries are only just wider than one single blood cell. Each capillary consists of a

This resin cast shows the vital network of vessels which supply blood to the brain. Brain cells die within a few minutes if starved of oxygenated blood.

very thin layer of tissue rolled up into a tube and surrounded by an equally thin membrane. All the capillary walls are thin enough to allow certain substances to pass in and out of the blood. Control of the capillaries is provided by muscles.

In addition to the exchange of substances, the capillaries located in the skin play a special role – they help to regulate body temperature.

When the body is hot, the skin capillaries get wider, making it possible for a larger-than-usual volume of blood to reach the skin where it can be cooled.

Being thin-walled, the capillaries can be damaged and those which are most at risk are the capillaries in the skin.

If the skin is cut or scratched, or receives a blow, the capillaries release their blood. A bruise is the after-effect of the capillary blood collecting in the skin.

Capillaries can be destroyed by burning, but they do have some ability to renew themselves. In old age, or as the result of excess alcohol over a long period, the capillaries may collapse, leaving purple patches or reddish lines.

After passing through the capillaries the blood returns towards the heart in the veins.

Veins

Veins are similar to arteries in that they are similarly distributed — the arteries and veins associated with a particular organ or tissue often run together. However, there are major differences. For example, many veins have valves in them which the arteries do not, and the walls of an artery are always thicker than those of a vein of corresponding size, while the central channel, or lumen, will be much bigger in the vein than the artery.

Veins are tubes of muscular and fibrous tissue. The wall of a vein is divided into an outer layer – the tunica adventitia; a middle layer of muscular fibre – the tunica intermedia; and an inner lining – the tunica intima. Veins contain only a very thin layer of muscle.

Right: The coronary arteries supply the heart muscle with the oxygen and nutrients it needs. There are essentially three main arteries – the two branches of the left coronary artery, and the right coronary artery.

Below: The arterial walls are made up of several muscular layers which propel the blood smoothly along the arteries with each heartbeat. This action can be felt most easily at the radial pulse which is located in the wrist.

Coronary arteries

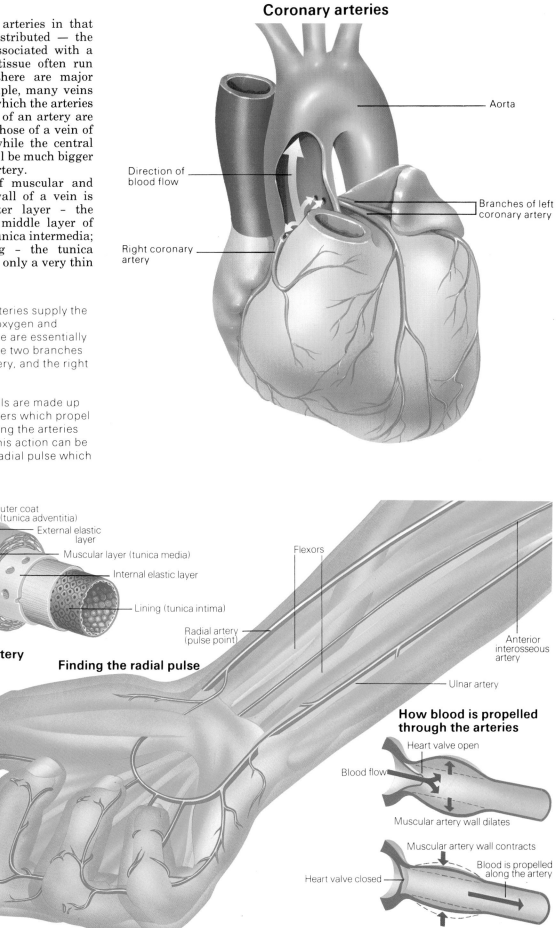

Aorta

Direction of blood flow

Branches of left coronary artery

Right coronary artery

The structure of an artery

Outer coat (tunica adventitia)
External elastic layer
Muscular layer (tunica media)
Internal elastic layer
Lining (tunica intima)

Finding the radial pulse

Flexors

Radial artery (pulse point)

Anterior interosseous artery

Ulnar artery

How blood is propelled through the arteries

Heart valve open

Blood flow

Muscular artery wall dilates

Muscular artery wall contracts

Blood is propelled along the artery

Heart valve closed

Structure and function of the arteries

Blood Circulation

Blood starts its journey around the body by leaving the left ventricle through the aorta. At this stage the blood is rich in oxygen, food broken down into molecules and other important substances such as hormones.

After giving rise to the coronary arteries, the aorta passes upward before doubling back on itself in an arch. Originating from this arch are the two main arteries to the head, the left and right carotid arteries, and one artery to each arm. The aorta descends down the chest and into the abdomen.

In the abdomen there are three main arteries to the intestines and the liver, and one to each kidney before the aorta divides into the left and right iliac arteries which supply blood to the pelvis and the legs.

From the arteries the blood flows into the smaller arterioles which lead to every organ and tissue in the body including the heart itself, and then enters the vast network of capillaries.

In the capillaries, the blood cells jostle along in single file, giving up oxygen and other substances and taking in carbon dioxide and other waste products.

When the body rests, blood tends to flow through so-called preferential, or preferred, channels. These are capillaries that have become larger than average. But if extra oxygen is needed by any particular part of the body, blood flows through nearly all the capillaries in that area.

After passing through the capillaries from the arteries, blood enters the venous system. It first passes into very small vessels called venules which are the venous equivalent of arterioles. It then makes its way into small veins and back towards the heart along veins which are large enough to be seen under the skin. Veins of this size contain valves which prevent blood from flowing back towards the tissues. The valves have little half-moon shaped cups projecting into the lumen of the vein that make the blood flow in only one direction.

All the veins from the various parts of the body eventually merge into two large blood vessels, one called the superior, the other called the inferior vena cava. The first collects blood from the head, arms and neck and the second receives blood from the lower part of the body. Both veins deliver blood to the right side of the heart and from here it is pumped into the pulmonary artery (the only artery to carry blood with no oxygen). This artery takes the blood to the lung.

The final stage of the journey is for the now oxygen-rich blood to flow through the pulmonary vein (the only vein to carry oxygenated blood) into the left side of the heart.

The circulation to the lungs is called the pulmonary circulation and the one to the rest of the body is called the systemic circulation. There are pulmonary and systemic arteries which carry the blood outwards from the heart and pulmonary and systemic veins which return it.

Short cuts

On leaving the intestines, blood does not flow directly back to the heart but is drained into what is known as the hepatic portal system of veins. This allows the blood, which may be rich in digested food, to be carried directly to the liver.

Once blood from the intestines reaches the liver, it passes in among the liver cells, in special capillaries called sinusoids, and then enters another system of veins called the hepatic veins. These eventually lead on to the inferior vena cava, and thus into the heart. This system ensures that food passed into the venous system from the intestines is brought to the liver in the most efficient way.

Other areas where there are special kinds of venous structure are in the extremities: the hands, feet, ears and nose. Here it is possible to find direct

The arterial system

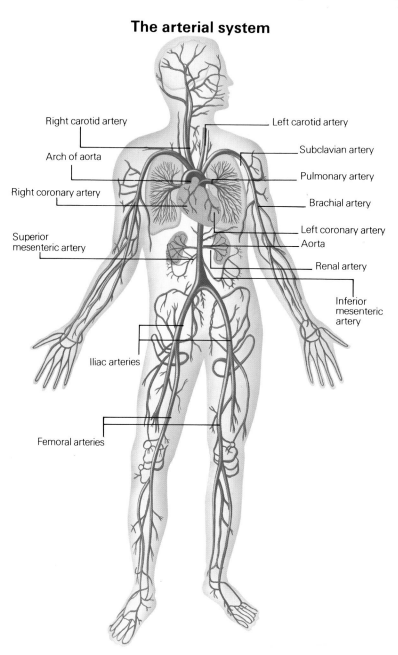

Right carotid artery

Arch of aorta

Right coronary artery

Superior mesenteric artery

Iliac arteries

Femoral arteries

Left carotid artery

Subclavian artery

Pulmonary artery

Brachial artery

Left coronary artery

Aorta

Renal artery

Inferior mesenteric artery

Vein networks

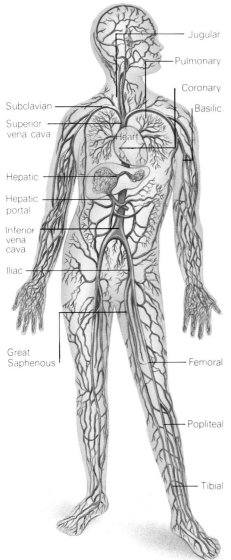

communications between the small arteries and veins, where blood may flow through from one to the other without having to go through a system of capillaries in the tissues. The main function of these arterio-venous connections is to do with control of body temperature. When they are open, heat loss increases and the body cools.

Failsafe mechanism
In some parts of the body, such as the arms and legs, arteries and their branches are joined so that they can 'double up' on each other and form an alternative route for the blood if one is damaged: this is called a collative circulation.

When there is damage to an artery, the branch of the adjoining artery which has taken over grows wider to give a greater degree of blood circulation. If the body is put under physical stress, such as when suddenly breaking into a run, blood vessels in the leg muscles increase in size and those in

the intestine shut down so that the blood is directed to the site at which it is most needed. When you are resting after a meal the reverse process occurs. This is assisted by a series of circulatory by-passes called anastamoses.

Distribution and flow
The blood is not evenly spread throughout the system. At any given moment, about 12 per cent is in the arteries and veins which carry it to and from the lungs. About 59 per cent is in the veins, 15 per cent is in the arteries, 5 per cent in the capillaries and the remaining 9 per cent in the heart. Nor does the blood flow at the same rate in all parts of the system. It spurts from the heart and through the aorta at a brisk 33 cm (13 in) per second, but by the time it has reached the capillaries it has slowed down to a gentle 0.3 cm (about a tenth of an inch) per second.

The flow back through the veins gradually increases in speed so that blood is delivered back to the heart at 20 cm (about eight inches) per second.

Control of circulation
There is an area in the lower part of the brain, called the vasomotor centre, which controls blood circulation and hence the blood pressure. The blood vessels which are responsible for controlling the situation are arterioles and lie between the small arteries and the capillaries in the blood circuit. The vasomotor centre receives information about the level of your blood pressure from pressure-sensitive nerves in the aorta and the carotid arteries, and then sends out instructions to the arterioles.

Below: In the diagram, the deep leg veins are shown in dark blue and the superficial veins in light blue. A series of valves, opening and closing (rather like canal locks) in response to continual changes in the pressure of the circulating blood, ensure a constant flow (below). This counteracts the effects of gravity. The cross-section of the lower leg (bottom) shows the relative positions of the deep and superficial veins.

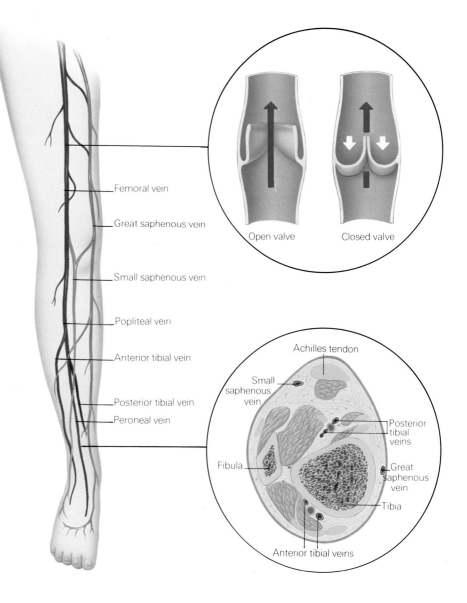

CHAPTER 8

LYMPH-VASCULAR SYSTEM

The lymph-vascular system is another of the body's systems of vessels that carry fluid around the body. Lymph vessels are concerned with conveying excess fluid, foreign particles and other materials from the body's tissues and cells. This system is therefore involved in dealing with waste and potentially harmful particles. In this it works closely with the blood, particularly with the white blood cells known as lymphocytes that are so essential to the body's defence against disease.

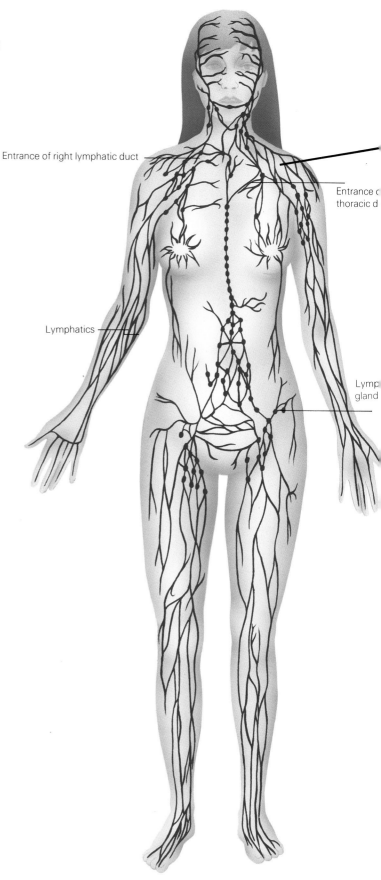

Entrance of right lymphatic duct

Entrance of thoracic d

Lymphatics

Lymp gland

Right: The lymphatic system consists of a network of fine vessels which collect surplus fluid (lymph) from the body's cells and tissues and return it to the bloodstream. The lymph vessels drain into special veins near the heart via the right lymphatic duct and the thoracic duct. The inset shows a section of a lymph node, a collection of tissue distributed in various parts of the body along the route of the lymph vessels.

Lymph Vessels

The lymph-vascular, or lymphatic system, is composed of lymph vessels and highly specialized lymphoid organs and tissues including the thymus, spleen and tonsils.

The small lymph vessels – the smallest are called lymph capillaries – run alongside the body's arteries and veins. They collect surplus fluid, known as lymph, from the tissues. The walls of lymph capillaries are very thin and highly permeable, so that large molecules and particles, including bacteria, that cannot enter the blood capillaries are also carried away in the lymph.

Some lymph vessels contain an involuntary muscle which contracts rhythmically in one direction, driving the lymph forwards. They also have valves to prevent the lymph from flowing backwards.

Lymph vessels are found in all parts of the body except the central nervous system, bone, cartilage and teeth. The constituents of lymph contained in the vessels is dependent on their location. For example, the vessels draining the limbs contain fluid surplus to body needs which is leaked from cells or blood vessels; the lymph is therefore rich in protein. However, the lymph in the intestines is full of fat called chyle which it has absorbed from the intestines during digestion. This lymph has a milky colour.

At various points along their pathways the lymph vessels join with a knot of tissue known as a lymph node (sometimes referred to as a lymph gland). It is from here that the white blood cells known as lymphocytes circulate around the body in both the blood and lymph vessels. The lymph nodes are found around major arteries and can be felt at those points where the arteries run close to the surface of the skin. For example they occur in the groin, the armpits and the neck.

In the lymph nodes, bacteria and other foreign particles that are present in the lymph entering the node are filtered off and destroyed. As the lymph leaves a node it picks up lymphocytes and antibodies – protein substances that inactivate foreign particles.

All the lymph vessels join together to form two large ducts, the thoracic duct and the right lymphatic duct, which drain into the innominate veins near the heart. Lymph is therefore drained from the tissues into the blood by the lymphatic system.

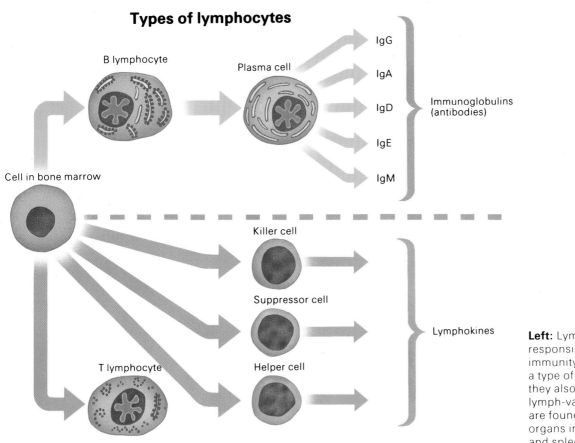

Types of lymphocytes

B lymphocyte

Plasma cell

IgG

IgA

IgD

IgE

IgM

Immunoglobulins (antibodies)

Cell in bone marrow

Killer cell

Suppressor cell

Lymphokines

Helper cell

T lymphocyte

Left: Lymphocytes are responsible for the body's immunity. Although they are a type of white blood cell they also have a role in the lymph-vascular system and are found in many lymph organs including the tonsils and spleen.

Organs and Tissues

The spleen is an integral part of the lymphatic system. Its main function is to act as a filter for the blood and to make antibodies; in addition, an enlarged spleen, which doctors can feel by palpating the walls of the abdomen, is often an indication of disease somewhere in the body and means further tests should be done.

The spleen lies just below the diaphragm at the top of the left-hand side of the abdomen. It is normally about 13 cm (5 in) long, and it lies along the line of the 10th rib. The spleen usually weighs about 200gm (about ½lb) in adults, but in cases where it is enlarged it can weigh up to 2kg (4½lb) or more.

If a spleen is examined with the naked eye, it will look like a fibrous capsule surrounding a mass of featureless red pulp. It may just be possible to make out little granulations which are called Malpighian corpuscles; in fact, these granulations actually are collections of lymphocytes.

The organ is supplied with blood via the splenic artery, which, like any other artery, splits first into smaller arteries and then into tiny arterioles. However, the arterioles of the spleen are unusual in that they are wrapped in lymphatic tissue as they pass through the pulp of the spleen. The arterioles are unique in one other way: instead of being connected to a network of capillaries, they seem to empty out directly into the substance of the spleen itself.

The odd way in which the spleen is supplied with blood is what enables it to perform two of its basic functions. First, the fact that the arterioles are wrapped with lymphatic tissue means that the lymphatic system comes into immediate contact with any abnormal protein in the blood, and forms antibodies to it. Second, the way that the blood empties directly into the pulp of the spleen also allows the reticular cells of the organ to come into direct contact with the blood which should be discarded. At the same time, it filters the blood of any old or worn out cells.

Functions of the spleen

The spleen is one of the main filters of the blood. Not only do the reticular cells remove the old and worn-out blood cells, but they will also remove any abnormal cells. This applies in particular to red blood cells, but white cells and platelets are also filtered selectively by the spleen when it is necessary.

The spleen will also remove abnormal particles floating in the bloodstream. It therefore plays a major part in ridding the body of harmful bacteria, to give just one example. It is also instrumental in making antibodies – proteins circulating in the blood which bind on to and immobilize a foreign protein, so that white blood cells called phagocytes can destroy it. The Malpighian corpuscles make the antibody.

In some circumstances the spleen has a very important role in the manufacture of new blood cells. This does not happen in the normal adult, but in people who have a bone marrow disease the spleen and the liver are major sites of red blood cell production. In addition to this, the spleen manufactures a great deal of the blood of a foetus while it is in the uterus during gestation.

Feeling the spleen

The spleen cannot be felt in normal healthy people, but there is a large range of diseases that cause enlargement of the spleen, which can then be felt through the walls of the abdomen. The procedure is simple: with the patient lying on his back, the doctor starts to feel (or palpate) the bottom of the abdomen, and then works up towards the top left-hand corner. The spleen moves as the patient breathes, so he is asked to take deep breaths so that this movement can be felt.

Enlargement of the spleen can also be detected on X-rays or by using a radioactive isotope scan.

The thymus

Over the last two decades it has become clear that the thymus sits at the centre of the remarkable web of interconnected organs and tissues that make up the lymphatic system and are involved in the immune response – that is, defending us from attack by sources of infection.

There is still considerable ignorance about exactly how the thymus does its

Below: The spleen is situated in the top left-hand corner of the abdomen, just below the diaphragm. It is in a relatively exposed position, which is why it is frequently damaged in accidents and has to be removed.

Position of the spleen

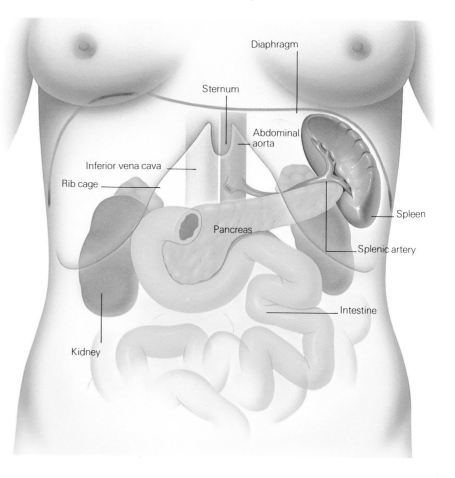

Size and location of the thymus

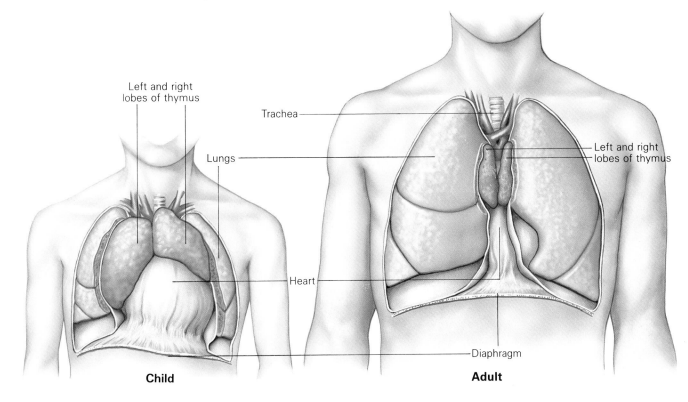

Left and right lobes of thymus

Trachea

Lungs

Left and right lobes of thymus

Heart

Diaphragm

Child

Adult

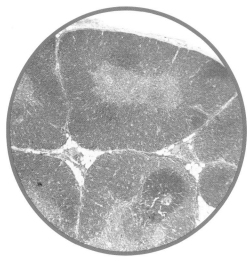

Top: The relative sizes of the thymus in an adult and a child graphically demonstrate its importance in establishing the body's immune system early on. In adulthood it actually shrinks. **Above:** A low-power magnification of a section through a normal thymus shows up some of its structure. The large purple masses which you see are the lobes of this vital organ.

job, but it is now known that it is essential for the proper running of the lymphatic system, and that it has really carried out its major function during the first few years of life.

The thymus is found in the upper part of the chest, where it lies just behind the breastbone. In a young adult it is a few centimetres long and weighs about 15 gm (½ oz). However, this simple statement conceals the most remarkable thing about the thymus, and that is the way that, quite unlike any other organ, it is at its largest at about the time of puberty when it may weigh up to 45 gm (1½ oz).

In a baby, the thymus is really very large compared to the rest of the body, and it may extend quite a long way down the chest behind the breastbone. It grows quite quickly until about the age of seven; after this the thymus continues to grow, but much more slowly until puberty.

After the age of puberty the thymus starts to shrink in size – a process called involution – until in an elderly person there may be no more thymus tissue present apart from a bit of fat and connective tissue.

Structure and function

The thymus contains many of the lymphocytes that are important in the body's defence against disease. These cells are found in the blood, the bone marrow, the lymph glands and the spleen, and they can be seen travelling into the tissues in an inflammatory reaction. (See page 89.)

The outer layer of the thymus, called the cortex, has many lymphocytes. Inside this is an area called the medulla which contains lymphocytes

in addition to other types of thymus cells.

There seems to be little doubt that in the early years of life the thymus is concerned with programming the way in which the body resists infection, and in particular, it seems that the thymus is responsible for making sure that the system does not turn its activities against the body's own tissues.

There are two main types of immune cells in the body and they are both different sorts of lymphocytes. The T or 'thymus' cell lymphocytes are under the control of the thymus and are responsible for the recognition of foreign substances and for many of the ways in which the body attacks them. The other sort of immune cell – the B lymphocyte – is responsible for actually manufacturing anti-bodies to foreign substances.

The exact ways in which the thymus goes about controlling its T lymphocytes are not known, but one important mechanism has come to light. It seems that about 95 per cent of the new types of lymphocyte that are made in the thymus are in fact destroyed there, before they ever have an opportunity to get out into the rest of the body. The probable reason for this is that they would have the potential for turning against the body itself, and the only cells that the thymus allows to develop are those which will attack outside or foreign substances.

Tonsils and adenoids

The tonsils are part of a ring of lymphoid tissue (Waldeyer's ring) which encircles the entrance to the food and air passages in the throat. Although they are present at birth they are relatively small, but grow rapidly during the first few years of life, only to regress after puberty. However, they do not disappear completely.

The tonsils' exact function is not known but it has been suggested that they play a significant role in maintaining the body's defence against disease. They are ideally situated to scrutinize ingested material and to react to those which pose a threat to the body. This immunity is given by the lymphocytes processed by the tonsils. In addition, the tonsils produce antibodies which deal with infections locally.

Almost everyone will have suffered an attack of tonsillitis at some time in life. The organism producing the infection is usually a streptococcus (a certain type of bacterium). When the tonsils are infected they become enlarged and inflamed with specks of pus exuding from their surfaces. Fortunately, the infection responds well to common antibiotics and improvement can be expected within 36 to 48 hours. Symptoms can be alleviated by eating soft foods and lots of liquids, and pain-killers such as aspirin both relieve the pain and reduce the body temperature.

Adenoids are lymph glands situated at the back of the nose just where the air passages join those of the back of the mouth or pharynx. The lymph involved in this system is the body's defence against infection and the lymph nodes, such as the adenoids, are full of infection-fighting cells, the white blood cells. The adenoids are so placed that any infection breathed in through the nose is filtered by them and - hopefully - killed. Sometimes, however, things can go wrong.

Adenoids are present from birth, but on the whole they disappear before puberty. They are most obvious from the age of one to four. This is because between these ages the child is continually exposed to new types of infection by bacteria and viruses.

Not a great deal is known about how the adenoids become infected, but any respiratory germ can affect them. Once they become damaged, chronic infection may set in. If the adenoids are recurrently inflamed, they tend to swell and this can give rise to ill-effects.

The immune response

The immune response is the body's reaction to the invasion of foreign substances by the mobilization of the white blood cells known as lymphocytes. While lymphocytes are initially produced in bone marrow they circulate through the body in both the blood and lymph vessels and are also present in the lymph nodes. They are

Position of the tonsils and adenoids

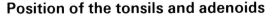

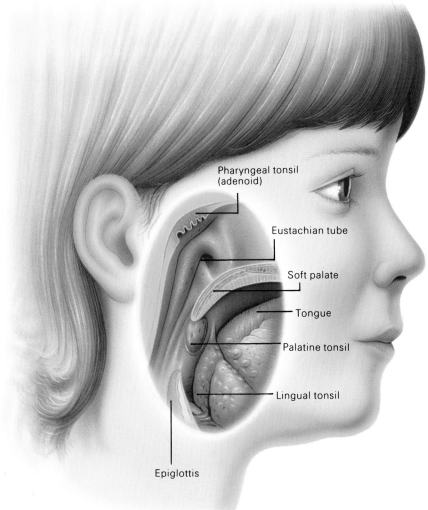

Pharyngeal tonsil (adenoid)

Eustachian tube

Soft palate

Tongue

Palatine tonsil

Lingual tonsil

Epiglottis

Left: The tonsils encircle the entrance to the food and air passages (above), suggesting a role of defence against infection. But when infected – the most common infection being tonsillitis – they become swollen and inflamed, making swallowing, and even breathing, difficult and painful.

How immunity-producing cells function

B Lymphocytes

T Lymphocytes

B lymphocyte (plasma cell) cell factory in bone marrow

Helper cell carries message to plasma cell

Attack by bacteria, microbes or viruses

Globulin 'tailor made' to kill or neutralize invader

Invader neutralized by globulin

Bloodstream

Attacking lymphocyte

Invader engulfed and destroyed by lymphocyte

Helper cell carries message to lymph node

T lymphocyte cell factory in lymph node

---

therefore constituents of two systems: the cardio-vascular and the lymphatic-vascular.

Lymphocytes develop into two types of cells. The first type, which makes antibodies, is known as the B lymphocyte, or B cell. The second, identical in appearance but with a different functin, is known as the T (thymus) cell, or T lymphocyte. There are two different types of T cells: those which assist B cells in the production of antibody, known as helper cells; and those called suppressor cells that prevent B cells from producing antibodies. B and T cells which destroy any invading tissue or organism are sometimes referred to as killer cells.

Much is yet to be learned about the nature and working of the immune response but some new information has come to light in recent years. It appears that when an invading organism enters the body it is taken either to a nearby lymph node or to the spleen by the lymph vessels.

Here monocytes differentiate, or develop, into cells called macrophages which surround and engulf (phagocytose) the organism and in some way present it to T and B cells. The T and B cells acquire a 'chemical memory', of the specific protein, or antigen, in the invading organism. Thereafter

these cells are said to be immunocompetent.

The immunocompetent T and B cells are therefore able to recognize the antigen the next time a similar invasion occurs. When this happens the T and B cells multiply to produce other T and B cells which have the ability to combat the antigen and render it harmless. In this way the body builds by an immunity to specific foreign substances.

B lymphocytes capable of dealing with foreign organisms differentiate to plasma cells, which produce gamma globulins, or antibodies. These combine with the antigen of the organism and destroy it. This process is known as the humoral (chemical) immune response. The production of T cells with the ability to deal with foreign organisms is called the cellular immune response.

Allergies and tissue rejection

The cellular immune response can produce adverse effects in cases where tissue from another individual is grafted on to or transplanted into the body. Here the introduced tissue is recognized as foreign by the lymphocytes, which react by invading the tissue and destroying it, a process often referred to as tissue rejection. Attempts

Above: Plasma cells, which arise from B lymphocytes, produce immune globulins which enter the bloodstream to ward off attack by bacteria, microbes and viruses. Like B lymphocytes, T lymphocytes, made in the lymph nodes, are alerted to attack foreign tissue and viruses by helper cells, which carry messages of invasion to developing lymphocytes. These develop a chemical memory of the specific protein, or antigen, of the invader, and, should they enter the body again, the lymphocytes can recognize and then destroy them. In this way the body builds up an immunity to specific viruses.

are made to overcome this problem in patients who have transplants by trying to match donor tissues with those of the recipient, or by treating with hormones.

Similarly, the humoral immune response can also work against the body. It will sometimes give rise to allergies. In such cases, normally harmless substances such as pollen grains incite the production of antibodies which are harmful because they bring about the release of certain substances, such as histamine, in the tissues. Once released these substances have disruptive effects on blood vessels and muscular tissues.

CHAPTER 9

DIGESTIVE SYSTEM

Digestion makes nutrients and energy-producing substances available to the body tissues and cells. The digestive system depends on a number of different organs, glands and their enzymes to change the food we put into our mouths into the separate components that can be readily taken up by the blood from the small intestine, to be carried away for immediate use or for storage.

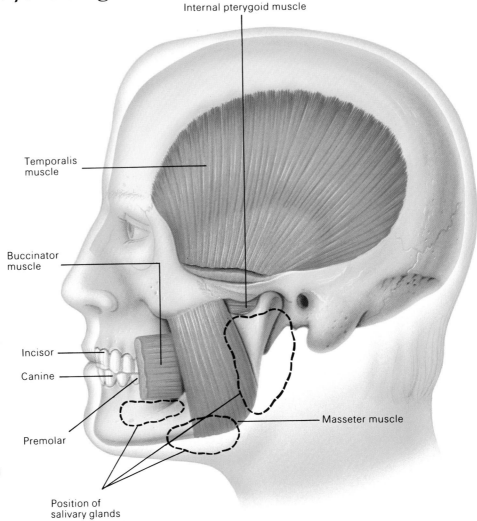

Internal pterygoid muscle

Temporalis muscle

Buccinator muscle

Incisor

Canine

Premolar

Position of salivary glands

Masseter muscle

Right: Mastication, or chewing, involves a series of facial muscles working in conjunction with the teeth, tongue and salivary glands. Biting is controlled by two muscles, the masseter and the temporalis; chewing by contractions of the buccinators which compress the cheeks and position the food in the mouth. The internal ptergoid muscles move the jaw sideways while the external ptergoids move it back and forth.

Digestion

Digestion is the process which breaks down food into substances that can be absorbed and used by the body for energy, growth and repair.

The digestive system depends on the action on the things we eat of substances called enzymes. These are produced by the organs attached to the digestive tract and they are responsible for many of the chemical reactions involved in digestion.

These changes begin in the mouth. When food is chewed, the salivary glands beneath the tongue step up secretion, and the enzyme ptyalin they produce starts breaking down some of the carbohydrates into smaller molecules known as maltose and glucose.

Food then travels down the oesophagus and into the stomach where the mixture of chemicals - mucus, hydrochloric acid and the enzyme pepsin - is poured on to it. Ptyalin stops working, but a new series of chemical reactions begins, triggered off by nerve impulses.

The amount of stomach juices released is governed both here and in the intestine by nerve impulses, the presence of food itself and the secretion of hormones.

The hormone gastrin stimulates the stomach cells to release hydrochloric acid and pepsin after food is in the stomach, so that it can be broken down into peptones. Mucus secretion prevents the stomach lining from becoming damaged by acid. When the acidity reaches a certain point, gastrin production ceases.

In the small intestine

The food leaving the stomach - a thickish, acidic liquid called chyme - then enters the duodenum, the first part of the small intestine. The duodenum makes and releases large quantities of mucus, which protects it from damage by the acid in the chyme and other enzymes. The duodenum also receives digestive juices from the pancreas, and considerable quantities of bile, which is made in the liver and stored in the gall bladder until needed.

Right: The alimentary canal is a muscular tube about 10m (33ft) long which starts at the mouth and ends at the anus. The canal is actually a part of two different systems. The first, the digestive system, involves the structures from the mouth to the end of the small intestine. The second, from the large intestine to the anus, is concerned with expelling undigested wastes from the body and is part of the excretory system.

Alimentary canal

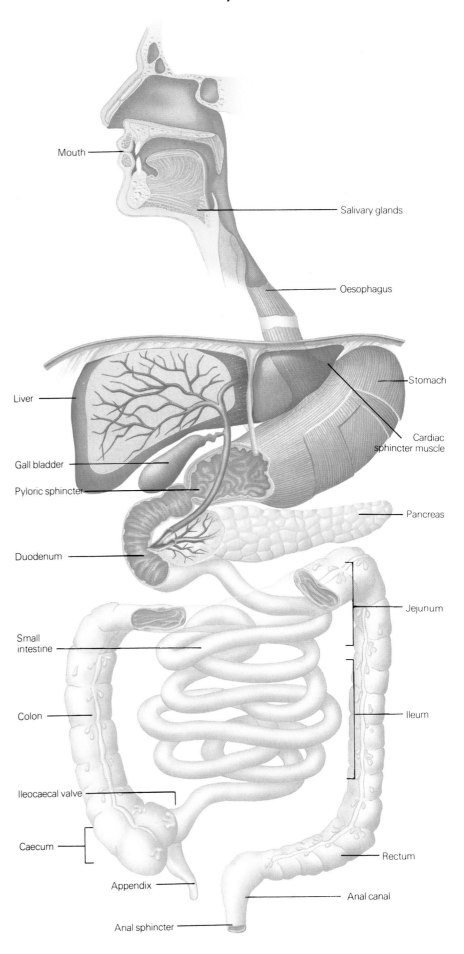

Mouth
Salivary glands
Oesophagus
Liver
Stomach
Cardiac sphincter muscle
Gall bladder
Pyloric sphincter
Pancreas
Duodenum
Small intestine
Jejunum
Colon
Ileum
Ileocaecal valve
Caecum
Rectum
Appendix
Anal canal
Anal sphincter

Two hormones trigger the release of pancreatic juices. The hormone secretin stimulates the production of large quantities of alkaline juices which neutralize the acidic, partially digested chyme. Pancreatic enzymes are produced in response to the release of a second hormone, pancreozymin. Bile is also released into the duodenum from the gall bladder in order to break down fat globules.

Pancreatic enzymes help the digestion of carbohydrates and proteins, in addition to fats. These enzymes include trypsin, which breaks the peptones into smaller units called peptides; lipase, which breaks fat down into smaller molecules of glycerol and fatty acids; and amylase, which breaks down carbohydrates into maltose.

The digested food then enters the jejunum and ileum, further down in the small intestine, where the final stages of chemical change take place. Enzymes are released from cells in small indentations in the walls of the jejunum and ileum which are known as the crypts of Leiberkühn.

Most food absorption takes place in the ileum which contains millions of minute projections called villi on its inner wall. Each villus contains a capillary, and a tiny blind-end branch of the lymphatic system known as a lacteal. When digested food comes into contact with the villi, the glycerol, fatty acids and dissolved vitamins enter the lacteals, are carried through into the lymphatic system and they are then poured out into the bloodstream.

Amino acids from protein digestion and the sugars from carbohydrates, plus vitamins and important minerals such as calcium, iron and iodine are absorbed directly into the capillaries in the villi. These capillaries lead into the hepatic portal vein which transports the food directly to the liver. This, in turn, filters out some substances for its own use and storage, and the remainder of these substances passes out into the body's general circulation.

Breaking down starch

One of the tasks of the digestive system is to break down starch-based carbohydrates, such as potatoes and bread, into individual sugar molecules. This process starts in the mouth, where there is a starch-splitting enzyme (or chemical ferment) called amylase, which is found in saliva. More amylase is mixed with food when it has passed down through the stomach into the intestine.

Amylase breaks the starch down into pairs of sugar molecules, which are then split by another series of enzymes in the small intestine, so

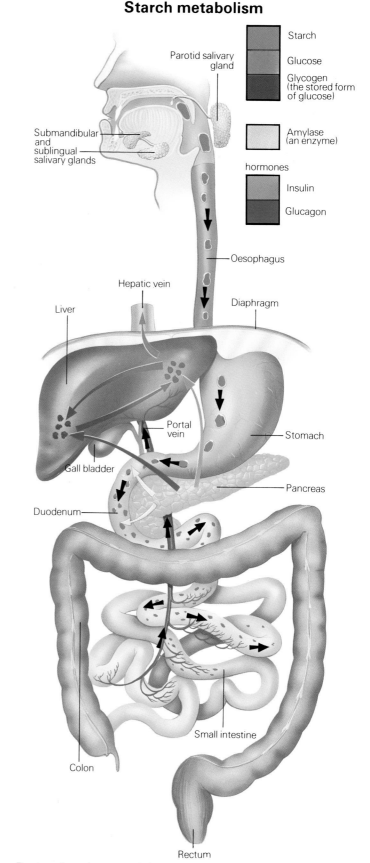

Starch metabolism

Starch

Glucose

Glycogen (the stored form of glucose)

Amylase (an enzyme)

hormones

Insulin

Glucagon

Parotid salivary gland

Submandibular and sublingual salivary glands

Oesophagus

Hepatic vein

Liver

Diaphragm

Portal vein

Stomach

Gall bladder

Pancreas

Duodenum

Small intestine

Colon

Rectum

Above: During digestion, starch is broken down into glucose by the enzyme amylase. Glucose is carried by the blood to the liver. If the level of glucose is high, insulin, a hormone from the pancreas, causes the free glucose to be converted into glycogen which is stored in the liver. When blood glucose levels become low, the pancreas releases another hormone, glucagon, which causes the stored glycogen to be released as glucose.

How the body uses glucose

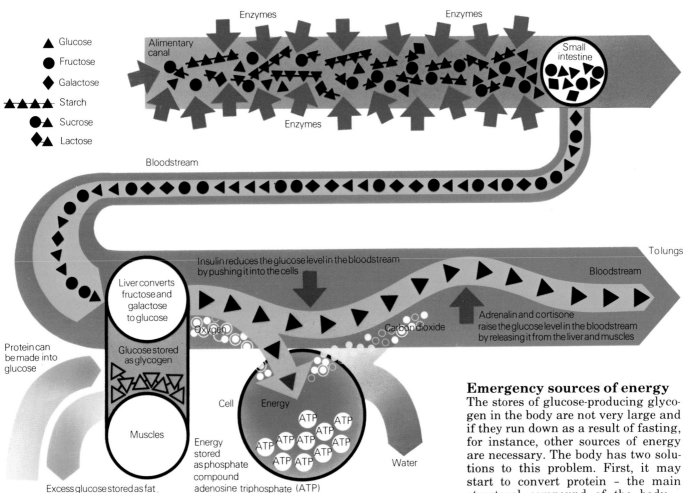

- ▲ Glucose
- ● Fructose
- ◆ Galactose
- ▲▲▲▲ Starch
- ●▲ Sucrose
- ◆▲ Lactose

Enzymes

Enzymes

Alimentary canal

Small intestine

Enzymes

Bloodstream

To lungs

Bloodstream

Insulin reduces the glucose level in the bloodstream by pushing it into the cells

Liver converts fructose and galactose to glucose

Oxygen

Carbon dioxide

Adrenalin and cortisone raise the glucose level in the bloodstream by releasing it from the liver and muscles

Protein can be made into glucose

Glucose stored as glycogen

Cell

Energy

Muscles

Energy stored as phosphate compound adenosine triphosphate (ATP)

ATP ATP ATP ATP ATP ATP ATP ATP

Water

Excess glucose stored as fat.

In digestion, enzymes break down carbohydrates into glucose, fructose and galactose, which are absorbed into the bloodstream in the small intestine. The liver transforms all these into glucose; it is stored as glycogen in the liver and muscles and released into cells to be used as energy (water is a by-product) or stored as ATP. Hormones control glucose in the blood.

that only individual sugar molecules are absorbed. Finally, the sugars are all carried to the liver in the bloodstream. The liver changes all the fructose and other similar compounds into glucose.

The body has many mechanisms which make sure there is an adequate level of glucose in the bloodstream to supply its needs. These depend on switching on or off the release of glucose that is stored in the liver. Glucose is stored as a compound called glycogen, which is a loose-knit mesh of glucose molecules. Glycogen is also stored in the muscles.

Once glucose is released into the blood, it is taken up by the cells. To do this, insulin is essential. Insulin, like

amylase, also comes from the pancreas, from special islands of tissue called islets of Langerhans. But, unlike amylase, it is secreted into the blood, not into the intestine.

When the glucose is inside the cells, it is burnt with oxygen to produce energy. Carbon dioxide and water are the waste products of this process. The carbon dioxide is carried in the blood to the lungs, where it is excreted back into the air, while the water simply joins the pool making up 70 per cent of the body weight.

Just as the liver stores glucose, in the form of glycogen, so the energy made from burning glucose has itself to be stored in each cell, to be used little by little to provide power for the chemical reactions on which the cell depends. The cells do this by creating high-energy phosphate compounds that are easily broken down to release the energy. These phosphate compounds (adenoisine triphosphate or ATP is the chemical name for the commonest) are like a battery that can be used and recharged at will, to supply small amounts of energy as they are needed. The recharging comes from burning glucose.

Emergency sources of energy

The stores of glucose-producing glycogen in the body are not very large and if they run down as a result of fasting, for instance, other sources of energy are necessary. The body has two solutions to this problem. First, it may start to convert protein – the main structural compound of the body – into glucose. Secondly, it may start to burn fat in the tissues instead of glucose. The fat provides just as good a source of energy as glucose, but in doing so produces extra waste products called ketones. (See page 116).

Control of glucose levels

Since glucose is such an important fuel, its level in the blood needs to be kept within fairly definite limits, if we are to remain in good health. Too high a level of blood glucose produces diabetes. If the glucose level falls too low, the brain can no longer function properly and loss of consciousness results – this is known as hypoglycaemia.

The blood glucose level in our bodies is kept constant by balancing the effect of insulin (which lowers blood glucose by pushing it into cells) with a whole range of other hormones, all of which tend to push the blood glucose up, by releasing glucose from the liver. The most important are adrenalin and cortisone, both of which come from the adrenal gland. Another, called growth hormone, comes from the pituitary gland in the brain. This also tends to increase the amount of glucose in the blood.

The Mouth

The human mouth is a kind of cavern containing the tongue and the teeth. It is bounded by the lips, while at its exit it links up with passages leading to the digestive tract and to the lungs. Because of this connection with two of the most vital body systems, the mouth is inevitably involved both in digestion and the process of breathing. It is also concerned with speech.

It is the lips that give the mouth its expression. They are made up of muscle fibres interspersed with elastic tissues and copiously supplied with nerves giving the lips their extreme sensitivity.

Covering the lips is a modified form of skin which is a kind of structural halfway house between the true skin which covers the face, and the membrane that lines the inside of the mouth. Unlike true skin the skin of the lips has no hairs, sweat glands or oil-secreting glands.

The mouth is lined with mucous membrane that contains glands which produce the slightly sticky clear fluid known as mucus. The continuous secretion of these glands keeps the inside of the mouth permanently moist, helped by the action of the salivary glands. The membrane lining the cheeks receives an enormous amount of wear and tear and has a remarkable capacity for regeneration.

Towards the front of the mouth, at the top, is the hard palate, with the soft palate towards the back. The hard palate, formed by the bottom of the upper jawbone or maxilla, allows the tongue to press against a firm surface and so enables food to be mixed and softened. The softness of the soft palate is essential as it enables it to move upwards as food is swallowed, and so prevents the food from being forced up into the nose, whose passages enter the back of the mouth.

Hanging down from the centre of the soft palate is a piece of tissue called the uvula or 'third tonsil'. Its true function is a mystery but some think that it forms an effective seal at the air passages when food is swallowed, so preventing choking.

The tongue

The tongue is shaped rather like a triangle – wide at the base and tapering almost to a point at its tip. It is attached at its base or root to the lower jaw, or mandible, and to the hyoid bone of the skull. At its sides the root is joined to the walls of the pharynx, the cavity that forms the back of the mouth.

The middle part of the tongue has a curved upper surface, while its lower surface is connected to the floor of the mouth by a thin strip of tissue, the frenulum. The tongue's tip is free to move but, when a person is not eating or speaking, it normally lies neatly in the mouth with its tip resting against the front teeth.

The actions of the tongue are determined by the muscles of which it is composed and to which it is joined, and by the way the tongue is fixed into position in the mouth.

The tongue itself contains muscle fibres running both longitudinally and from side to side, and these are capable of producing some movement, but the actions of the tongue are given a huge versatility by the contractions of a variety of muscles situated in the neck and at the sides of the jaws. The styloglossus muscle in the neck, for example, is responsible for bringing the tongue upward and backward, while the hyoglossus, also in the neck, brings it back down again into the normal resting position.

In eating, one of the tongue's main jobs is to present the food to the teeth for chewing and to mould softened food into a ball, or bolus, ready for swallowing. These actions are performed by a range of curling and up and down movements. When the task has been completed (or sooner in someone who gulps his food) the tongue pushes the bolus into the pharynx at the back of the mouth from where it enters the oesophagus and is swallowed into the stomach.

Salivary glands

Each day we all usually produce about 1.7 l (3 pt) of saliva – a watery secretion consiting of mucus and fluid. It contains the enzyme ptyalin that aids digestion and a chemical called lysozyme that acts as a disinfectant to help protect the mouth from infection. Saliva is therefore slightly antiseptic.

Saliva is produced by three pairs of glands sited in the face and neck: the parotids, the submandibulars and the sublinguals. There are also many smaller glands scattered around the mouth. Each salivary gland is composed of branching tubes that are packed together and lined with secretory cells. The function of the secreting cells varies between the glands and the fluids they produce are different.

The parotids are the largest of the salivary glands and are in the neck, sitting at the angle of the jaw and stretching up to the level of the cheekbone just in front of the ear. Saliva from the parotids empties into the cheeks from ducts that run forward from the glands themselves. Compared with the other salivary glands, the parotids produce a secretion that is watery and contains an increased amount of ptyalin – the enzyme that digests starch.

Section through tongue

Right: These illustrations demonstrate how the tongue is attached within the mouth (far right) and also show a close-up of its structure (right), including the papillae on its surface and the taste buds, salivary glands and muscle tissue below.

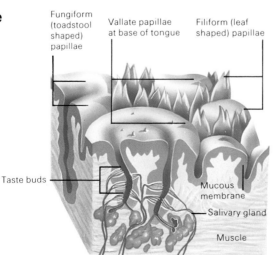

Fungiform (toadstool shaped) papillae

Vallate papillae at base of tongue

Filiform (leaf shaped) papillae

Taste buds

Mucous membrane

Salivary gland

Muscle

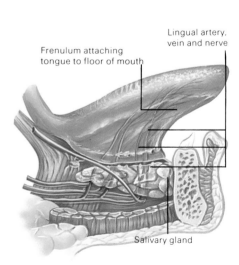

Frenulum attaching tongue to floor of mouth

Lingual artery, vein and nerve

Salivary gland

Structure of the mouth

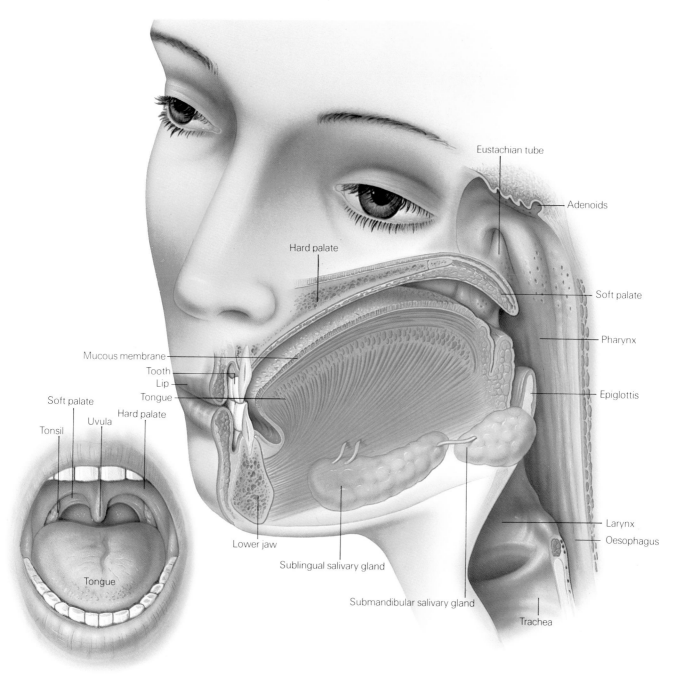

Eustachian tube

Adenoids

Hard palate

Soft palate

Pharynx

Mucous membrane

Tooth

Lip

Epiglottis

Tongue

Soft palate

Hard palate

Uvula

Tonsil

Tongue

Larynx

Oesophagus

Lower jaw

Sublingual salivary gland

Submandibular salivary gland

Trachea

Although the parotids are the largest glands they produce only about a quarter of the total volume of saliva. The submandibular glands, as their name suggests, lie under the jaw below the back teeth, and the sublinguals (also aptly named) lie under the tongue in the floor of the mouth. Both these pairs of glands discharge their contents at either side of the frenulum of the tongue (the small strip of tissue that sticks out from the base of the tongue and joins with the floor of the mouth). The sublingual glands mostly secrete a very sticky, mucus-filled saliva. The submandibulars produce a saliva that is about half-and-half

mucus and ptyalin-containing fluid and this makes up the bulk of the total volume of saliva secreted into the mouth over any period of time.

The role of saliva

The major function of saliva is to help in the process of digestion. It keeps the mouth moist and comfortable when we eat and helps to moisten dry food allowing it to be chewed and swallowed more easily. The mucus in saliva coats the bolus, and acts as a lubricant to help us to swallow.

The enzyme ptyalin secreted in saliva begins the first stage of digestion. It begins to break down starchy food

Above: The front view (left) shows what you see when you open your mouth and look in a mirror. Shown above are the deeper physical structures.

into simpler sugars, but its action is stopped by acid in the stomach. However, if the balls of food are large enough and well chewed then the acid fails to penetrate to the centre for some time and breakdown of starch continues.

Saliva also allows us to taste our food and drink. The sensation of taste is created by the many thousands of taste buds that are mainly situated in the mucous membranes of the tongue.

The salivary glands

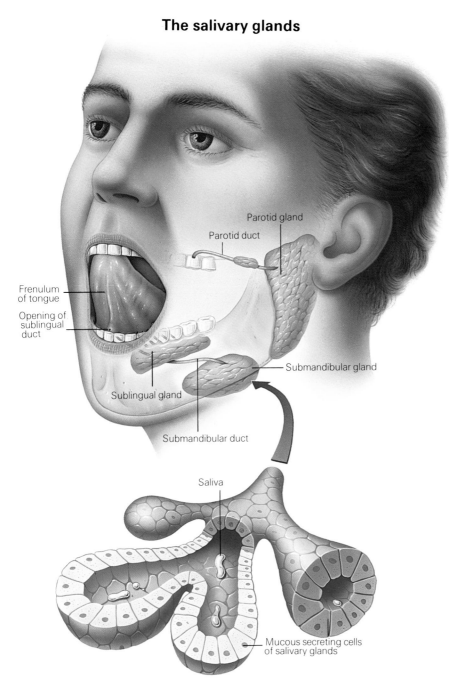

Parotid gland

Parotid duct

Frenulum
of tongue

Opening of
sublingual
duct

Submandibular gland

Sublingual gland

Submandibular duct

Saliva

Mucous secreting cells
of salivary glands

Above: Saliva enters the mouth along ducts leading from the glands. These empty into the upper part of the cheek and the floor of the mouth at a number of points. Saliva helps to keep the mouth moist and also moistens dry food. The enzyme ptyalin is present in saliva and this starts the process of digestion by breaking down starchy food. The effect of the enzyme on the breakdown of food usually stops in the stomach when acted upon by the stomach acids.

These taste buds, however, can only respond to liquids, and solid food in a dry mouth will produce no sensation of taste at all; it is essential for saliva to dissolve some of the food first. This fluid, containing food particles, can then wash over the taste buds which are chemically stimulated to send messages to the brain; the brain then interprets the flavour of the food.

Saliva is produced continually throughout the day and night at a slow rate; the amount being controlled by the autonomic nervous system that controls all our unconscious activity. But at various times the rate of salivation is altered by nervous stimulation. Stimulation of the sympathetic system reduces the flow of saliva; this is demonstrated by our mouths going

dry when we are nervous – speech can become difficult because our lips and tongue are not lubricated enough to move freely. On the other hand, increased salivation is a reflex action carried by the parasympathetic nervous system: the nerves that carry the sense of taste to the brain stimulate the flow of saliva when food is in the mouth. This is known as an inborn reflex but increased flow of saliva can also be created by the mere thought of food. So it is true that just looking at food can make your mouth water, and this is known as a conditioned reflex.

Teeth
The teeth are hard bone-like structures implanted in the sockets of the jaws. Two successive sets occur in a lifetime.

Each tooth consists of two parts: the crown, which is the portion visible within the mouth, and the root, which is the part embedded within the jaw-bone. The roots of the teeth are usually longer than the crowns. Front teeth have only one root, while those placed further back generally have two or three roots.

The major structural element of a tooth is composed of a calcified tissue known as dentine. Dentine is a hard bone-like material which contains living cells. It is a sensitive tissue and gives the sensation of pain when stimulated either thermally or by chemical means. The dentine of the crown is covered by a protective layer of enamel, an extremely hard cell-free and insensitive tissue. The root is covered with a layer of cementum, a substance that is somewhat similar to dentine and which helps anchor the tooth in its socket.

The centre of the tooth is in the form of a hollow chamber filled with a sensitive connective tissue known as the dental pulp. This extends from within the crown right down to the end of the root, which is open at its deepest part. Through this opening, minute blood vessels and nerves run into the pulp chamber.

Support of teeth
Each tooth is attached by its root to the jaw-bone; the part of the jaw which supports the teeth is known as the alveolar process. The mode of attachment is, however, complex and teeth are attached to the jaw by fibres known as the periodontal ligament. This consists of a series of tough collagen fibres which run from the cementum covering the root to the adjacent alveolar bone. These fibres are interspersed with connective tissue which also contains blood vessels and nerve fibres.

The mode of attachment of the teeth results in a very small degree of natural mobility. This serves as a kind of buffer which may protect the teeth and bone from damage when biting.

A zone of crucial importance in this system is at the neck of the tooth where the crown and root merge. In this region a cuff of gum is tightly joined to the tooth and serves to protect the underlying supporting tissues from infection and other harmful influences.

Types of teeth

There are two series of human teeth. Deciduous teeth are those present during childhood and all are usually shed. Deciduous teeth can be divided into three categories: incisors, canines (eye teeth) and molars. The permanent teeth are those which replace and also extend the initial series. These teeth can be divided into the same types as the deciduous teeth, and in addition there is a further category known as the premolars, which are intermediate both in form and position between canines and molars.

Incisors are characterized by a narrow blade-like incised edge. and the incisors in opposite jaws work by shearing past each other like the blades of a pair of scissors. Canines and pointed teeth are well adapted for a tearing action, while molars and premolars are effective at grinding food rather than cutting it.

Teeth form an even, oval-shaped arch with the incisors at the front and the canines, premolars and molars progressively placed further back. The dental arches normally fit together in such a way that on biting, the teeth opposite interlock each other.

Development of teeth

The first sign of the development of the teeth occurs when the foetus is only six weeks old. At this stage the epithelial cells of the primitive mouth increase in number and form a thick band which has the shape of the dental arch. At a series of points corresponding to individual teeth, this band produces bud-like in-growths into the tissue which the epithelium covers. These buds then become bell-shaped and gradually grow in such a way as to map out the shape of the eventual junction between enamel and dentine. Certain cells then go on to form the dentine, while others give rise to enamel.

The edges of the bell continue to grow deeper and eventually map out the entire roots of the teeth, although this process is not complete until about one year after the deciduous teeth have emerged. At birth the only sign of the occlusion is provided by the 'gum pads', which are thickened

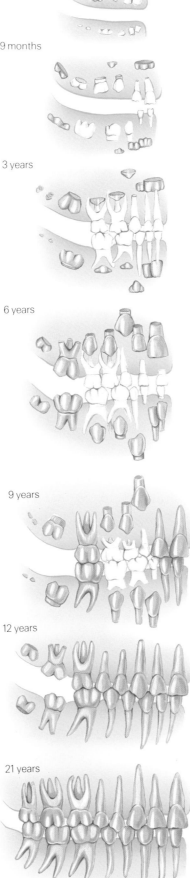

Birth

9 months

3 years

6 years

9 years

12 years

21 years

The deciduous, or milk teeth begin to erupt about half-way through the first year of life – a painful process for many infants. These first teeth are the lower incisors (cutting teeth), which are followed shortly by the upper incisors, canine teeth and molars, to make a full set of 20 deciduous teeth. Of the permanent teeth, the molars erupt before the others – around the age of six – and as the deciduous teeth are gradually lost the permanent teeth erupt behind them. By the early twenties, most people have a full set of permanent teeth. However, some 25 per cent of adults never develop wisdom teeth.

bands of gum tissue. Around the age of six months, the first of the lower incisors begins to come through the gum, a process known as dental eruption. The age at which this occurs is variable: a very few babies have teeth at birth, while in others they may not emerge until the age of one.

After the lower incisors have emerged, the upper incisors begin to erupt, and these are followed by canines and molars, although the precise sequence may vary. Teething problems may be associated with any of the deciduous teeth.

By the age of two-and-a-half to three, the child will usually have a complete set of 20 milk teeth. Ideally they should be spaced in such a way that provides room for the larger permanent teeth.

Subsequently, after the age of six, lower then upper deciduous incisors become loose and are replaced by the permanent teeth. The permanent molars develop not in the place of the deciduous molars but behind them. The first permanent molars come through at the age of 6, the second molars at the age of 12, and the third molars, or wisdom teeth, around the age of 18. There is, however, considerable variation in the timing of the emergence of all the teeth. About 25 per cent of people never develop one or more wisdom teeth. The reason for this may be an evolutionary one: as the jaw has got smaller, the number of teeth has lessened. Some wisdom teeth may never erupt through the gum and if they become impacted (wedged closely together under the gum) they may need to be removed. This happens in 50 per cent of people.

Deciduous and permanent teeth

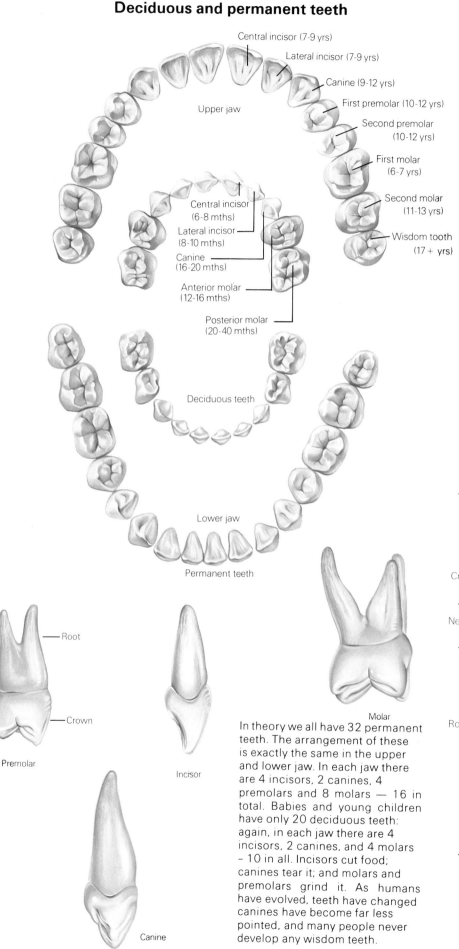

Central incisor (7-9 yrs)

Lateral incisor (7-9 yrs)

Canine (9-12 yrs)

First premolar (10-12 yrs)

Second premolar (10-12 yrs)

First molar (6-7 yrs)

Second molar (11-13 yrs)

Wisdom tooth (17+ yrs)

Upper jaw

Central incisor (6-8 mths)

Lateral incisor (8-10 mths)

Canine (16-20 mths)

Anterior molar (12-16 mths)

Posterior molar (20-40 mths)

Deciduous teeth

Lower jaw

Permanent teeth

Root

Crown

Premolar

Incisor

Molar

Canine

In theory we all have 32 permanent teeth. The arrangement of these is exactly the same in the upper and lower jaw. In each jaw there are 4 incisors, 2 canines, 4 premolars and 8 molars — 16 in total. Babies and young children have only 20 deciduous teeth: again, in each jaw there are 4 incisors, 2 canines, and 4 molars – 10 in all. Incisors cut food; canines tear it; and molars and premolars grind it. As humans have evolved, teeth have changed canines have become far less pointed, and many people never develop any wisdom teeth.

Changes in teeth arrangement

The part of the jaw that supports the milk teeth increases very little in size from the age when all the milk teeth have erupted. Milk teeth tend to be smaller than their permanent replacements and only when the large permanent incisors have erupted does the final form of the dental arches become apparent. The upper permanent incisors often appear out of proportion to the child's face when they first come through, but this naturally becomes less apparent as the face grows while the teeth remain the same size. Any tendency for the upper incisor teeth to protrude usually only becomes obvious when the milk teeth are replaced: the larger permanent teeth will exaggerate any discrepancy in their position. Similarly, crowding often only becomes clear when the permanent teeth erupt.

During the six years or so that it takes for the milk teeth to be entirely replaced by their 32 permanent successors, it is very common for a gap to appear between the upper incisors. This gap usually tends to close when the permanent canines erupt as they push the incisors together.

Cross-section of a molar

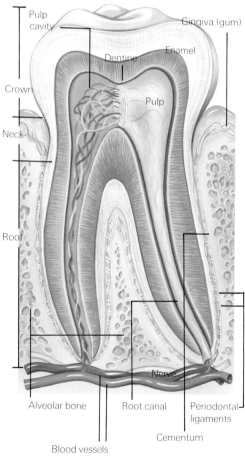

Pulp cavity

Gingiva (gum)

Dentine

Enamel

Crown

Pulp

Neck

Root

Nerve

Alveolar bone

Root canal

Periodontal ligaments

Cementum

Blood vessels

The Oesophagus and Stomach

The oral phase of digestion ends with the tongue pushing the bolus of food up against the roof of the mouth and into the muscle-lined cavity at the back of the throat – the pharynx – before entering the oesophagus.

The lowermost or laryngeal section of the pharnyx is involved entirely with swallowing. This section lies directly behind the larynx and its lining is joined to the thyroid and cricoid cartilages whose movements help to produce the sounds of speech. Squeezing actions of muscles help to propel mouthfuls of food through this part of the pharynx on their digestive journey.

The first part of swallowing is a voluntary act over which we have conscious control. Once the food has passed the back of the tongue, however, the continuation of the act of swallowing is an involuntary, automatic act.

The bolus of food does not just slide down the oesophagus into the stomach, it is actively pushed down by a series of wave-like contractions – a process called peristalsis. The passage of food is therefore an active process and not just a passive mechanism depending on gravity, which is why we can eat and drink, if we want to, just as well standing on our heads as sitting down.

Once food is in the pharynx, several activities take place within the space of a couple of seconds to prevent swallowing from interfering with breathing. The muscles of the pharynx contract, forcing the bolus of food towards the upper end of the oesophagus. At the same time, other throat and face muscles raise the tongue up against the roof of the mouth so that food does not go back into the mouth; they also move the soft palate (the non-bony part of the roof of the mouth) upwards to prevent food getting into the space at the back of the nose, and close the epiglottis over the raised larynx so that food can not get into the trachea and lungs and cut off the oxygen supply. Occasionally the epiglottis does not close in time and food or liquid does get into the larynx. When this happens the substance swallowed is immediately expelled by forceful coughing – the sensation we know as 'food going down the wrong way'.

The oesophagus

The top of the oesophagus lies immediately behind the trachea or windpipe. Just below the level of the notch at the top of the chest, the tube bends slightly to the left and passes behind the left bronchus. It then goes through the diaphragm and connects with the upper end of the stomach.

The oesophagus is an elastic tube about 25 cm (10 in) long and about 2.5 cm (1 in) in diameter. Like the rest of the alimentary tract, the oesophagus is made up of four layers – a lining of mucous membrane to enable food to pass down easily, a submucous layer to hold it in place, a relatively thick layer of muscle consisting of both circular and longitudinal fibres, and finally an outer protective covering.

The pharynx during swallowing

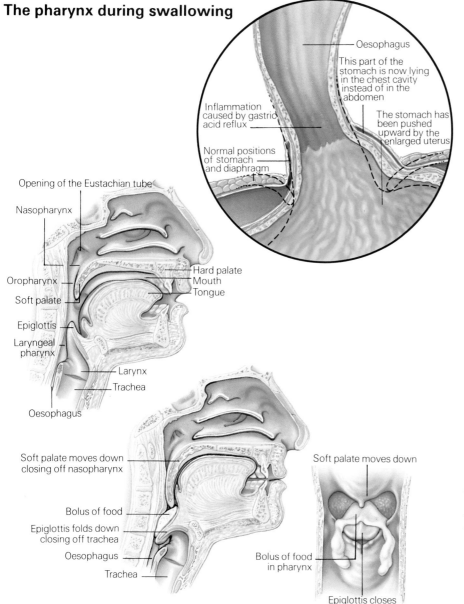

Oesophagus

This part of the stomach is now lying in the chest cavity instead of in the abdomen

The stomach has been pushed upward by the enlarged uterus

Inflammation caused by gastric acid reflux

Normal positions of stomach and diaphragm

Opening of the Eustachian tube
Nasopharynx
Oropharynx
Soft palate
Epiglottis
Laryngeal pharynx
Oesophagus
Hard palate
Mouth
Tongue
Larynx
Trachea

Soft palate moves down closing off nasopharynx
Bolus of food
Epiglottis folds down closing off trachea
Oesophagus
Trachea

Soft palate moves down
Bolus of food in pharynx
Epiglottis closes

Left above: Oesophageal reflux in pregnancy is most common during the last few months of gestation; the enlarged uterus pushes the top of the stomach up into the chest cavity causing the stomach contents to back up into the oesophagus.

Left below: When we swallow, food is pushed towards the oesophagus by the muscles of the oropharynx. The soft palate moves upwards to block off the entrance to the nasal passage and the epiglottis closes over the wind-pipe.

The stomach: site and structure

The stomach is situated higher up in the body than most people think – in fact, it is found just under the diaphragm. It is a muscular bag that acts as a reservoir for food, with a smooth, slippery outer coat and corrugated inner lining that is protected from its own acidic digestive juices by layers of mucus. The digestive juices reduce the food in the stomach to a mushy pulp, which then passes into the duodenum through a ring of muscle, the pyloric sphincter.

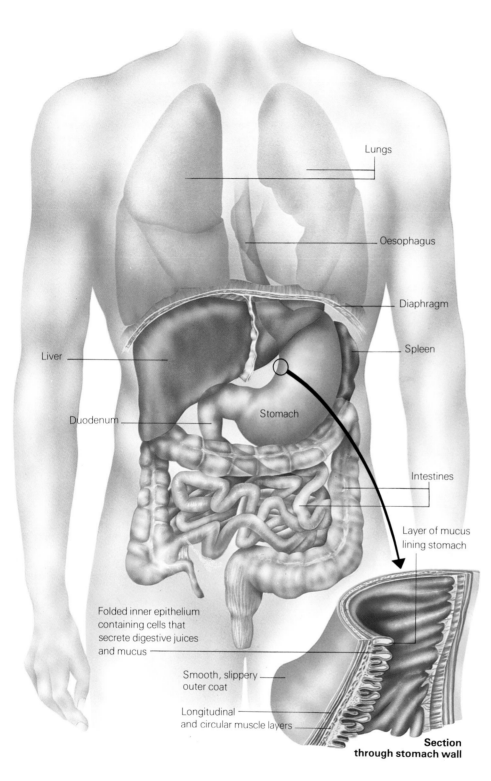

Lungs

Oesophagus

Diaphragm

Spleen

Liver

Duodenum

Stomach

Intestines

Layer of mucus lining stomach

Folded inner epithelium containing cells that secrete digestive juices and mucus

Smooth, slippery outer coat

Longitudinal and circular muscle layers

Section through stomach wall

There is no clear sphincter (constricting muscle ring such as that at the anus) that separates the oesophagus from the stomach; the stomach juices are normally kept in place by a combination of the muscular lining of the oesophageal walls and the fact that the tubular oesophagus gets pinched off as it passes through the diaphragm on its way from the chest to the abdomen. When this mechanism is inadequate then reflux will result.

Doctors use the word reflux to describe any circumstance where some sort of fluid in the body flows the wrong way. Although the reflux of acid contents of the stomach is perhaps the commonest problem of this sort, similar conditions can occur in various other systems.

It is very common for the acid contents of the stomach to flow back into the oesophagus, or gullet. In fact because it is so common it can be thought of as a normal event, but if it is excessive it can give rise to problems such as indigestion.

Reflux is actually commonest in infancy and old age although it also frequently occurs in the middle years of life. It may also cause a problem in pregnancy, because the womb tends to push the abdominal contents upwards.

The stomach

The stomach is a muscular bag situated in the upper part of the abdomen. It is connected at its upper end to the oesophagus (the gullet), and at its lower end to the duodenum (the first part of the small intestine). The wall of the stomach consists of a thick layer of muscle, lined with a special membrane called the epithelium.

First, the stomach acts as a reservoir for food. The lining membrane then produces a special juice which contains acid and enzymes to break down the food and thereby aid digestion. In the stomach the food is mixed together with the digestive juices until it has formed a pulp, which is then forced out into the duodenum. At the junction between the stomach and the duodenum there is a ring of muscle, the pyloric sphincter, which relaxes from time to time to allow the food to pass into the duodenum. The food is then pushed along the intestines to be further digested and absorbed.

The stomach exit is guarded by a muscle known as the pyloric sphincter, very like the mechanism at the stomach entrance, except that it is never completely closed. As the waves of peristalsis push chyme through the stomach, the sphincter lets out chyme in small amounts, which passes into the small intestine.

The Small Intestine

Joined to the lower part of the stomach, the duodenum is the first part of the small intestine and is important in the efficient digestion of food. It is a horseshoe-shaped tube curled round the head, or top, of the pancreas gland.

Two layers of muscle in the wall of the duodenum alternately contract and relax and so help to move food along the tube during digestion. Inside the muscle layers is the submucosa, containing many glands (called Brunner's glands) which secrete protective mucus. This helps to prevent the duodenum from digesting itself and from being eaten away by the acid mixture arriving from the stomach.

In the innermost layer of the duodenum, the mucosa, are glands which secrete an alkaline juice containing some of the enzymes needed for digestion. The juice also works to neutralize stomach acid. The cells of the mucosa are in constant need of replacement. They multiply faster than any other cells in the body: of every 100 cells, one is replaced every hour throughout life.

Digestion

The partially digested, liquefied food reaching the duodenum contains much hydrochloric acid. In the duodenum this acidity is neutralized by the secretions of the duodenum itself, and by the actions of bile and pancreatic juice which pour into the duodenum from the gall bladder and pancreas

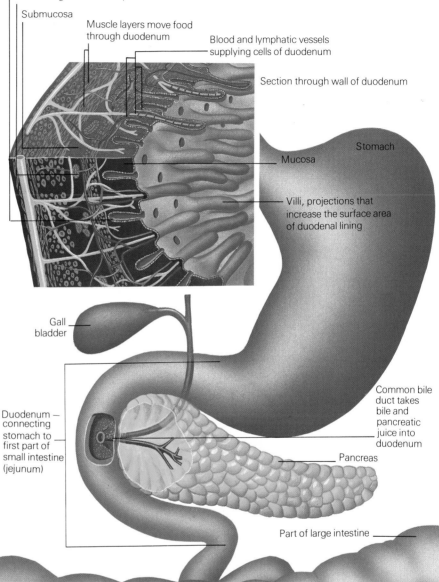

The duodenum

Crypts of Lieberkühn secrete digestive enzymes and alkaline juice to neutralize stomach acid

Brunner's glands secrete protective mucus

Submucosa

Muscle layers move food through duodenum

Blood and lymphatic vessels supplying cells of duodenum

Section through wall of duodenum

Stomach

Mucosa

Villi, projections that increase the surface area of duodenal lining

Gall bladder

Duodenum — connecting stomach to first part of small intestine (jejunum)

Common bile duct takes bile and pancreatic juice into duodenum

Pancreas

Part of large intestine

The small and large intestines

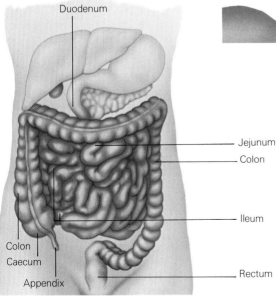

Duodenum

Jejunum

Colon

Ileum

Colon

Caecum

Appendix

Rectum

Above: A tube-like structure, the duodenum is the first part of the small intestine, receiving food from the stomach and carrying on the process of digestion by secreting enzymes which further break down food.

Left: The duodenum, jejunum and ileum make up the small intestine, the final structure of the digestive system. The large intestine is part of the alimentary canal, but is active only in the process of excretion.

through the common bile duct. These three juices continue the process of digestion.

The duodenum measures about 25 cm (10 in). Leading on from the duodenum is the jejunum which is about 2.5 m (8 ft) long before it merges with the ileum. There is no sudden break between the jejunum and the ileum, more of a gradual change. The jejunum has a diameter of about 3.8 cm (1½ in) while that of the ileum is slightly smaller. The jejunum also has thicker walls than the ileum, although they both consist of two muscular layers on the outside, and inner layers of mucosa which line the intestinal cavity or lumen.

The jejunum is attached to the back of the abdominal wall by a fan-like structure called the mesentery which is made up of two layers of peritoneum. It is while food is in the jejunum that its nutritive elements are absorbed into the blood. For this reason the jejunum has a highly efficient blood supply carried in numerous arteries and veins.

Position of the jejunum

The mesentery

Unlike the duodenum, which is more or less fixed firmly to the back of the abdominal wall, the jejunum and the ileum are supported on a membrane called the mesentery.

This fan-like structure consists of two layers of peritoneum. It is about 15 cm (6 in) long and is attached to the back wall of the abdomen. The end which supports the intestine is about 5.5 m (6 yd) long. The depth of the mesentery, measured from its base all the way out to the intestines is about 20 cm (8 in) – this allows both the jejunum and ileum some room in which to float about quite freely within the abdominal cavity.

Role of the jejunum

The jejunum provides the site where the useful nutritional elements of food are absorbed, leaving mainly water and food waste behind. The absorption process is then completed in the ileum.

In order to carry out this role, the jejunum has a very specialized interior designed to ensure that the greatest possible area is in contact with the lumen so that greater absorption can take place.

The interior of the jejunum consists of a series of circular folds. And if you were to look at this inner surface under a microscope, you would see that the whole surface is made up of delicate finger-like projections, called villi. Each villus measures approximately 1 mm. The surface in contact with digested food is increased yet further because the cellular surface of each villus is gathered into what is known as the 'brush border'.

Absorption of food

Since the jejunum is designed to allow the passage of food from the intestine into the blood, it needs an efficient blood supply. The arteries and veins which carry the blood to and from the walls of the jejunum run in the mesentery. The veins which drain the jejunum, like the veins draining the rest of the intestine, do not go straight back to the heart, but are gathered together to form the portal vein which drains into the liver. This means that food absorbed into the blood is delivered to the liver for processing before it goes into the rest of the body.

As well as absorbing food into the blood, some of the fatty constituents of the food are absorbed into the lymphatic system instead. Each villus has a central lymph channel or 'lacteal' which enables this to take place. This special fat-containing lymph fluid which drains from the intestine is called chyle.

The ileum

The ileum is the lower part of the small intestine, and is the part which the food reaches last on its way from the stomach to the colon, or large bowel. It is a 3.5 m (12 ft) long tube – leading on from the duodenum and the jejunum and connecting with the large bowel – and accounts for just over half the total length of the small intestine.

The ileum is similar in structure to the other two segments of the small intestine. The outer surface is protected by the peritoneum – the membrane which lines the abdominal cavity. Its interior consists mainly of muscular layers, responsible for moving the digested food along the intestines, layers of mucosa and, finally, an inner lining of cells which borders on the central cavity.

Position and structure of the ileum

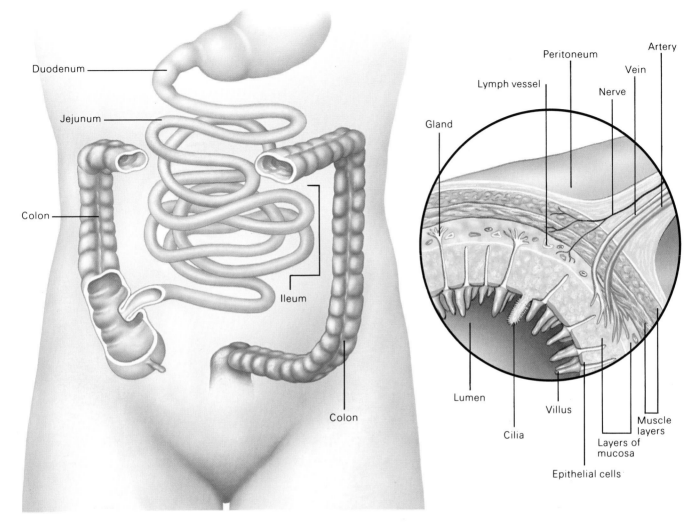

The ileum (above) is the last part of the small intestine food passes through on its way to the colon. Its inner surface or lining (inset) is covered with small finger-like projections which are called villi (below left). The effect of this is to increase the surface area of the ileum, allowing food to be absorbed quickly into the capillaries (below right).

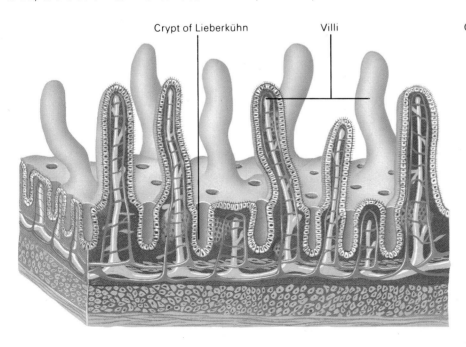

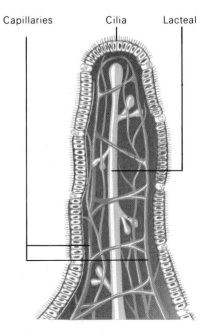

The Liver

The liver has two vital roles: making (or processing) new chemicals, and neutralizing poisons and wastes.

The organ stands four-square in the way of every drop of blood coming away from our intestines – blood which carries all the nutrients absorbed from the food we eat. In other words, blood can only get back to the heart and lungs from the stomach by first passing through a system of veins into the liver, known as the portal system.

The liver is the largest organ in the body, weighing between 1.36 and 1.81 kg (3 and 4 lb). It is tucked underneath the diaphragm, protected from damage by the lower ribs. There are two projecting parts, or lobes, called the left and right lobes, the right being the largest, occupying the whole of the top of the abdomen's right side. The left is smaller, reaching the midpoint of this left area. It is not usually possible to feel the liver, but when it enlarges – as a result of disease – it protrudes from behind the rib cage, and can then be felt if the abdomen is pushed in.

Functions

As in any other part of the body, it is cells that do the real work, at a microscopic level, of maintaining life's processes.

Medical science calls the 'creative' cells of the liver hepatocytes. They are specialized to handle the basic substances our bodies run on – proteins, carbohydrates and fats.

Protein processing: proteins are essential for renewal and creation of cells all over the body, for the formation of hormones, the body's chemical 'messengers', and for making enzymes.

We eat protein in various forms, both vegetable and animal in origin, and from 'raw' proteins, the liver has to create proteins acceptable to the body by first breaking them down, and then actually re-building them.

Put simply, this process, called synthesis, means raw proteins being taken or absorbed from the blood flowing through the portal veins into the surrounding hepatocytes, being synthesized by the liver's enzymes, and then being handed back in their new form. Waste, however, does not return to the bloodstream.

Carbohydrate processing: these are the large class of chemical substances made of three atoms – basic building blocks of all physical matter: carbon, hydrogen and oxygen.

They occur most typically in sugary or starchy foods, and we need them for energy. Our muscles literally burn sugar, or sugar-like substances whenever they work – a process assisted by oxygen. The liver plays a vital role in organizing this fuel into forms which can be used.

This it does by turning carbohydrates into two forms, closely akin to pure sugar. One is 'instant energy', glucose. The other is storable energy, a substance similar to glucose and called glycogen. Sugar shortage rapidly causes brain damage, and so the level of sugar in the blood must be precisely maintained, hence the need to store sugar for times of need, such as sudden exertion, or starvation. Equally, if too much sugar is present in the blood, a hormone made by the liver can store the excess as glycogen.

Conversion of fats: fats are essential to the body, too. They are turned by the liver into forms which can actually be built into or renew existing fatty tissue, typically the subcutaneous layer beneath the skin which acts as insulation and shock absorber. Fat, in addition, is a means of storing energy.

Waste disposal: lining the veins of the liver are highly specialized cells, called Kuppfer cells after the man who identified them, which 'vacuum clean' the blood of impurities, such as bacteria. These cells also weed out excess red blood cells manufactured (our bodies always over-produce these) and hand them across to the hepatocytes for processing.

From all the sources mentioned – blood itself, proteins, fats and to a much lesser extent carbohydrates – by-products are produced during the rebuilding that goes on in the hepatocytes. Some, such as ammonia (produced during the breakdown of protein), is poisonous, and the liver cells neutralize this, sending the harmless waste product urea back into the main circulation. Fat and blood waste products pass out as bile.

The same applies to actual poisons we consume – such as alcohol – and indeed medicines. If a drug is to be long-lasting in its effects, it needs either to be resistant to the liver's enzymes or to by-pass the liver completely.

Ketones

We need a continuous supply of glucose in the bloodstream to carry out all the body's functions and to supply tissues with energy. When glucose intake is low – for example, during dieting – proteins and carbohydrates are broken down to make more glucose. However, because all our reserves of protein (mainly muscle) would quickly dwindle away, many tissues switch over to using the products of fat breakdown as an alternative source of fuel. These are known as ketones.

There are three types of ketones: two ketone bodies (aceto-acetic acid and betahydroxy-butyric acid) and acetone. Acetone, which is a waste product of fat breakdown, is produced at the same time as the ketone bodies, but has no useful function. Ketone bodies, on the other hand, are readily utilized as a source of energy.

When glucose is scarce, ketones are produced and transported into the bloodstream from fatty tissue to the liver, where ketone bodies are formed. The ketones are then released into the circulation, to be taken up and used for energy by the muscles, the heart, the brain and the many other tissues.

In health and disease

Ketones do not appear in the blood until several hours after a balanced meal. By the time most of us wake up in the morning, we are slightly ketotic: small amounts of ketones are present in the blood and urine. Much of the energy for an early morning jog would be supplied to the muscles by these ketones, which disappear from the bloodstream after a good breakfast.

During a weight-reducing diet, or more extreme food deprivation, a moderate amount of ketosis will occur.

Pregnant women in labour often become ketotic. However, high levels of ketones in the blood may delay the progress of labour by interfering with the womb's ability to contract effectively, and so glucose is given by an intravenous drip to inhibit ketone formation.

When glucose is scarce, fatty tissue is broken down into fatty acids and carried in the bloodstream to the liver, where ketone bodies are formed.

The liver has a marvellous capacity to renew itself – a whole lobe cut away in an operation can be replaced in a few weeks. However, on rare occasions, destruction of liver cells outstrips the rate of replacement, and this leads to acute liver failure.

The results of liver failure are easy to imagine by considering the jobs the liver performs. Blood sugar falls, and without a proper level, brain damage can result. Failure of protein production, including manufacture of those which cause clotting in the blood, make the patient bleed easily; it also leads, for various technical reasons, to complications such as accumulation of fluid in the abdomen, called ascites.

How the liver works

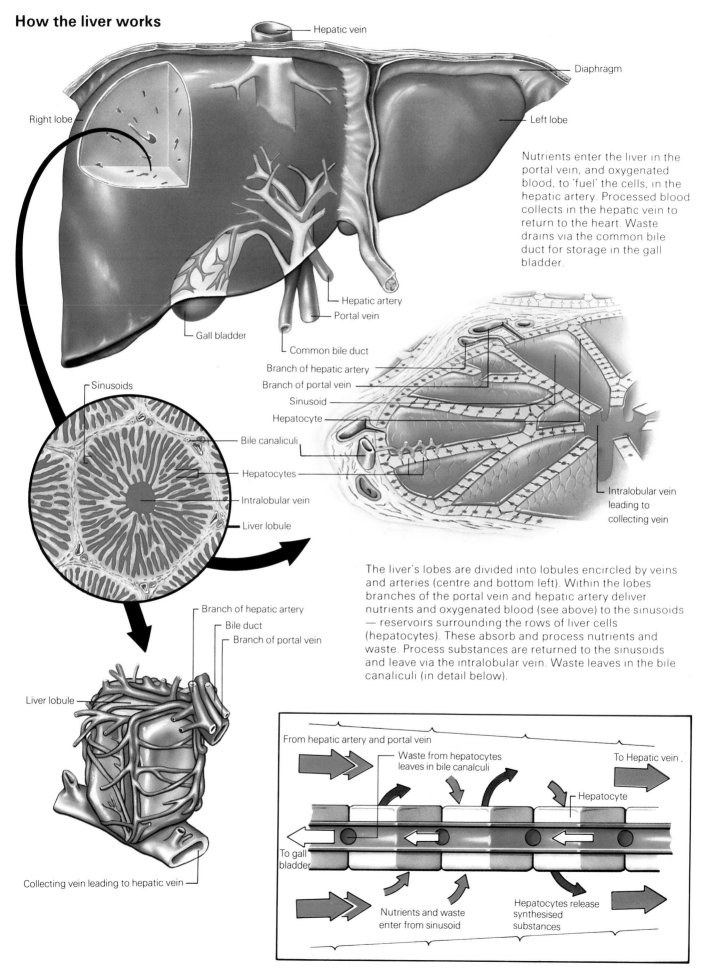

Nutrients enter the liver in the portal vein, and oxygenated blood, to 'fuel' the cells, in the hepatic artery. Processed blood collects in the hepatic vein to return to the heart. Waste drains via the common bile duct for storage in the gall bladder.

The liver's lobes are divided into lobules encircled by veins and arteries (centre and bottom left). Within the lobes branches of the portal vein and hepatic artery deliver nutrients and oxygenated blood (see above) to the sinusoids — reservoirs surrounding the rows of liver cells (hepatocytes). These absorb and process nutrients and waste. Process substances are returned to the sinusoids and leave via the intralobular vein. Waste leaves in the bile canaliculi (in detail below).

Bile

Bile is a thick, bitter, yellow or greenish fluid made in the liver and stored in the gall bladder. Released from the gall bladder into the small intestine in response to the presence of food, it is essential to the digestion of fats.

It is also part of the body's excretory, or waste-disposal system, because it contains the remnants of worn-out blood cells.

Every day, the liver produces about a litre (1.76 pints) of bile. Although over 95 per cent water, it contains a wide range of chemicals including bile salts, mineral salts, cholesterol and bile pigments which give the bile its own characteristic colour.

It is made continuously and in small quantities by every cell in the liver. As it flows from the cells, it collects in minute channels between groups of liver cells called bile caniculi, which empty into bile ducts or tubes placed between the lobes, or projecting parts of the liver.

From the bile ducts, bile drains into exit tubes known as the hepatic ducts. Unless bile is needed immediately for digestion, it flows into the gall bladder, which is a storage sac under the liver.

The bile stays in the gall bladder until given the cue to play its part in the digestive process. As food – but particularly fatty food – enters the duodenum (the first portion of the intestine) from the stomach, the duodenum makes a hormone called cholecystokinin.

This hormone travels in the bloodstream to the gall bladder and makes its walls contract so that bile is squeezed out. The bile then flows down another tube, the common bile duct, and through a narrow gap, the Sphincter of Oddi, which allows the bile to pass into the small intestine.

Bile at work

Bile's mineral salts, which include bicarbonate, then neutralize the acidity of partly digested food in the stomach.

The bile salts, which are chemicals called sodium glycocholate and sodium taurocholate, break down fats so the digestive chemicals (enzymes) can go to work.

As well as this detergent-like action, the bile salts are also believed to act as 'ferries' further down the intestine,

Without bile our bodies could not digest fats. It is made in the liver, stored in the gall bladder and does its work in the intestines. Every day the liver produces about 1 litre (1.76 pints) of bile, which exits from the liver via the hepatic ducts. Bile salts return to the liver in the blood of the portal vein, twice during the process of digestion.

enabling digested fats to get through the intestine wall. They are also carriers of vitamins A, D, E and K.

The body is very conservative in its use of bile salts. They are not destroyed after use, instead 80-90 per cent of them are carried back to the liver in the blood where they stimulate the secretion of more bile and are put to use once again by the body.

The colouring

Bile gets its colour from the presence of a pigment called bilirubin. One of the many jobs of the liver is to break down worn-out red blood cells. As this happens, the red pigment haemoglobin in the cells is chemically split and forms the green pigment biliverdin, which is quickly converted to the yellow-brown bilirubin.

Passage of bile

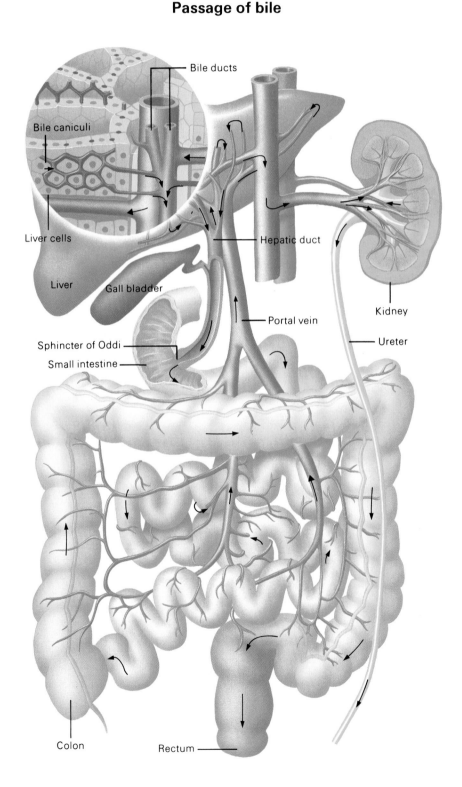

Bile ducts
Bile caniculi
Liver cells
Liver
Gall bladder
Hepatic duct
Portal vein
Kidney
Ureter
Sphincter of Oddi
Small intestine
Colon
Rectum

The greenish tinge of bile is given by remnants of unconverted biliverdin. As well as pigmenting the bile, bilirubin colours and partially deodorizes the faeces, and also encourages the intestine to work effectively.

Bile pigment is also responsible in part for the yellow colour of urine. In the intestine, bilirubin is attacked by bacteria permanently stationed there and converted to a chemical known as uribilinogen, which is carried to the kidneys and released in the urine.

When something is wrong with the liver or gall bladder, bilirubin tends to accumulate in the blood and the skin and whites of the eyes look yellow.

And because too little bile is reaching the intestines, the faeces may be pale and greyish in colour.

Gall stones

Even if the liver's bile production system is working normally, things can go wrong in the gall bladder. Most notorious of gall bladder problems is gall stones.

These are hard lumps of a chemical substance called cholesterol, which actually form in the gall bladder.

There are three different kinds of gall stones. The most common is known as mixed stones because these contain a mixture of the green pigment in bile and cholesterol, one of the chemicals produced in the body by the breakdown of fats. They develop in clutches, up to 12 at a time, and have facets so that they fit together in the gall bladder.

Cholesterol stones, as their name implies, are formed largely from cholesterol. They seldom occur in more than ones or twos, and can grow up to 1.25 cm (½ in) in diameter, which

Position of the gall bladder

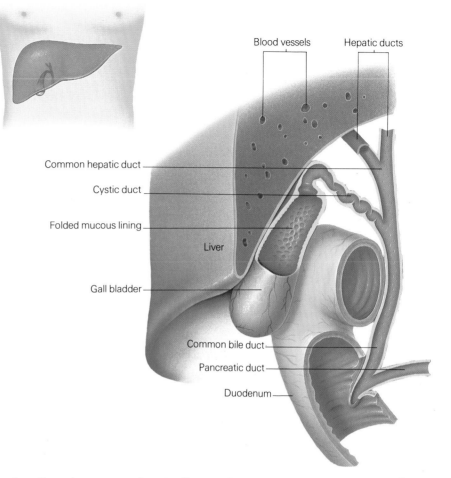

Blood vessels
Hepatic ducts
Common hepatic duct
Cystic duct
Folded mucous lining
Liver
Gall bladder
Common bile duct
Pancreatic duct
Duodenum

makes them large enough actually to block the common bile duct.

Pigment stones are made largely of the green bile pigment, occur in large numbers, and are usually small. They tend to form as a result of illnesses affecting the composition of the blood.

The gall bladder can store up to 0.41 litres (¼ pint) of bile. This is emptied into the intestine, through an opening in the side of the duodenum, whenever fatty foods arrive from the stomach. Bile can break down or emulsify fat, very much as detergent does.

Left: Bile is a greenish fluid simulated here to show how its emulsifying salts act like detergents. They physically break down globules of fat during digestion.

CHAPTER 10

EXCRETORY SYSTEMS

The body has several methods of getting rid of waste products — products which must be removed so that the body is not poisoned. This is done through the various excretory systems which depend on several organs and glands for waste removal: the urinary system whose main components are the bladder and kidneys; the bowel, or large intestine; the gall bladder; and the sweat glands in the skin.

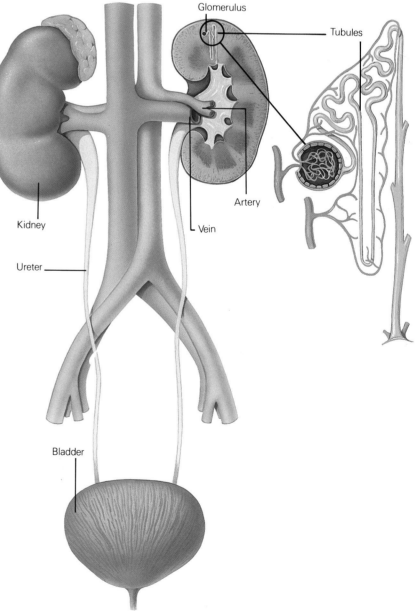

Glomerulus

Tubules

Kidney

Vein

Artery

Ureter

Bladder

Right: The urinary system is one of the body's main systems of excretion. It consists of the kidneys, bladder, and the urethra, the tube that carries urine from the bladder to the opening in the body from where it is released.

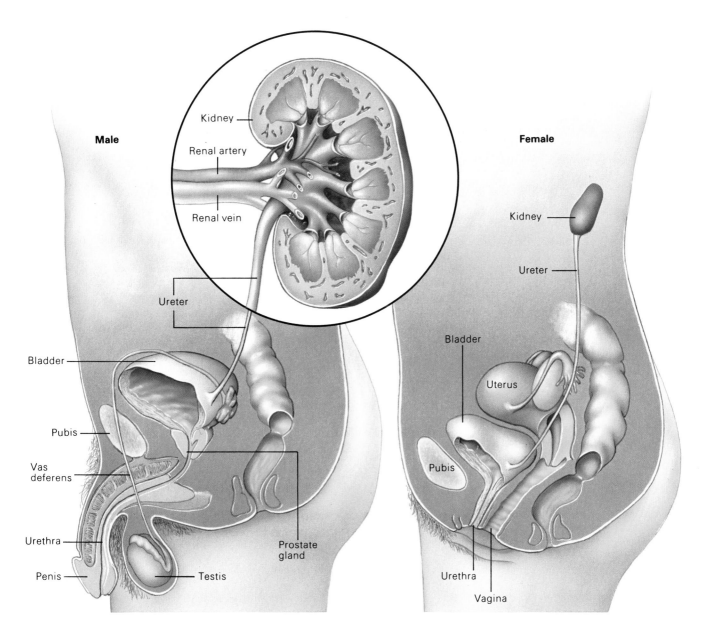

Male and female urinary systems. In both sexes the bladder is a funnel-shaped sac, resembling an upside-down pyramid. The base of the pyramid provides a surface on which, in women, the uterus rests, and in men, the coils of the intestine. The male urethra — the channel down which urine passes — measures about 20 cm (8 in) in length, but in females it is considerably shorter.

Excretion

Excretion is the process by which the body rids itself of waste products. Different constituents of the body continuously produce their own by-products and these must be eliminated if the body is not, in effect, to poison itself. Various organs - including the lungs, the kidneys, the liver and the bowel - ensure that this does not happen.

It may seem odd to think of the lungs as organs of excretion, but carbon dioxide is the most important waste product to be excreted by the body. If carbon dioxide starts dissolving in the blood in greater quantities than normal, then the blood becomes very acidic. This in turn paralyzes many chemical activities in the body and death can occur. This is known as respiratory failure and may be the final stage in chronic bronchitis.

The urinary system

Most body cells use some protein in their chemical activities and whenever protein is broken down the waste products contain nitrogen. The kidneys are responsible for filtering this nitrogen-containing waste - the most common compound of which is urea - out of the bloodstream. The kidneys also regulate the amount of water passed out of the body and keep the correct balance of salt in the body.

The action of the kidneys is complex. The kidneys receive about one litre (one and three quarters of a pint) of blood every minute. This blood eventually reaches a filter at the end of one of the kidney tubules - of which there are two million in each kidney - and is separated out so that the watery element of blood (the plasma) passes into the tubule while most of the rest stays in the bloodstream. The filtered fluid passes down the long kidney tubule and most of the water, salt and other valuable substances are absorbed back into the bloodstream. Some water, urea and other waste substances are passed in the form of urine down two tubes into the bladder.

The kidneys produce urine continually during the day and night. About two litres (3½ pints) of urine are passed in 24 hours, but this can vary greatly. The delicate control of the body's water balance is brought about by the kidney tubule which may absorb more or less of the filtered fluid journeying down it. The instructions to absorb extra water if the body is becoming dehydrated come from the hormone ADH (antidiuretic hormone) which is secreted from the pituitary gland in the brain. The total amount of urea which is passed out remains about the same, but it is dissolved in more or less water and gives rise, therefore, to stronger or weaker urine.

A very similar system exists for the management of the balance where a hormone called aldosterone, secreted from the adrenal gland just above the kidneys, acts on the tubule and makes it reabsorb more or less salt according to the body's needs.

The gall bladder

Bile is stored in the gall bladder which squeezes it out into the intestines from the stomach. The reason for this is that bile contains substances that break down large droplets of fat into smaller droplets - a process called emulsification - and makes them easier to absorb. So the bile system not only provides a useful way of eliminating waste products fom the liver but also plays an important role in the digestion of food. (See page 118.)

The bowels

When food enters the stomach it is churned around and broken down by acid until it is liquid. It then enters the small intestine where the true process of digestion takes place and all the desirable nutrients in the food are absorbed. Finally it enters the colon or bowel. This is a long, wide tube which starts in the lower right-hand corner of the abdomen, then works up and round in a horseshoe shape before coming to an end at the anus.

It is during this passage through the large bowel that what remains of the original food gradually solidifies, as water from it is absorbed into the bloodstream through the bowel wall. The final hardness of the food waste - the faeces - depends upon how much water is absorbed.

Most of the substance of the faeces is simply food residue after the nutrients have been removed. It is arguable whether this should be called excretion, but the bowel certainly does contain some true excretions, since it contains the waste products of cell chemistry in the form of bile.

The sweat glands

On a hot day the body loses a large amount of salt and water in sweat. Sweat is the product of the sweat glands in the skin and its sole purpose is to regulate the body heat since heat is lost as the sweat evaporates from the skin.

However, if someone were not to sweat at all for a day, then any excess salt or water would easily be excreted by the kidneys. So sweat does not fulfil any essential function in the clearing of waste products.

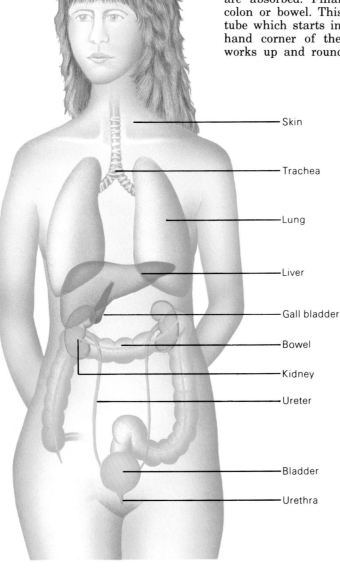

Skin — Trachea — Lung — Liver — Gall bladder — Bowel — Kidney — Ureter — Bladder — Urethra

How the body clears itself of waste

These are the methods, or systems, by which the body rids itself of waste products — mainly the result of digestion and various chemical processes necessary for the maintenance of life.

Skin excretes water and salt, derived from food, through the pores via the sweat glands

Lungs excrete carbon dioxide, from the burning of glucose as fuel, and some water via the wind pipe (trachea) and mouth

Liver and gall bladder excrete bilirubin, from the breakdown of haemoglobin from red blood cells in the liver, via bile passed out with faeces

Kidneys excrete urea — from the use of proteins by the cells - water and mineral salts via the bladder and urethra

The bowel excretes faeces, the remains of food after nutrients have been removed, via the anus

The Large Intestine

Anatomists divide the large intestine into four parts: the caecum, colon, rectum and anal canal, or anus. The caecum and the worm-like appendix that extends from it are both blind alleys with no known function in humans.

The first part of the large intestine is known as the ascending colon. It runs straight up the right side of the abdominal cavity. About two to three centimetres from the lower end there is a T-junction where the ileum (the last part of the small intestine) enters.

At the top right-hand side the colon makes a bend to the left, just under the liver. It then crosses the body below the stomach and runs down the left side of the body into the pelvic area, where it continues as the rectum.

The first bend of the colon from the right is called the hepatic flexure; the second bend, as it descends, is known as the splenic flexure. The portion of the colon that crosses the body is the transverse colon and, not surprisingly, the section that runs down the body is the descending colon.

The colon is by far the largest section of the large intestine, measuring 1.3 m (4½ ft). The function of the colon is to move solid material to the anus by the process of peristalsis, and to absorb salt and water delivered to it from the small intestine. The water is absorbed by the blood from the liquid remains of digestion.

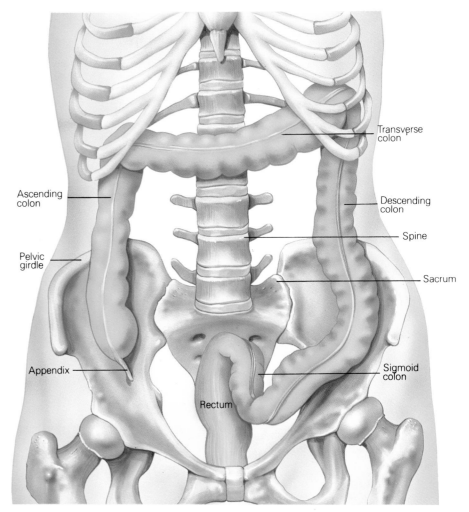

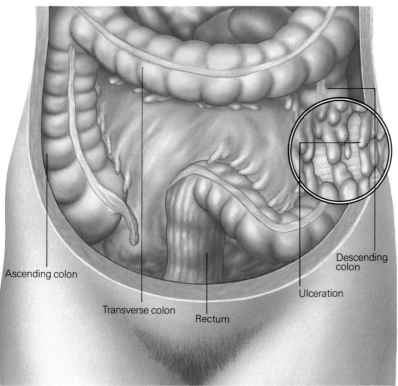

Above and left: The colon and rectum. The colon moves waste matter towards the anus, via the rectum. This part of the excretory system is rather prone to inflammation which may result in ulcerative colitis (inset left).

The ascending colon, along with the last part of the small intestine, is supplied with blood by the superior mesenteric artery. From there the inferior mesenteric artery brings blood to the rest of the bowel. Both blood vessels are branches of the aorta. Branches of the portal vein takes blood from the intestines to the liver.

Colitis

Colitis is an inflammation of the colon's mucous membrane. There are two kinds: acute colitis is often a result of an infection or an allergy and lasts only a short while; chronic, or ulcerative colitis is much more serious. It can have serious complications and requires prolonged treatment. Chronic colitis is more prevalent in the 20-40 year group but it can occur at any age.

Anatomy of the anal canal and rectum

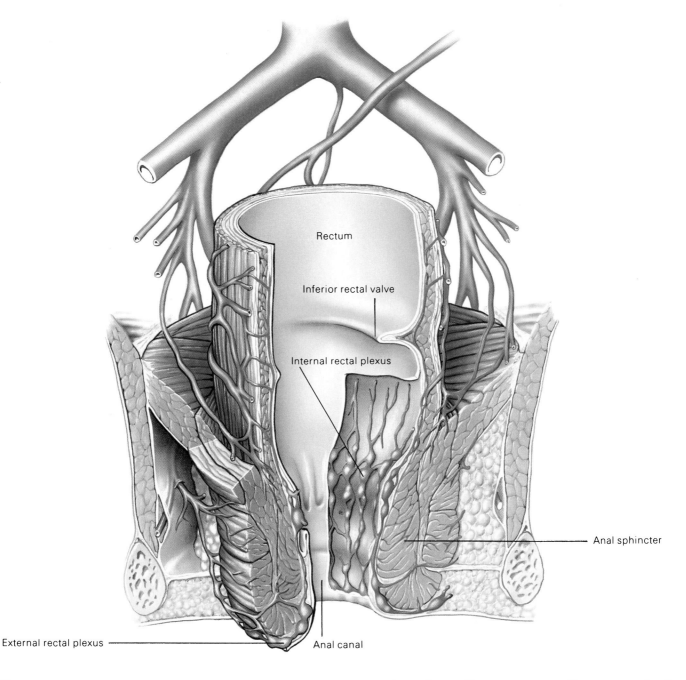

Rectum

Inferior rectal valve

Internal rectal plexus

Anal sphincter

External rectal plexus

Anal canal

The rectum

There is much confusion among lay people about the difference between the rectum and the anus. The anus is only the short narrow tube surrounded by a ring of muscle which joins the rectum, the lowermost part of the large bowel, to the outside. The main function of the anus is to maintain continence of faeces while the rectum acts as a reservoir for them. With a normally functioning anus and rectum a person can evacuate his bowels when it is socially convenient and not just when faeces happen to have passed through the whole of the large bowel.

The rectum itself, like the rest of the bowel, consists of a muscular tube lined with a special membrane which is known as epithelium. In the rectum, this epithelium contains glands which produce mucus to lubricate the faeces and make their passage easier. The muscular part of the rectum contracts during defecation to expel the faeces, but at other times is capable of stretching. It is this potential for increasing in size which enables the rectum to act as a reservoir.

The anus

The anus or anal canal is about 10 cm (4 in) long and is the opening through which the body's solid waste products – known as faeces – are excreted.

Faeces are usually composed of about 75 per cent water and 25 per cent solid material. Some of the water is mucus which lubricates the alimentary canal and eases the passage of faeces from the body. Of the solids, about a third is bacteria, a third is undigested fats and proteins, and a third is cellulose or roughage, the part of plant foods which is undigested.

The colour of faeces is due to bile pigments (chemical breakdown products of red blood cells) called stercobilin and bilirubin. These bile pigments also help to sterilize and deodorize faeces.

Faecal odour is mainly due to bacterial action in the intestine which pro-

Controlling the bowel

Wall of bowel

Faeces

Nerve pathway

Involuntary bowel action

Voluntary bowel action

Spinal cord

Internal sphincter

External sphincter

Anus

Bowel control comes from the brain, which sends out signals to the external sphincter muscles to stay closed until it is convenient to defecate. The signals 'kill' the desire to defecate and it remains suppressed for some hours.

end joins on to the large intestine. It can be up to 10 cm (4 in) long and about 1 cm (5/8 in) in diameter.

It is found only in humans, certain species of apes and in the wombat. Other animals have an organ in the same position as the appendix that acts as an additional stomach, where cellulose, the fibrous part of plants, is digested by bacteria. It seems that as we evolved through the ages and began to eat less cellulose in favour of more meat, a special organ was no longer needed for its digestion. The appendix could therefore be described as a relic of evolution.

Appendicitis

Facts about the appendix appear to contradict one another. On the one hand, nature appears to have adapted it to act as a watchdog for infection at the lower end of the gut. Like the tonsils and adenoids, it contains a large collection of lymph glands for this purpose; but if the appendix does become inflamed, a condition called appendicitis results and the organ may have to be removed. On the other hand, the appendix seems by no means essential to health. It can be dispensed with at an early age, making no apparent difference, and has nearly shrivelled up completely by the age of 40 or so.

duces a variety of nitrogen compounds and also hydrogen sulphide, which imparts a typical 'bad egg' smell.

How it works

As the faeces near the end of their journey down the intestines, they gradually harden as liquids are absorbed by the body and the solid waste is pushed into the rectum. At the end of the anus are two rings of muscle, known as the internal and external sphincters. Normally the two sphincters keep the anus closed, but during defecation – the passing of faeces – they relax to allow it to escape. The internal sphincter (which is under the control of the nervous system) senses the presence of the faeces and relaxes, allowing them to enter the anal canal. The external sphincter is kept closed deliberately (a skill we learn in babyhood) until a convenient moment presents itself when the faeces can be passed. To ease the passage of the faeces from the anus, the tissue in the lining of the canal secretes a lubricating fluid called mucus.

The appendix

The appendix is a narrow tube-like piece of gut resembling a tail, which is located at the end of the large intestine. The tip of the tube is closed; the other

Below: The only time we are aware of the appendix is when it becomes infected (inset). For the most part it is a useless part of the large intestine with no known function.

The position of the appendix

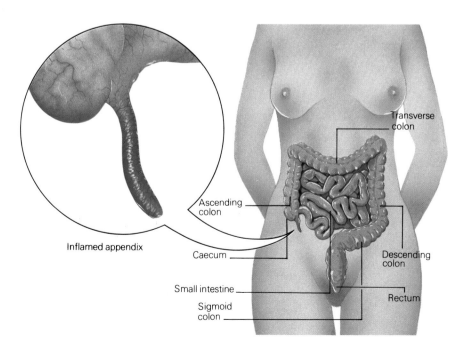

Inflamed appendix

Transverse colon

Ascending colon

Descending colon

Caecum

Rectum

Small intestine

Sigmoid colon

The Kidneys

We have two kidneys, lying on the back wall of the abdomen. From the inner side of each kidney a tube called the ureter runs down the back of the abdominal cavity and enters the bladder. The tube leading from the bladder is called the urethra. In women, its opening is in front of the vagina, and in men at the tip of the penis.

The kidneys contain thousands of tiny filtering units, or nephrons. Each nephron can be divided into two important parts – the filtering part, or glomerulus, and the tubule, where water and essential nutrients are extracted from the blood.

The glomerulus consists of a knot of tiny blood capillaries which have very thin walls. Water and the waste dissolved within it can pass freely across these walls into the collecting system of tubules on the other side. So large is this network of blood capillaries that it may contain – at any one moment – almost a quarter of the circulating blood throughout the whole body, and filters about 130 ml (4.6 fl oz) from the blood each minute.

The holes in the capillary wall form a biological sieve, and are so small that molecules beyond a certain size cannot pass. When the kidneys become infected, the glomeruli inflame and the sieve fails to be so selective, allowing larger molecules to escape into the urine. One of the smallest protein molecules to find its way into the urine is albumin. This is why your doctor tests your urine for protein to see whether the kidneys are functioning properly.

The tubules run between the glomeruli to a collecting system which ultimately drains into the bladder. Each glomerulus is surrounded by a Bowman's capsule, which is the beginning of its tubule. It is here that almost all the filtered water and salt is reabsorbed, so that the urine is concentrated. To reabsorb all this water, the body has a highly sophisticated system in which a hormone secreted into the blood from the pituitary gland in the brain changes the permeability of the tubule (its ability to reabsorb water).

While the hormone is in the blood, the tubule allows a great deal of water to be reabsorbed. When the hormone is 'turned off', however, the tubule becomes less permeable to water and more is lost in the urine – this is called diuresis and the hormone concerned is known as antidiuretic hormone (ADH). In certain conditions, such as diabetes insipidus (not to be confused with 'sugar diabetes' or diabetes mellitus), this hormone may be totally lacking. When this happens the patient cannot conserve water, and so loses large quantities in the urine, which have to be replaced by drinking.

Another hormone, aldosterone, secreted by the adrenal glands just above the kidneys, is responsible for exchanging sodium salt for potassium salt – so helping to control blood pressure and the balance of salt in the body. Parathormone, another hormone made by four small glands buried behind the thyroid gland, regulates the reabsorption of the essential mineral calcium, from which our bones and teeth are made.

High blood pressure

The kidneys regulate the amount of salt in the body and produce a hormone called renin. The level of renin depends upon the level of salt, which in turn is controlled by the action of the adrenal hormone, aldosterone, on the tubules. Renin activates another hormone, angiotensin. This has two effects: firstly, it constricts the arterioles and raises the blood pressure; secondly, it causes the adrenal gland to release aldosterone, making the kidneys retain salt and causing the blood pressure to rise.

Left: Kidneys secrete renin which produces angiotensin when pressure is low; this constricts the arteries and raises pressure. At the same time, adrenal glands produce aldosterone; this causes salt retention which also raises pressure and stops renin production.

Right: A kidney and its components. The renal artery carries blood to the kidney, splits into arcuate arteries and finally into afferent arterioles. Each of these ends in a glomerulus (inset). Blood is filtered through the glomerular wall and enters the renal tubule. The basic components of blood (plasma, protein, red and white corpuscles) are too large to cross the semi-permeable membrane of the glomerulus, but most of the other materials (e.g. water, salts and hormones) can pass across it. The next stage is called selective reabsorption (far right). Materials essential to the body are reabsorbed into the efferent arterioles, across the tubule wall. Once the blood has been thoroughly filtered, it leaves the kidney in the renal vein; waste products are excreted in the urine.

How the kidneys control blood pressure

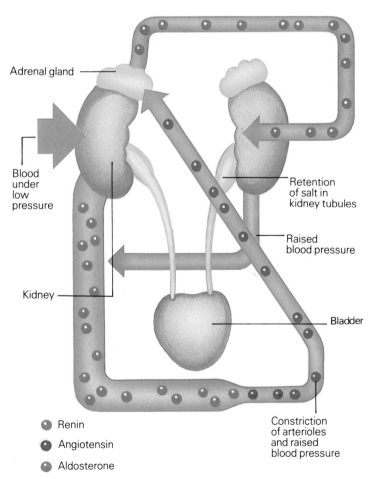

- Adrenal gland
- Blood under low pressure
- Kidney
- Retention of salt in kidney tubules
- Raised blood pressure
- Bladder
- Constriction of arterioles and raised blood pressure

- ● Renin
- ● Angiotensin
- ● Aldosterone

The kidney's filtering system

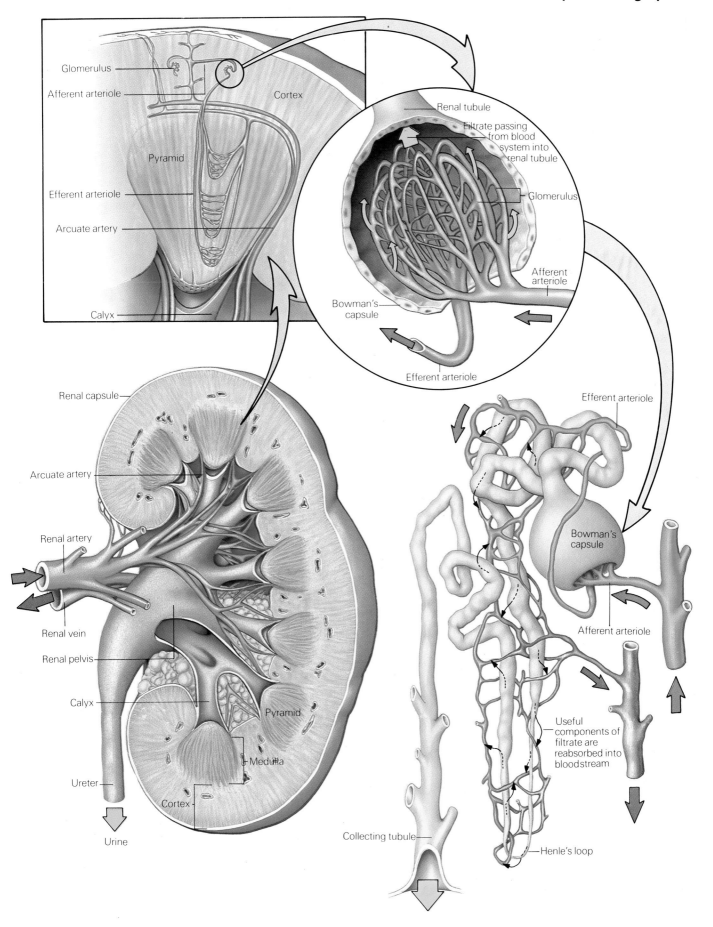

Glomerulus

Afferent arteriole

Cortex

Pyramid

Efferent arteriole

Arcuate artery

Calyx

Renal tubule

Filtrate passing from blood system into renal tubule

Glomerulus

Afferent arteriole

Bowman's capsule

Efferent arteriole

Renal capsule

Arcuate artery

Renal artery

Renal vein

Renal pelvis

Calyx

Ureter

Medulla

Cortex

Pyramid

Urine

Efferent arteriole

Bowman's capsule

Afferent arteriole

Useful components of filtrate are reabsorbed into bloodstream

Collecting tubule

Henle's loop

The Bladder

The urinary bladder is a hollow, thick-walled, muscular organ which lies in the lower part of the pelvic basin between the pubic bones and the rectum. It is a four-sided, funnel-shaped sac resembling an upside-down pyramid. The base of the pyramid provides a surface on which the small intestine or, in women, the uterus, rests.

The walls of the bladder consist of a number of muscular layers which are capable of stretching while the bladder fills, and then contracting to empty it. The kidneys pass a nearly continuous trickle of urine down the ureters from the kidneys to its walls. However, rather than the bladder acting like a balloon, with the pressure constantly increasing when it is filled, the muscle fibres of the bladder allow considerable expansion by adapting to the volume of urine until the bladder is nearly full. When it begins to resist, the need to pass urine is felt.

The two ureters – the tubes through which urine passes from the kidneys to the bladder – enter near the rear corners at the upper surface. There are one-way valves in the openings where they join the bladder to prevent urine from flowing back towards the kidneys if the bladder is too full.

Urine is passed out of the body via the urethra, which opens from the lowest point of the bladder. Normally this opening is kept closed by a sphincter, a circular muscle which contracts to seal the passageway. While urinating, this sphincter relaxes simultaneously as the muscles of the bladder wall contract to expel the urine.

The mature male urethra averages 20 cm (about 8 in) in length and consists of three sections. The first or prostatic section is about 2.5 cm (1 in) long and passes from the sphincter, or valve, at the outlet of the bladder through the middle of the prostate gland. The middle part of the urethra in the male is only about 12 mm (½ in) long and is often called the membraneous urethra.

The final – and, at over 15 cm (6 in), the longest – section is called the spongy or cavernous urethra. This is within the penis and opens at the urethral meatus (the slit in the tip).

In women the urethra is much shorter and its only function is to be a channel for the disposal of urine. It is about 1 cm (⅓ in) in diameter and is also surrounded with mucous glands. The fact that it is so short and opens into a relatively exposed, contaminated area explains why women frequently get urinary infections.

Urine

The contents of the fluid inside cells are kept within very strict limits. Certain toxic substances such as urea and acids are constantly being formed, and these must be eliminated to keep their concentrations in the blood acceptably low. Certain other substances such as salt and water must also be kept within strict limits, and this process, homoeostasis, is a major function of the kidneys. Clearly a very flexible system is needed – particularly since fluid intake varies from zero to as much as 10 litres (2½ gal) a day.

The composition of the urine finally excreted depends on what toxic products the body is producing. Virtually everything found in urine is also present in the blood: only the concentrations differ, those in urine being enormously varied so as to keep those in the blood within narrow limits. The foul odour often associated with urine is due to its decomposition by bacteria from the air. The smell of fresh urine is not as disagreeable.

The whole picture is immensely subtle and complex, but the end result is that a fluid is formed within which waste products and variable amounts of other substances such as sodium can be removed from the body. About 1200 litres (250 gal) of blood pass through the kidneys daily, and about 110 litres (25 gal) of filtrate is formed. Nearly all of this is reabsorbed, leaving just 1 litre (2 pt) of urine. This passes continuously from the kidneys via the ureters to the bladder, and is the average amount of urine passed per day.

Bladder control

Normally the adult bladder will hold up to half a pint of urine before any discomfort is felt, and emptying (micturition) occurs before a full pint has been stored. As the bladder fills, the stretching of the muscle walls passes signals to the spinal cord.

In a small child, this prompts automatic emptying by reflex action. With toilet training, this reflex is gradually suppressed by control from higher centres in the brain. If signs of fullness occur at an inconvenient time, the brain sends orders to the bladder walls to relax and thus allow further filling before the signal is felt again.

Cross-section of the urethra

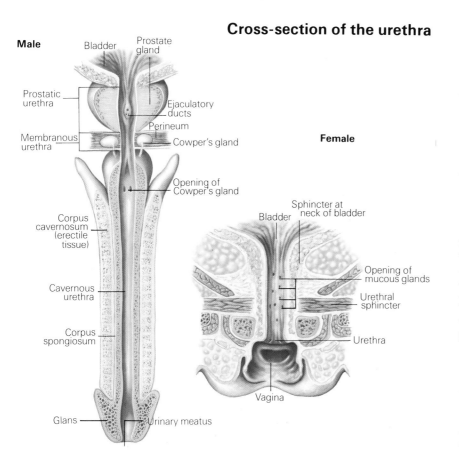

Male
Bladder
Prostate gland
Prostatic urethra
Ejaculatory ducts
Perineum
Membranous urethra
Cowper's gland
Opening of Cowper's gland
Corpus cavernosum (erectile tissue)
Cavernous urethra
Corpus spongiosum
Glans
Urinary meatus

Female
Sphincter at neck of bladder
Bladder
Opening of mucous glands
Urethral sphincter
Urethra
Vagina

Left: The male and female urethras, drawn to scale. Notice the proximity of the bladder to the urethral opening in each: in the female the urethra is much shorter and therefore more exposed and vulnerable to infection.

The Sweat Glands

Normal body temperature is, by tradition, 37°C (98.6°F), though there are variations and daily fluctuations from person to person. It is essential, however, that the normal temperature or core temperature is kept more or less constant. If the outside temperature rises too much, the core temperature is maintained by losing heat through the sweat glands as perspiration.

A small amount of body heat is lost each day directly through the lungs and through the skin without involving the sweat glands at all. But, as can be imagined, this is a fairly inefficient way of losing heat. It is not a very flexible method, because you cannot increase your breathing – like a panting dog – if you get very hot.

In fact, most of the heat loss that occurs every day results from perspiration. However, the liquid sweat usually evaporates from the skin before it can be noticed and for this reason it is known as 'insensible perspiration'. It is this evaporation that allows heat to be lost. It works on the principle that liquid needs energy to evaporate – like turning boiling water into steam. In humans that energy comes from the surface of the skin, and the effect of evaporating sweat is to use up some of the heat and energy in the skin, thereby leaving you cooler. Once you have become so hot that the sweat is beginning to pour off your skin, the system has actually reached the stage where it can only just cope – it is working at its most efficient at the so-called 'insensible' stage.

Types of sweat gland
The body is covered in sweat glands that produce liquid. Before puberty only one set is functioning – the eccrine glands which are all over the body except in the lips and some parts of the sexual organs. There are many of these glands in thick-skinned areas such as the palms of hands and the soles of the feet, and their activity is controlled both by the nervous system and some hormones. This means that as well as responding to changes in temperature, they also react under other conditions, hence the sweaty hands of excitement and the unexpected hot flush of the menopause.

The other glands, the apocrine glands, are much more complicated than the eccrine glands. Under a microscope they look like worm casts – highly complicated coils. They develop and start to function during adolescence and are found in the armpits, the groin and the areola of the breast. They are not associated with the

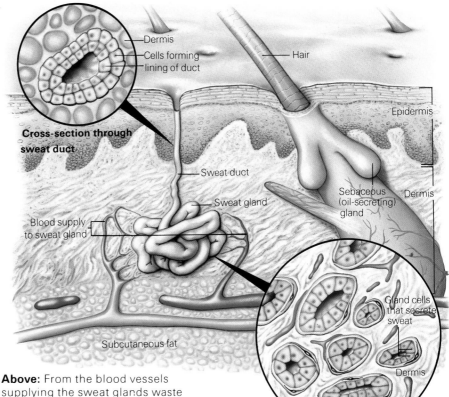

Above: From the blood vessels supplying the sweat glands waste products are removed and secreted as perspiration through the glands' cells. The sweat is then evaporated — unless, of course, things get too hot and the skin becomes saturated.

Cross-section through sweat gland

nervous system, but the thick milky substance which they produce does cause body odour, if the body is not washed regularly. This is because the milky substance reacts with the bacteria present in the skin and the by-product of this reaction is an unpleasant, offensive smell or 'body odour'.

Overheating
Sweat from the eccrine glands is not simply water – it consists of a wide range of chemicals found in the body, the most important of which is salt. People who sweat very heavily from working or living in a hot environment may lose up to five litres (9 pt) of liquid a day. In this case, they not only have to replace the lost fluid, but the lost salt, too - salt tablets are usually recommended. Failure to do this can result in severe muscular cramps and headaches, a condition known as heat exhaustion. It is possible, however, to adapt to living in a hot environment; the body itself adjusts and excretes less salt.

If the body does not adapt fully to very hot weather, a person can run the risk of suffering from heat stroke. This is a very serious condition in which the body stops sweating completely, and the core temperature rises dramatically. If the person is not quickly cooled down, brain damage may occur and ultimately death – fortunately this is an exceedingly rare condition.

Overheating can also be seen when people have a fever. Bacteria and viruses produce toxic substances which the body reacts to by turning the thermostat control higher. This raises the core temperature so feverish people sweat a lot.

Keeping cool
The principle of perspiration as the body's own cooling system works most efficiently in a reasonably dry atmosphere. If it is humid as well as hot, sweat has no chance of drying off and the film of perspiration that covers the skin stops the cooling off process. This is why hot humid climates are so uncomfortable to live in, compared with hot dry climates, because it is impossible to stay cool. Likewise, tight-fitting clothes make you feel hot and sticky – your skin is bathed in a film of sweat just as if you were in a tropical rain forest.

CHAPTER 11
REPRODUCTIVE SYSTEM

Sexual activity is a basic drive and one that humans share with all other animals. It is necessitated by the need to reproduce in order for the species to survive. In humans, the reproductive organs and glands begin to develop during the phase of growth known as puberty. In women, a finely-tuned timing mechanism controls the major physical processes of reproduction and this is evident in the processes of menstruation, conception and pregnancy.

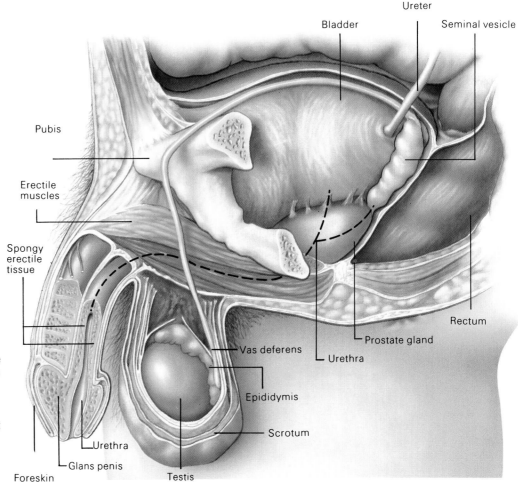

Right: The male genital organs are comprised of the penis, the scrotum, prostate gland, seminal vesicles and various tubes linking the genital tract. The testes (singular, testis) are not part of the genitalia but form the gonads where the male sex hormone testosterone is produced.

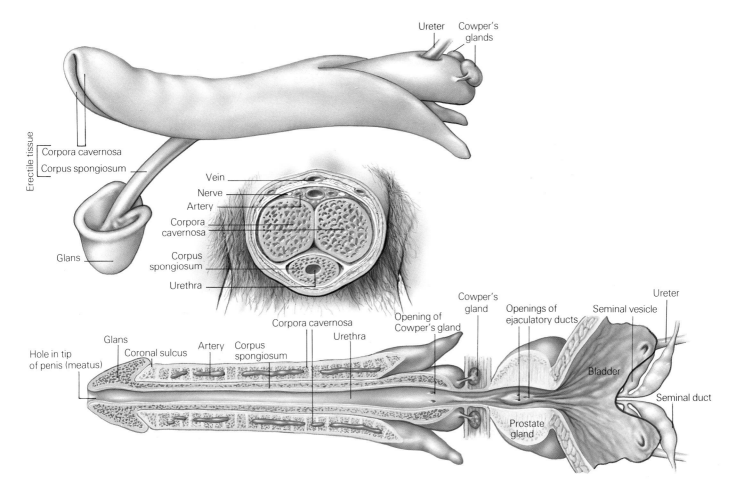

Labels on illustrations: Ureter, Cowper's glands, Erectile tissue, Corpora cavernosa, Corpus spongiosum, Glans, Vein, Nerve, Artery, Corpora cavernosa, Corpus spongiosum, Urethra, Corpora cavernosa, Cowper's gland, Openings of ejaculatory ducts, Ureter, Seminal vesicle, Opening of Cowper's gland, Bladder, Glans, Coronal sulcus, Artery, Corpus spongiosum, Urethra, Hole in tip of penis (meatus), Seminal duct, Prostate gland

The Reproductive Organs

The reproductive organs of the male and female are divided into two parts: the external and internal genitals; and the gonads. The gonads are represented in the male by the testes and in the female by the ovaries.

It is during puberty that the gonads begin to grow and become active, under the influence of the gonadotropic hormones which are produced in the pituitary gland. These hormones in turn stimulate the production of the sex hormones: testosterones, or androgens, in males and oestrogens and progesterones in females. These sex hormones promote the growth of the genitalia as well as secondary sexual characteristics such as the growth of the larynx in the male (which produces the breaking of the voice), and the onset of menstruation, or the menarche, in the female.

The male
In men, the genitals consist of the penis and scrotum, which are situated outside the body, and the prostate gland, seminal vesicles and various tubes of the genital tract, which are found inside the abdominal cavity.

The male genital system is designed to produce sperm and deposit them in the female.

The penis consists of a central tube – the urethra – down which urine passes when a man relieves himself (urination or micturition), or down which semen passes during intercourse. The urethra connects the bladder, where urine is stored, to a hole at the tip of the penis (the meatus). Semen enters the urethra during intercourse through a pair of tubes called the seminal ducts or vas deferens which join it shortly after it leaves the bladder. A tight ring of muscle at the opening from the bladder into the urethra keeps the passage closed so that urine only emerges when this is intended.

The penis usually hangs down in front of the scrotum, the wrinkled bag that contains the testes, in a slack or flaccid state. Its length varies from 6-12 cm (2½-5in). When sexually stimulated it becomes stiff and erect, usually pointing slightly upwards. It is then 10-20 cm (4-8 in) long. The tip of the penis – the glans or 'helmet' – is the most sensitive area. The valley behind

Above: A detailed view of the penis (top) showing all its parts. The illustration in the centre is a section through the internal shaft of the penis and shows the three groups of tissue responsible for erection. The bottom illustration shows a longitudinal section of the penis, in which the path of the urethra can be clearly seen.

the glans is the coronal sulcus, the main length of the penis is the body or shaft, and the area of the penis where it joins the lower abdomen is called the root.

Erection
The greater part of the penis is made up of three groups of tissue which are responsible for erection. These areas are supplied with a rich network of blood vessels, and when a man is sexually excited the amount of blood flowing into these areas increases enormously, while at the same time it is prevented from leaving. This en-

Structure of the testis

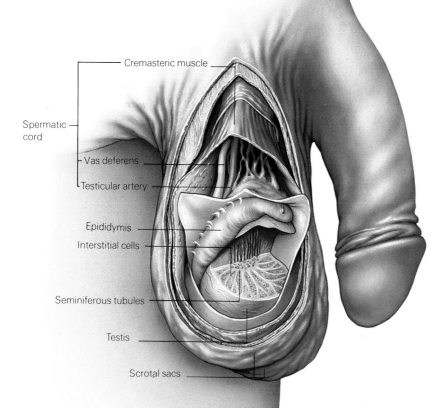

Cremasteric muscle

Spermatic cord

Vas deferens

Testicular artery

Epididymis

Interstitial cells

Seminiferous tubules

Testis

Scrotal sacs

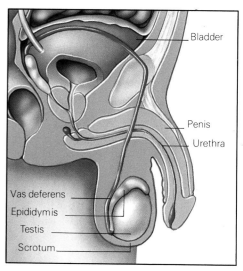

Bladder

Penis

Urethra

Vas deferens

Epididymis

Testis

Scrotum

Above: The testes consist of seminiferous tubules where sperm is made, and interstitial cells which produce the male hormone testosterone. Sperm is stored in the epididymis before passing along the vas deferens to be ejaculated. The inset is a simple diagram demonstrating how the testes link with the penis itself.

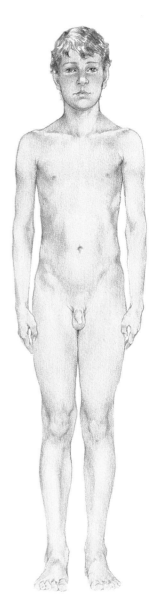

gorgement with blood makes the penis longer, thicker and rigid; it also rises as the internal pressure increases. After ejaculation has taken place and sexual excitement has subsided, the blood flow diminishes to normal levels and the penis returns to its flaccid state as the extra blood causing the erection drains away.

The foreskin and the glans

The delicate glans is protected by a loose fold of skin called the foreskin or prepuce. As the penis enlarges during erection this peels back to leave the glans exposed to the stimulation that eventually leads to orgasm. The skin on the glans and foreskin make a greasy substance called smegma, which acts as a lubricant facilitating the movement of the foreskin over the glans. It is important to wash this away regularly: in some men smegma tends to accumulate, forming a smelly, cheesy mess which can cause soreness or inflammation of the foreskin - a condition called balanitis. Repeated or persistent balanitis is sometimes a medical reason for carrying out circumcision - which is normally a social or religious practice.

The testes

The normal human male has two testes which develop in the embryo from a ridge of tissue at the back of the abdomen. When the testes have formed, they gradually move down inside the abdomen so that at the time of birth, each testis has usually arrived in its final position within the scrotum.

The function of the testes is twofold. First, they provide the site where sperm is manufactured; each sperm contains all the genetic information for that particular male. Second, the testes contain cells which produce the male sex hormone testosterone and consequently the male characteristics such as the deep voice, male hair distribution and typical distribution of fat. These two functions are carried out by completely separate sets of cells within each of the testes; one function can fail without the other

Below: These male figures pinpoint five stages in male physical development and highlight the appearance and growth of secondary sex characteristics, such as pubic hair. It is also interesting to note the difference of the penis and scrotum in proportion to one another from youth and puberty. The gradual change of body shape can also be seen.

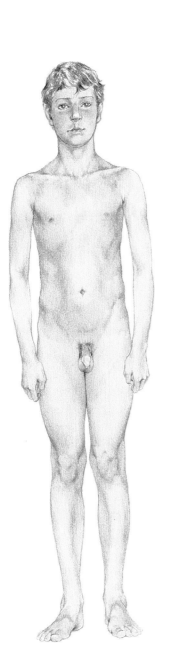
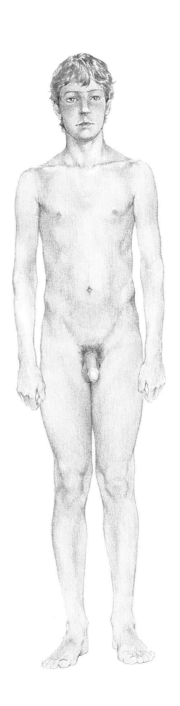
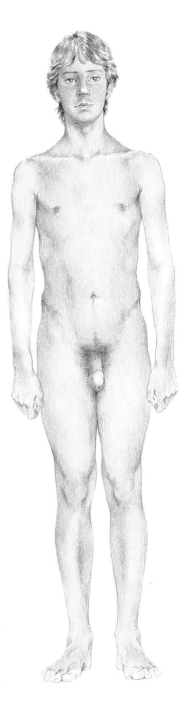

How sperm mature

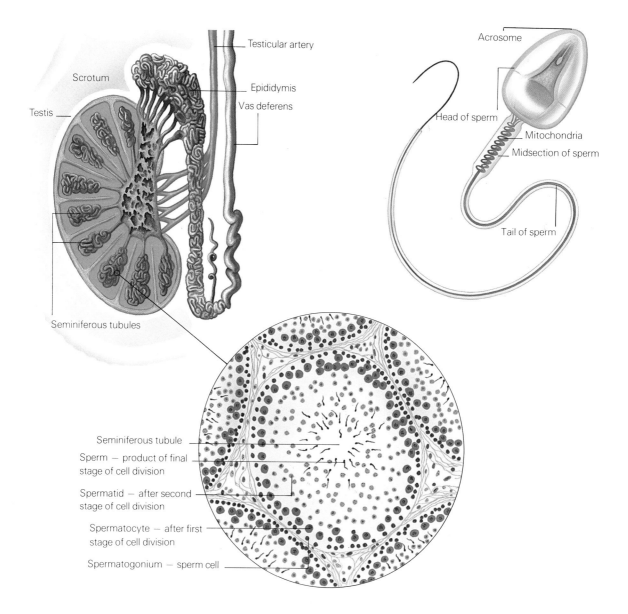

one necessarily doing so.

The testes are oval structures. Attached to the back of each one is a smaller structure which is shaped like a long comma and is called the epididymis. The epididymis consists of a series of microscopically tiny tubes which collect sperm from the testis. These tubes connect together to form one tube, called the vas deferens, which transfers the sperm towards the base of the bladder. All these structures, with the exception of the vas deferens, are microscopic in size.

Each testis is suspended in the scrotum by the spermatic cord, which consists of the vas deferens, the testicular artery and the testicular vein. These three structures are surrounded by a tube of muscle, called the cremasteric muscle. The spermatic cord, therefore, serves two purposes: first, to provide a blood supply to the testis; and second,

to conduct the newly-formed sperm away from the testis.

Sperm

Sperm is the name given to the male reproductive cell. Its only purpose is to achieve fertilization by union with the female cell, the ovum.

Each sperm is about 0.05 mm in length and is shaped like a tadpole. It has three main sections which consist of a head, a mid-section and a tail. The front of the head – the acrosome – contains special enzymes which enable the sperm to penetrate into the ovum and so achieve fertilization. The mid-section contains structures called mitochondria, which hold the vital source of energy needed by the sperm on its journey to the ovum.

The tail's only function is to propel the sperm, which it does by moving in a whip-like fashion, generating a speed

Above: From puberty sperm are constantly produced in the seminiferous tubules. To become sperm, the basic sperm cells go through three stages of cell division (inset) before passing through the tubules and into the epididymis, where they are stored. A mature normal sperm (above right) has a head, midsection and tail.

of about 3-3.5 mm per minute.

The sperm is made up of a number of chemicals and genetic material. These are the chomosomes which carry the genetic blueprint of the father, and which will determine the paternally inherited characteristics of the child. It is the sperm which carries the genetic message that determines the sex of the child.

The manufacture of sperm

The successful manufacture of sperm necessitates a temperature of about three degrees Centigrade lower than the rest of the body. Consequently, manufacture takes place outside the body, within the scrotum. Surrounding tissue helps to regulate the temperature of the testicles inside the scrotum by pulling them upwards to the body in cold conditions, and by a rich supply of blood vessels which dissipate the heat when the temperature gets too high.

Sperm production - at the rate of 10 to 30 billion a month - takes place in the seminiferous tubules in the testicles. The newly formed sperm then pass through the seminiferous tubules into the epididymis which is located behind the testicles. This serves as a storage and development area, the sperm taking between 60-72 hours to achieve full maturity. In fact, the epididymis can be emptied by three or four ejaculations in twelve hours; it takes about two days to be refilled. If there is no ejaculation, the sperm disintegrate and are reabsorbed.

Ejaculation

Before ejaculation occurs, the sperm move along the vas deferens - two

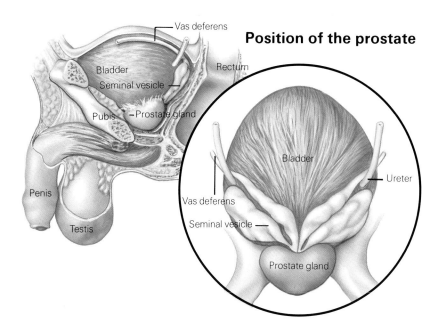

Position of the prostate

Above: The diagram shows a side view, showing the prostate gland and its position in relation to other organs. The inset shows it more clearly in relation to the bladder. Note the position of the vas deferens and the ureter.

Below: This diagram shows a rectal palpation. This is the simple medical examination technique used to check the prostate for any obvious problems.

tubes connecting the testicles to the prostate gland - and into a further storage area, the ampulla. Here, the sperm receive a secretion from the seminal vesicles, two coiled tubes adjoining the ampulla. This secretion, called seminal fluid, stimulates the motility - the ability to move spontaneously - of the sperm, and helps them survive in the vaginal secretion. The prostate gland - through which the sperm pass during ejaculation - produces a small amount of a similar fluid, giving the sperm full motility.

At the moment of ejaculation the sperm and seminal fluid are forced out of the ampullae, and epididymes, into the urethra by a series of muscular contractions.

If the sperm have been ejaculated into the vagina of a woman, they move as fast as they can through the cervix and into the uterus, where they make their way into the Fallopian tubes. It is in these tubes that fertilization may occur if an egg is present.

The prostate gland

The prostate gland is a walnut-shaped structure found only in males. It is situated at the base of the bladder and surrounds the urethra. This gland produces the fluid that mixes with semen to make up part of the seminal fluid. Although the exact function of the prostatic fluid is unknown, it is thought that one of its roles is to help keep the sperm active so that fertilization can occur more easily.

Owing to its position in the body, problems associated with this gland can often affect the normal functioning of the bladder - although this particular problem is more common among elderly men.

Rectal palpation

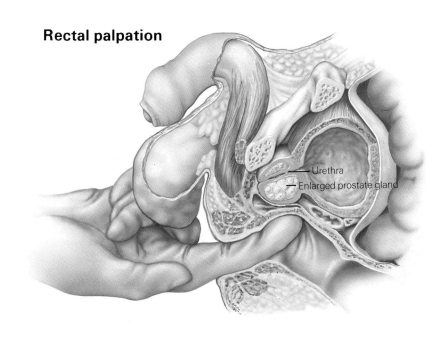

Structure of the vulva

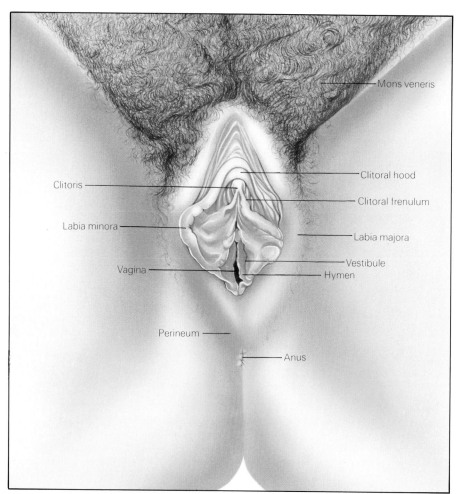

Labels on illustration:
Mons veneris
Clitoral hood
Clitoral frenulum
Clitoris
Labia majora
Labia minora
Vestibule
Vagina
Hymen
Perineum
Anus

The female
The female's reproductive system must not only receive the sperm but also must produce ova (eggs) for fertilization and eventually nurture one egg if it is fertilised, so that a baby can develop.

The external female genitals are the clitoris and the labia, which together are known as the vulva. Most prominent among the parts of the vulva are the two pairs of 'lips' or labia. The outer and larger - labia majora - consist of thick folds of skin that cover and protect most of the other parts. They become thinner at the base and merge with the perineum (the skin over the area between the vulva and the anus). At the top the outer lips merge with the skin and hair on the pad of fatty tissue that covers the pubic bone, the mons pubis or mons veneris - often referred to as the Mount of Venus.

Within the labia majora are the labia minora or 'lesser lips'. They join at the top to form a protective hood over the sensitive clitoris, dividing into folds which surround it. They also protect the opening to the urethra or water passage. The area between

Above: Situated at the entrance to the vagina the vulva consists mainly of outer and inner lips known as the labia. These folds of skin cover and protect the sensitive interior, including the main organ of sexual excitement — the clitoris.

the labia minora is largely taken up by a space called the vestibule. Before a women is sexually active, the space is mostly covered by the hymen, also known as the maidenhead. This varies in shape, size and toughness. The tags of skin which many women have around the vestibule are the remains of the hymen, and are called the carunculae myrtiformes. At the back, the labia minora join to form the fourchette, which is often ruptured during the first childbirth.

The clitoris and glands
The clitoris is actually similar in structure to the penis, even to the extent of having a hood of labia equivalent to the foreskin and a small connecting band of tissue called the frenulum. It is primarily an organ of sexual excitement. It is extremely sen-

sitive, and when stimulated its spongy tissue fills with blood and becomes erect. Friction on the erect clitoris — either by movement of the penis during intercourse or by some other means — will usually lead to orgasm. Other parts of the vulva also respond to sexual stimulation: the labia contain erectile tissue and often become enlarged during love-making; and the Bartholin's glands become active.

There are two pairs of glands associated with the vulva. The first are Skene's glands which lie just below the clitoris and secrete an alkaline fluid which reduces the natural acidity of the vagina. The other, larger pair lies in the bottom of the vestibule. These are Bartholin's glands and they secrete fluid when a woman is sexually aroused, so that the entrance to the vagina becomes moist and can more easily accommodate the penis. These glands are normally about the size of a pea and not prominent. They are liable, however, to venereal and other infections, becoming swollen, red and tender. This condition (Bartholinitis) requires treatment with antibiotics. In some cases, an abcess forms in one of the glands - a Bartholin's abcess - and this may need to be incised to release the pus.

The vagina
The vagina is the channel which leads from the vulva to the uterus. During a woman's life the vagina undergoes several changes. The vagina of a child is obviously smaller than that of a mature woman. The lining of the wall of the vagina is thinner in a child or post-menopausal woman than that of a woman in the reproductive years of her life. These changes are largely influenced by a group of hormones released by the ovary; these are called oestrogens.

The vagina plays an important role during intercouse and childbirth. The role during childbirth is relatively passive when the vagina forms the lower portion of the birth canal and is capable of opening sufficiently to allow the birth of the baby. We have only relatively recently begun to understand some of the changes which occur in the vagina during intercourse.

Structure
The vagina is a canal 7 cm (2¾ in) to 9 cm (3½ in) long, surrounded by fibrous and muscular tissue, but lined with a layer of cells called squamous epithelium. The walls of the canal are normally collapsed onto one another and thrown into many folds. These properties make it easy for the vagina to be distended during intercourse or childbirth. The urethra lies on the

front wall of the vagina and the rectum lies on the upper third of the back of the vagina. The anus is separated from the vagina by a fibro-muscular tissue called the perineal body.

During the reproductive years of a woman's life the vaginal secretions are slightly acidic. This tends to inhibit the growth of harmful bacteria in the vagina, but during the pre-pubertal and post-menopausal years, the vagina becomes mildly alkaline. Under these circumstances the bacteria can thrive and occasionally make the vagina rather sore and uncomfortable – a condition called atrophic vaginitis.

The walls of the vagina are well lubricated with secretions from the cervical canal and Bartholin's glands. During intercourse, secretions also seep through the vaginal epithelium into the vaginal canal. A certain amount of discharge from the vagina is normal in all women. The amount increases during ovulation and sexual arousal.

The hymen, also known as the maidenhead, is named after the Greek god of marriage, Hymen.

The hymen has no known physiological function but has achieved great importance in nearly all cultures as an insignia of virginity. However, hymens come in all shapes and sizes, and there is no way in which a hymen can be a reliable indication of virginity.

It is usually thin, punctured by holes and can easily be broken by strenuous physical exercise such as running and horse riding. Heavy petting, masturbation or the insertion of tampons can also cause a rupture.

Although the condition of the hymen is no proof of virginity, very often the hymen is first broken during sexual intercourse. Contrary to popular belief, an intact hymen does not prevent pregnancy. A sperm that comes into contact with the genital area, perhaps as a result of heavy petting, can travel through a hole in the hymen and up into the vaginal canal.

Function of the vagina

During sexual arousal the genital organs, especially the labia minora and lower vagina, become engorged with blood and the amount of vaginal secretion increases. During an orgasm the muscles of the pelvis including those surrounding the vagina contract involuntarily.

If a woman is particularly tense or anxious during intercourse, the muscles surrounding the vagina will go into spasm. This makes the vagina narrower and also makes sex painful. This condition is called vaginismus. It can be cured by help from a psycho-sexual counsellor, but if often takes many months before the woman can fully enjoy sex.

The uterus

The uterus is composed of two main parts – the corpus or body of the organ, and its cervix or neck – and it is capable of undergoing major changes during a woman's reproductive life. From puberty to the menopause, the endometrium develops each month to provide nutrition for a fertilized egg. If the egg is not fertilized the endometrium is shed during menstruation, and is slowly replaced in the course of the next menstrual cycle.

The cervix is shaped like a cylinder and its lower part projects into the vagina. The cervix is about 2.5cm (1in) long, and has a fine canal running through it which opens into the cavity of the uterus above, and the vagina below. If a finger is inserted into the vagina, the cervix can be felt as a small dimple.

In a woman who has not had children, this opening into the vagina is circular and quite small. During childbirth this stretches to allow the passage of the baby, and after childbirth it reshapes into a cross-wise slit.

During pregnancy, the uterus expands to allow the foetus to grow, and provides it with protection and nutrition. At the same time, the large muscle fibres are prevented from contracting.

The uterus suddenly changes its role when the foetus is mature and begins to contract in order to open the cervix and allow the baby and placenta to pass through. The uterus then

Structure of the vagina

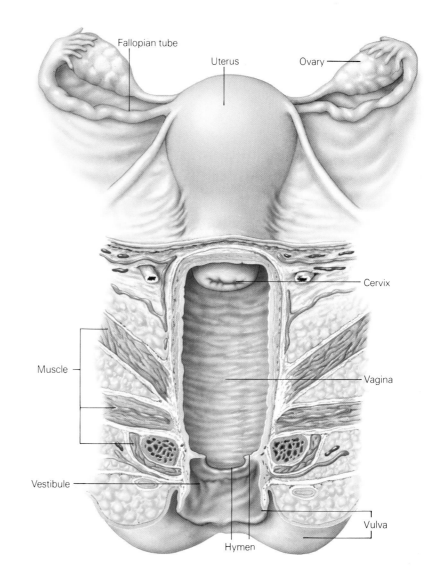

Right: The vagina is a tough muscular canal situated between the uterus and the vulva. Its corrugated structure is specifically designed to give it the amazing elasticity needed for the birth of a baby.

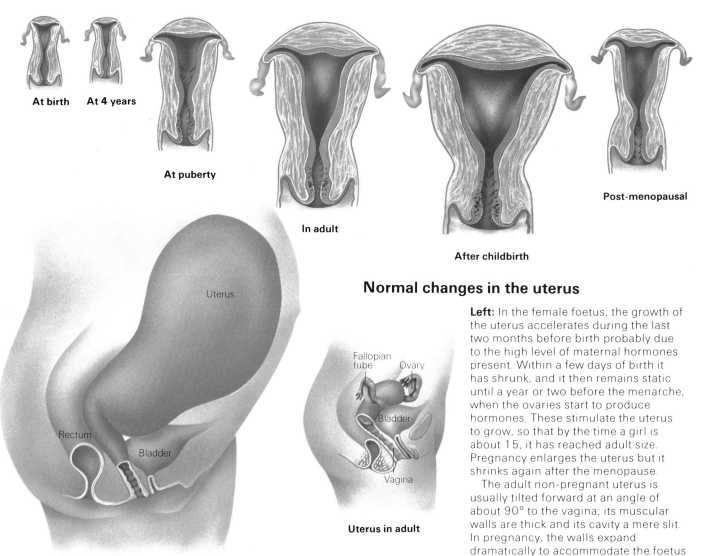

At birth **At 4 years**

At puberty

In adult

After childbirth

Post-menopausal

Uterus

Rectum

Bladder

Uterus in full-term pregnancy

Fallopian tube Ovary

Bladder

Vagina

Uterus in adult

Normal changes in the uterus

Left: In the female foetus, the growth of the uterus accelerates during the last two months before birth probably due to the high level of maternal hormones present. Within a few days of birth it has shrunk, and it then remains static until a year or two before the menarche, when the ovaries start to produce hormones. These stimulate the uterus to grow, so that by the time a girl is about 15, it has reached adult size. Pregnancy enlarges the uterus but it shrinks again after the menopause.

The adult non-pregnant uterus is usually tilted forward at an angle of about 90° to the vagina; its muscular walls are thick and its cavity a mere slit. In pregnancy, the walls expand dramatically to accommodate the foetus and the amniotic sac.

contracts tightly to close off the large blood vessels which have been supplying the placenta. After the birth it rapidly returns to its pre-pregnant state, ready to accept another fertilized egg. Rarely, this has been reported as happening as early as 36 days after the birth.

The uterus seems to have almost no function before puberty and after the menopause when it would obviously be unsuitable, mentally and physically, for a woman to have a baby.

All these changes in the functioning of the uterus are orchestrated by hormones released from the pituitary gland and from the ovaries, and by similar substances called prostaglandins which are released by the uterine tissue. The way in which these substances interact is still not fully understood.

Position
In an adult woman the uterus is a hollow organ approximately the size and shape of a small pear, and lies inside the girdle of pelvic bones. The narrow end of the pear is equivalent to the cervix which protrudes into the vagina – the remainder forms the body of the uterus. This is connected to the two Fallopian tubes which carry the monthly egg released from one of the pair of ovaries. In this way the uterus forms part of a channel between the abdominal cavity and the world outside the body.

Special mechanisms exist to prevent the spread of infection via this route into the abdominal cavity. Thus the lining of the uterus is shed when a woman menstruates, the cervix secretes protective antibodies and the natural acidity of the vagina inhibits the growth of harmful bacteria.

The front of the uterus sits on the bladder and the back lies near the rectum. The uterus is normally supported inside the pelvis by muscles – called the pelvic floor muscles – and by bands of connective tissue and blood vessels from the side wall of the pelvis which are attached to the cervix.

During pregnancy the uterus enlarges so that by the 12th week it can just be felt inside the abdominal cavity above the pubic bone. At about 38 weeks it usually reaches the lower end of the rib-cage, and about two weeks after the baby is born, the uterus can normally no longer be felt in the abdomen. After the menopause, the uterus shrinks in size.

The variations in size are controlled by the secretions of sex hormones, which also govern the nature of the endometrium. During the first half of a woman's menstrual cycle, the endometrium increases in thickness until the egg is released. It then stops growing but begins to secrete substances rich in nutrients to allow further growth of the egg if it is fertilized. If the egg is not fertilized, the endometrium is shed during menstruation.

The ovaries
The ovaries are the parts of the female reproductive system which are designed to make and release mature ova, or

eggs. When the ovum is fertilized by a sperm from a man it marks the start of a new human life. From the first period to the menopause, normal ovaries release one egg each month. They are also essential parts of the body's hormonal, or endocrine, system.

The ovaries are two grey-pink, almond-shaped structures each about 3 cm (1.2 in) long and about 1 cm (0.4 in) thick. They are found in the pelvis, the body cavity bounded by the hip or pelvic bones, and lie one on each side of the uterus. Each ovary is held in place by strong, elastic ligaments. Just above each ovary is the feathery opening of the Fallopian tube which leads to the womb, or uterus. Although they are very close to each other there is no direct connection between the ovary and the tube opening.

In a mature woman the ovaries have a rather lumpy appearance. The reason for this can be seen by looking at the internal structure under a microscope. Covering the ovary is a layer of cells called the germinal epithelium. It is from the cells in this border layer that the eggs or ova form; thousands of immature eggs, each in a round casing or follicle (the egg sac) can be seen clustered near the ovary edge.

Much more noticeable, however, are the follicles containing eggs in various stages of maturation. As these follicles enlarge, and after their eggs have been released, they produce the characteristic bumps on the ovary surface. The centre of the ovary is filled with elastic fibrous tissue which acts as a support for the follicle-containing outer layer.

Ovulation

Under a microscope, maturing follicles of the ovary can be seen as tiny balls enclosing a small mound of cells. In the centre of the mound is the egg cell in its final stages of maturation. When the follicle is ripe and the ovum matures, the cells at the follicle edge allow the ovum to leave. Exactly how this happens is still a mystery. The ovum is then wafted by the feathery ends, or fimbria, of the Fallopian tubes into the tube openings.

In their role as egg producers the ovaries also act as hormonal or endocrine glands. The ovaries function under the control of the pituitary gland at the base of the brain. The pituitary first makes a hormone, called follicle stimulating hormone (FSH), which travels in the bloodstream to the ovaries. FSH stimulates follicles and ovum development but it also brings about the secretion of the hormone oestrogen. Under oestrogen influence the lining of the uterus thickens in preparation for receiving a fertilized egg. Oestrogen also stimu-

lates the build up of body proteins and leads to fluid retention.

After a follicle has ripened and burst, another pituitary hormone, luteinizing hormone, or LH, goes into action and brings about the development of the corpus luteum (yellow body) in the empty follicle. (The job of corpus luteum is to help establish a pregnancy.) In turn, the corpus luteum makes and releases its own hormone, progesterone. If the egg is not fertilized within a fortnight the corpus luteum shrinks, progesterone production is turned off, and the lining of the uterus is shed as the monthly menstrual period. Now FSH production begins again and the whole cycle is repeated. If, however, the egg has been fertilized then the corpus luteum goes on working until the placenta is established and there is no bleeding.

Below: The ovaries are covered by a layer of cells. The cells which are destined to become ova (eggs) pass into the substance of the ovaries, where they are surrounded by a follicle membrane. Each month a single follicle matures, bursts in one ovary's surface and is released. If fertilized, the corpus luteum – which developes at the site of the egg's follicle – grows and secretes hormones that maintain pregnancy.

Site, structure and function of the ovaries

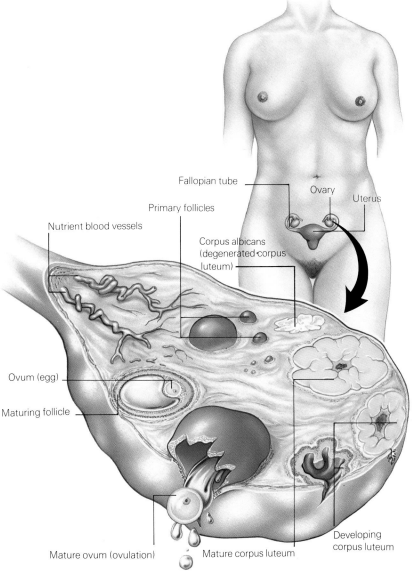

Fallopian tube
Ovary
Uterus
Primary follicles
Nutrient blood vessels
Corpus albicans (degenerated corpus luteum)
Ovum (egg)
Maturing follicle
Mature ovum (ovulation)
Mature corpus luteum
Developing corpus luteum

Menstruation

Ovary development is largely complete by the time the female foetus is in the third month of life in the womb, and few major changes will take place until puberty. By the time a baby girl is born her ovaries contain, between them, from 40,000 to 300,000 primary follicles, each containing an immature egg. At most only 500 or so of these eggs will ever be released, and probably no more than half a dozen – if that – will develop into new human beings.

When the ovaries first start to make the hormone oestrogen, they are not yet capable of releasing mature eggs. These early oestrogens bring about the physical changes of puberty such as growth of breasts, pubic hair, and widening of hips. These changes begin at least a year before a girl has her first period, and are a sign that the oestrogens have begun to stimulate the release of mature eggs.

Menarche

The start of periodic bleeding (menstruation) from the uterus is known as menarche and it is just one phase of the menstrual cycle which is governed by hormones from the pituitary gland in the brain and from the ovaries.

About four or five years before menarche the hypothalamus instructs the pituitary gland to secrete the growth hormone responsible for the sudden increase in a girl's height. This usually reaches a peak about two years before menarche and slows down just before her periods begin. Pituitary hormones also prompt egg cells in the ovary to secrete oestrogen, the sex hormone, which is largely responsible for enlarging the breasts, stimulating the growth of pubic hair and for building up the uterine lining.

In the year or so before menarche, girls may notice a light vaginal discharge. This accompanies other external and internal changes inside and outside the body as the body becomes sexually mature. Inside, the rise and fall in levels of oestrogen and pituitary hormones begin to form a pattern of interaction that will keep the menstrual cycle going. The first period arrives when the oestrogen level drops, leaving the built-up uterine lining without its vital support. This then crumbles and blood and cells fall into the uterus, out through the neck of the womb, and so to the outside.

Although menarche involves the same type of bleeding as subsequent menstrual cycles, the ovary is not yet

Pubescent development in the female. The girl below has developed pubic hair and breasts at the same rate. This is by no means always the case; a girl could be at the third stage of breast development and only at the first stage of pubic hair growth.

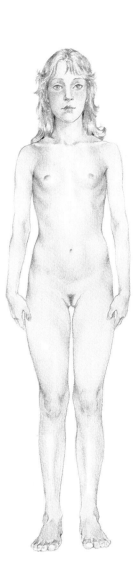
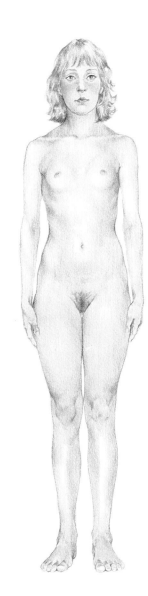
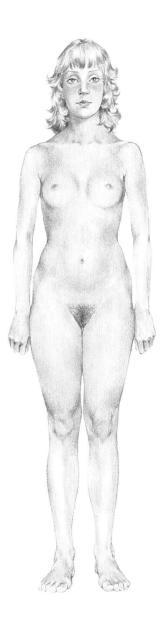

Oestrogen production and the developing egg

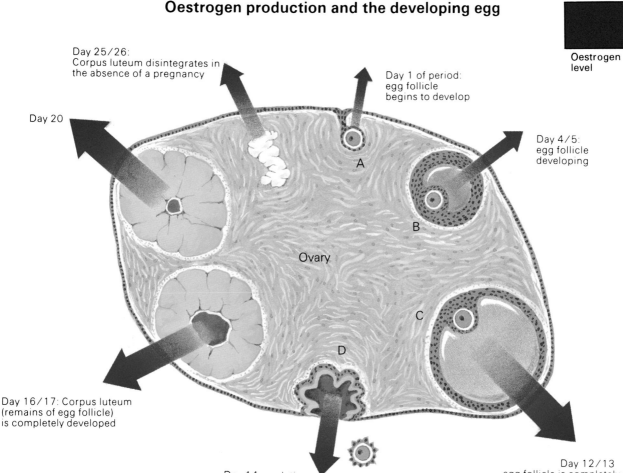

Day 25/26:
Corpus luteum disintegrates in
the absence of a pregnancy

Day 20

Day 1 of period:
egg follicle
begins to develop

Day 4/5:
egg follicle
developing

A

B

Ovary

C

D

Day 16/17: Corpus luteum
(remains of egg follicle)
is completely developed

Day 14: ovulation

Day 12/13
egg follicle is completely developed

Oestrogen
level

producing any ripe eggs. It takes several months, even a year, for the ovary to function fully and for the young girl to reach puberty, when her reproductive system is fully developed, although she still has to mature physically and emotionally.

The menstrual cycle

The time from the first day of one period to the first day of the next is known as the menstrual cycle. During this cycle the reproductive organs undergo a series of changes which make it possible for an egg to be released from the ovary and travel to the womb. If this egg is fertilized by a sperm, it will be nourished by secretions from the cells lining the womb until it burrows its way into the lining of the womb and is nourished from the mother's blood supply.

If the egg is not fertilized, the lining of the womb is shed in the menstrual flow. This allows a new lining to grow, ready to nourish the next egg.

This intricate cycle of activity is controlled by a centre in the brain called the hypothalamus, which acts as a menstrual clock. The clock operates through a small gland called the anterior pituitary gland, situated at the base of the brain. This gland

releases several hormones, two of which are particularly important for reproduction. One stimulates the growth and maturation of several small eggs in the ovary, while the other stimulates the release of these ripened eggs.

The eggs which mature during a menstrual cycle are surrounded by hormone-producing cells. The egg, together with these cells, is called the Graafian follicle. The main hormone produced by this follicle is oestrogen. During the cycle the surge in oestrogen production is responsible for stimulating the growth and formation of glands in the lining of the womb. It also changes the secretions at the neck of the womb, making it easier for sperm to swim into the womb and so meet the egg. Approximately 15 days before the next period is due, the pituitary gland releases a large amount of luteinizing hormone which stimulates the release of an egg from the ovary about 36 hours later. The egg then travels down a Fallopian tube into the womb. Fertilization usually takes place in the Fallopian tube.

The cells in the ovary which had formed the Graafian follicle now undergo changes, which include taking up fat. They are now referred to as the

The quantity of oestrogen that egg follicles produce varies during the menstrual cycle. Initially, the follicles produce very little oestrogen, but the level gradually builds up as the follicles develop (A and B) and reaches a peak on day 13 (C). At ovulation (D) the oestrogen level drops dramatically. It rises once more as the corpus luteum develops and drops after day 20, unless the egg has been fertilised.

corpus luteum. They still produce oestrogen, but now also produce a hormone called progesterone. Progesterone has two main functions in the menstrual cycle. The first is to alter the mucus at the neck of the womb, making it too thick for sperm to swim into the womb; the second is to make the glands lining the womb secrete a fluid which will nourish the newly fertilized egg.

If the egg is not fertilized, the corpus luteum degenerates. Small blood vessels in the area go into spasm so that cells lining the womb no longer receive oxygen and die. They are then shed together with some blood as menstruation, and the cycle is complete. All the hormones released during the cycle can influence the menstrual clock.

Conception and Reproduction

Conception is the union of a sperm and egg. It is a complex process in which a variety of conditions have to be right to ensure that it is successful.

If intercourse takes place around the time of ovulation, conception is very likely. A man produces around 400 million sperm in each ejaculation. These are surrounded by seminal fluid, which protects the sperm from the acidity of the vagina.

Once deposited in the vagina, the sperm immediately start their journey up the vagina through the cervix and into the uterus. They move by vigorously lashing their tiny 'tails'. Some of the sperm do not make this journey successfully, and will wither and die in the acid conditions of the vagina. This is nature's way of ensuring that damaged or unhealthy sperm do not manage to fertilize the egg.

Fertilization

The millions of sperm that have reached the uterus are nourished by the alkaline mucus of the cervical canal. They then travel up into the Fallopian tubes. This journey of about 20 cm (8 in) takes approximately 45 minutes – only about 2000 sperm may actually survive. The sperm will stay alive within the Fallopian tubes for up to three days, ready to fuse with an egg if ovulation takes place. If an egg is already present within the tube, fertilisation will take place immediately.

Fertilization is accomplished when a sperm penetrates the surface of the egg. Each sperm carries an enzyme (a substance responsible for causing life-supporting chemical processes) which helps liquefy the outer surface of the egg to make penetration of a single sperm easier. Once the egg is fertilized, the rest of the sperm die.

The egg and sperm (which has now discarded its tail) then fuse together to form a single nucleus (centre), which then begins to divide into two cells. Within 72 hours the cells continue to divide until a 64-celled egg is produced.

The fertilized egg then travels down to the uterus within approximately seven days (day 21 of a 28-day cycle). During this time it grows tiny projections which help it to burrow into the lining of the uterus, where it can be nurtured and a pregnancy can start. Once this process, called nidation, has occurred conception is complete.

The egg can now be nourished by the rich blood supply present in the uterine lining. From the moment of fertilization, the egg produces a hormone called human chorionic gonada-

Formation of the blastocyst

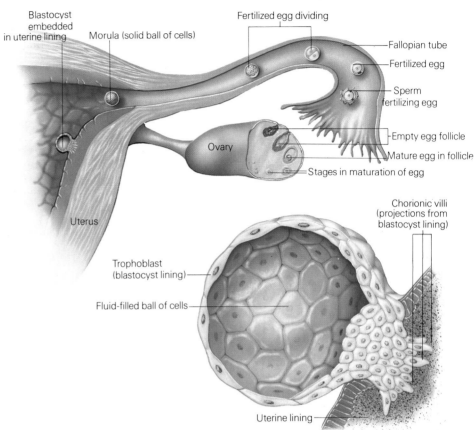

Above: The fertilised egg divides, forming the morula (ball of cells). This then divides to form the blastocyst, which embeds itself in the lining of the uterus.

trophin (HCG), which informs the ovary that fertilization has taken place, and which maintains the blood flow to the lining of the uterus so that the egg can continue its development.

The placenta

The placenta forms when a specialized part of the fertilized egg, called the trophoblast, embeds in the wall of the mother's uterus. By the 12th week of pregnancy the placenta is a separate organ; at the time of the baby's birth it weighs approximately 500 gm (a little over a pound) and is dark red, spongy and disc-shaped. Two layers of cells keep the circulation of the foetal blood in the placenta separate from the mother's blood, but many substances can pass from mother to baby.

Function

All the food and oxygen the foetus needs it receives from the mother, and it is able to eliminate any waste products back into her. This vital exchange function is carried out by the placenta, to which the foetus is attached by the umbilical cord. Carbon dioxide, waste products and hormones

pass from the foetus to the mother; oxygen, nutrients (simple carbohydrates, fats and amino acids) and hormones from mother to foetus.

The placenta also acts as a barrier to protect the foetus from potentially harmful substances, although many drugs can cross the placenta and harm the foetus. Some of the mother's antibodies, too, cross the placenta.

Finally, the placenta produces several hormones, some of which prevent the woman from releasing more eggs or having more periods while she is pregnant. They also encourage breast development in preparation for breast feeding, and the laying down of fat on the thighs, abdomen and buttocks as a future energy store. Other hormones also stimulate the growth of the womb and probably inhibit it from contracting before labour starts. There is also evidence to suggest that the amounts of these hormones released by the placenta may be an important factor in determining when labour starts.

Foetal development

The foetus is the name given to the unborn child from the time it is recognizable as a developing human being (from about two months after the egg has been fertilized). Prior to this the developing fertilized egg is known as the embryo.

A doctor will date the start of pregnancy from the first day of the last menstrual period, adding on nine calendar months and seven days to arrive at an estimate of the delivery date. Pregnancy is divided into trimesters (periods of three months in the life of the embryo or foetus), but in fact conception will probably take place between the tenth and fourteenth day of the menstrual cycle, when a woman is most likely to be ovulating and at her most fertile; therefore, pregnancy may actually begin during the second week of the first trimester. At this stage, the pregnancy consists of a single fertilised cell or egg. For three days or so after fertilization, this cell moves along the Fallopian tube towards the uterus, dividing and re-dividing to form a small group of cells called the morula.

The first trimester

For about another three days the morula floats in the uterus. It divides and re-divides to form a hollow clump of cells called the blastocyst, just visible to the naked eye.

Week 2: The blastocyst embeds itself in the endometrium: this is called implantation. Chorionic villi, projections from its covering, burrow into the lining of the uterus, to secure nourishment for the embryo.

The outer lining of the blastocyst called the trophoblast, begins to develop into the placenta. Blood cells start to form and the first heart cells are laid down.

Week 3: Hormonal changes cause the endometrium to thicken, and the blood from it nourishes the blastocyst.

Week 4: The amniotic sac is well developed. The embryo and later the foetus will stay in it throughout the pregnancy, comfortably suspended in the amniotic fluid, at a constant temperature and buffered against shocks.

The placenta consists of maternal blood vessels in the uterine wall, and foetal blood vessels rising from the umbilical cord. The exchange of food, oxygen and waste products takes place in the spaces between the blood vessels, which are not connected.
Deoxygenated (blue) blood leaves the foetus along the umbilical arteries, and oxygenated (red) blood reaches the foetus via the umbilical vein.

The heart is already beating, irregularly at first, but soon quite steadily and faster than the mother's.

The spine and the beginning of the nervous system are starting to form in the embryo, which is now about 7mm (0.28in) in length.

Week 5: The first organs form. The head is growing, enclosing the developing brain, which is linked to a rudimentary spinal cord. The arms and legs show as little buds, and the heart and blood circulatory systems are well established.

Blood vessels from the embryo join with others in the developing placenta to form the umbilical cord. The chorionic villi continue to increase in number and to branch, attaching the embryo firmly to the wall of the uterus.

In the embryo itself, now about 10mm (0.3in) long, the digestive system has begun to form, starting with the stomach and parts of the intestines. Although there is as yet no recognizable face, there are little depressions where the eyes and ears will be. The mouth and jaws also are starting to form, and the brain and spine continue to develop.

Week 6: The development of the head gets quicker. The internal parts of the ear and the eyes continue to form (the latter covered with the skin that will become the eyelids). The little holes that later become the nostrils start to develop. The brain and the spinal cord are nearly formed. The development of the digestive and urinary systems continues, although the liver and kidneys are not yet able to function. The arm and leg buds have

Anatomy of the placenta

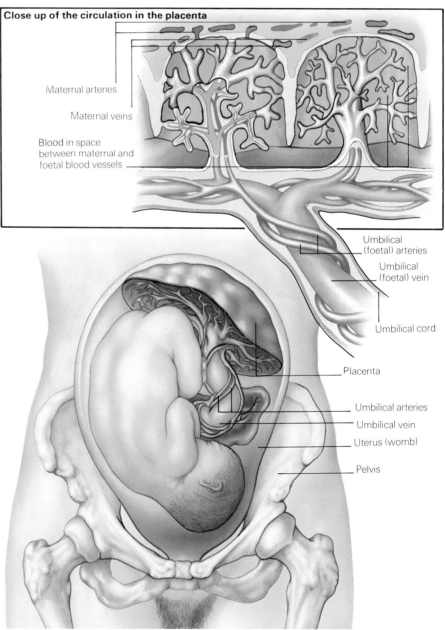

Close up of the circulation in the placenta

- Maternal arteries
- Maternal veins
- Blood in space between maternal and foetal blood vessels
- Umbilical (foetal) arteries
- Umbilical (foetal) vein
- Umbilical cord
- Placenta
- Umbilical arteries
- Umbilical vein
- Uterus (womb)
- Pelvis

The development of the hands

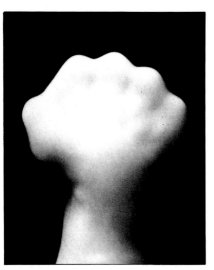

By the sixth week of pregnancy the arm buds are growing and the foetus has rudimentary hands.

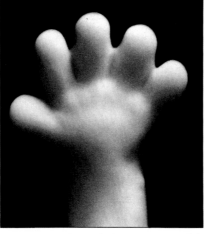

In the seventh week the structure of the hand begins to form; the finger ridges are visible.

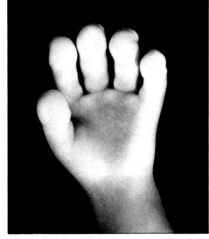

In the eighth week, the fingers and thumb, with their broad pads, are separate from one another.

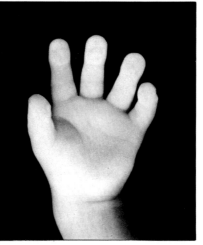

By the thirteenth week, the pads are smaller, the nail beds have begun to develop, and the hands curl.

grown and it is now just possible to see the rudiments of hands and feet. By the end of week 6 the embryo is about 1.3cm (0.5in) long.

Week 7: The placenta through which the embryo takes nourishment from its mother's circulation into its own and passes back its waste products to be excreted is now well developed. This is an important time for the growth of the eyes and parts of the inner ear, and the heart beats more powerfully. The formation of the digestive system continues, and many of the internal organs, although still in a very simple state, now exist. The lungs are growing, but they are solid at this point. There are small spinal movements and the face continues to form, to the point where it is possible to see the beginnings of the mouth. The arms and legs are growing and have developed hip, knee, shoulder and elbow joints.

Week 8: The eyes are almost fully developed, but are still covered with half-formed eyelid skin. The face continues to form and now has the beginnings of a nose. It is now possible to see separate toes and fingers and the limbs are able to move a little. The head, large in comparison with the rest of the body, leans downward over the chest. The foetus is now approximately 4cm (1.6in) long.

Week 9: The umbilical cord is completely formed and nourishes the foetus's circulatory system with blood. The inner part of the ear is complete; the outer part is starting to form. All the major inner organs of the body continue to develop, and the uterus has increased in size. By this point, the foetus is approximately 4.5cm (1.9in) long.

Week 10: The circulatory system is now pumping blood round the body of the foetus. The reproductive system

The foetus when 28 days old

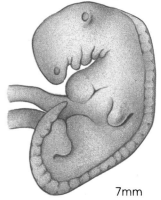

Right: The foetus from just over three weeks to seven weeks of development. In this short time, it triples in size and is recognizably human in its physical form.

The foetus when 24 days old

3mm

7mm

has begun to form, but only inside the body: the external genitals are not yet visible. The face continues to develop and the arms and legs are now very clearly formed, with tiny webbed fingers and toes. Movement of hands and feet is more vigorous, but still cannot be felt by the mother. By the end of week 10, the foetus measures 5.5cm (2.1in).

Week 11: The face is almost completely formed and the eyelids have developed. Muscles are starting to form and the development of the external sexual organs has begun. The placenta is by now a separate organ, a soft pad of tissue. The volume of fluid in the amniotic sac continually increases between the eleventh and the fortieth weeks of pregnancy.

Weeks 12-14: Nearly all the internal organs are now formed, but they cannot yet function independently of the mother. The uterus can now just be felt, rising above the pelvic bones, but the mother does not yet show her pregnancy.

The second trimester

Weeks 14-16: The limbs go on forming and the joints are able to move. Finger and toe nails develop, and a soft, fine hair, called langou, covers the whole foetus.

After week 14 the placenta is fully formed. Growth in size begins to be rapid: the foetus now weighs about 135g (4¾oz) and is approximately 12cm (5in) long.

After week 16 or thereabouts, the kidneys begin to produce dilute urine.

Week 20: By now, the foetus is able to make vigorous kicking movements, which the mother will be able to feel. The muscles are developing fast, and hair has begun to grow on the head. The foetus will now be about 21cm (8.4in) long.

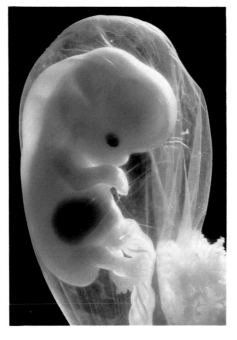

In this nine-week-old foetus, all the parts of the body are present, even though they are not all fully formed. The dark area will become the internal organs. Note the tiny toes and fingers.

Week 24: The muscles are almost completely formed. The placenta is growing continually: all necessary nutrients, including oxygen, pass through it from the mother to the foetus, and waste products go back through it into the mother's circulation and she excretes them. The circulation and blood of the mother and baby remain quite separate.

The foetus is still not able to exist independently of the mother, although, in very rare instances, babies born prematurely at this point and nursed with expert care have survived. The weight of the foetus is about 570gm (20oz) and the length about 33cm (12.7in).

Week 28: This is the point at which the foetus is said to become viable, because it would have a 5 per cent chance of survival if it were born prematurely. Covered with a grease called vernix, to protect it from the fluid in the amniotic sac, it is now approximately 37cm (14.5in) long.

The third trimester

The growth of the foetal body has now caught up with that of the head, and the foetus has the physical proportions of a baby. It is much thinner, however, because the subcutaneous (under the skin) fat has not yet developed. The amount of vernix has increased. The length of the body is now about 45cm (17.7in), and the baby born prematurely at this stage has a 15 per cent chance of survival.

Week 36: By this point, the chance of survival would be increased to 90 per cent, as the lungs are fully formed. In many cases, the baby has turned to rest head downwards in the womb,

The foetus when 7 weeks old

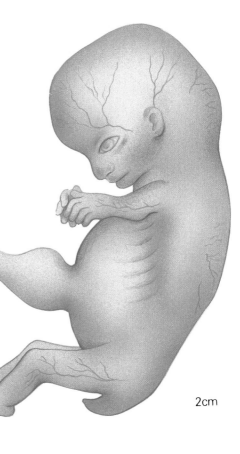

The foetus when 6 weeks old

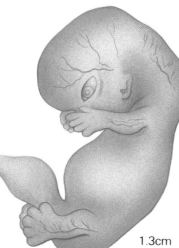

The foetus when 5 weeks old

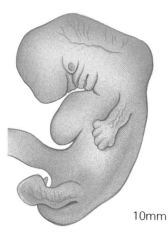

10mm

1.3cm

2cm

but in women who have already had a child, this may not happen until later.

The testicles of the male baby have come down into the scrotal sac, and the vernix has increased. The baby's weight goes up by about 28gm (1oz) per day. Some babies are born with the fine lanugo hair still on the arms, legs or shoulders, but it usually disappears in the final weeks of pregnancy.

Birth will take place at about the fortieth week, although some women go into labour later or earlier than this. When the baby is born, there will still be patches of vernix on the body, but not on the eyes and mouth. The child will be about 50cm (20in) long and have an average weight of about 3.4kg (7.7lb).

The mother

Since the first trimester is the three-month period in which the basic formation of the foetus takes place, it is important for the mother to avoid anthing which could cause foetal malformation. The doctor should be con-

sulted before any drugs are taken, and all women are advised to give up smoking and drinking alcohol as soon as they become pregnant.

Before starting a pregnancy, a woman should make sure that she is immune from rubella (German measles) and if she is not, should be vaccinated against it. Contracting it during pregnancy might cause the baby to be born with a number of grave abnormalities.

It is important for the mother to see a doctor at the beginning of the pregnancy for a thorough physical check-up and to arrange for antenatal care. Checking on the progress of the foetus is an important part of this. Methods of doing this range from simply measuring the size of the mother's abdomen to the use of ultrasound.

About a week before the normal menstrual period would start, there may be a little bleeding as new blood vessels are forming to nourish the growing embryo. The doctor should be

told of this and of any other symptoms, and he will also give advice on diet and the extra vitamins and iron which may be needed throughout the pregnancy. Regular blood pressure and urine tests should be made to check that the mother is fit and healthy.

During the second trimester, the mother will feel the foetus moving inside her, particularly just before she falls asleep. Her own blood circulatory system has changed, with a continual increase in the production of blood cells.

Many women find that they drink a great deal more liquid than usual in this period, and some may need iron supplements to help in the increased production of blood.

By week 20 the breasts are ready for breast feeding: some women find that the nipples produce a yellow fluid, called colostrum, but not all pregnant women experience this, and those who don't should not worry that their ability to breast feed will be affected in any way.

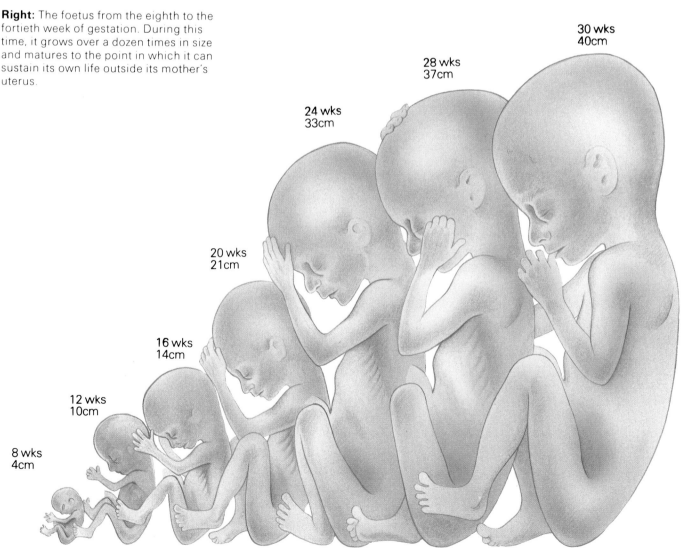

Right: The foetus from the eighth to the fortieth week of gestation. During this time, it grows over a dozen times in size and matures to the point in which it can sustain its own life outside its mother's uterus.

8 wks
4cm

12 wks
10cm

16 wks
14cm

20 wks
21cm

24 wks
33cm

28 wks
37cm

30 wks
40cm

At this stage of the pregnancy, some mothers have indigestion, heartburn and constipation, and they need to take these things into account when they are planning their diet. As the pregnancy advances, the increase of weight and pressure on the internal organs can cause haemorrhoids (piles) in the rectum and varicose veins in the legs. The haemorrhoids can partly be prevented by avoiding constipation, and the irritation they cause can be relieved by ointment or suppositories, obtained from the doctor. The wearing of elastic support stockings or tights can help to prevent the formation of varicose veins. But it is essential that these be put on *before* getting out of bed in the morning.

The third trimester

By the third trimester the uterus has expanded a great deal, and many women find that it is difficult to walk without leaning back a little, which can cause backache. There will be occasional painless contractions of the womb, which are normal and help with circulation through the placenta.

Lying on the stomach will become uncomfortable. However, once the baby's head has 'engaged' – descended into the pelvis – many women feel a great deal more comfortable, because the pressure on the stomach and diaphragm is much reduced. Some time in or about the fortieth week, labour will begin. The mother's pelvic bones have already become more separated in readiness for the delivery of the baby. Powerful contractions, rupture of the amniotic sac, or the passing of a little blood from the uterus, are among the first signs that the baby is about to be born. The cervix starts to dilate and the baby begins its journey.

At birth, the average baby weighs about 3.4kg (7.7lb), but a birth weight of anything between 2.8kg (6.2lb) and 4.0kg (8.8lb) is regarded as normal.

The hair on the newborn baby's head varies in length from scarcely visible to about 4cm (1.5in), the nails reach to the ends of the fingers and toes, or even a little beyond them, and the eyes are almost always blue in colour, because the eye colouring is not yet fully formed.

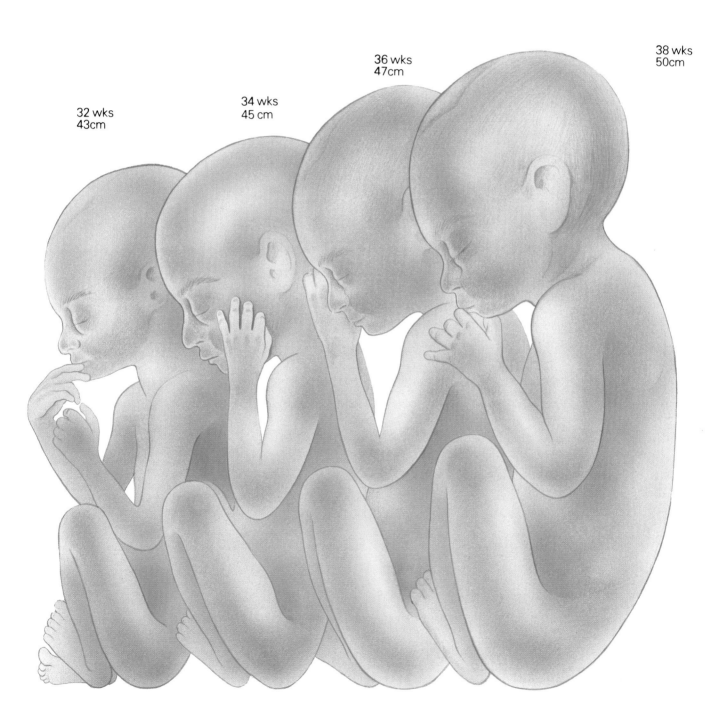

32 wks
43cm

34 wks
45 cm

36 wks
47cm

38 wks
50cm

Glossary

ABDOMEN The abdominal cavity which lies between the diaphragm and the pelvis and contains all the organs of digestion, the kidneys, liver and the pancreas. The front wall is a muscular sheet, and the internal surface is lined by the peritoneal membrane. (Compare with cranium and thorax.)

ACETYL CHOLINE Chemical released from the nerve endings and which is the 'transmitter' for the parasympathetic nerves. Among its functions, it causes muscles to contract and bronchial airways to constrict.

ACTH Adrenocorticotrophic hormone. A pituitary hormone which stimulates corticosteroid production. ACTH may be given by injection.

ADENOIDS Collections of lymph tissue (like the tonsils) found in the pharynx at the back of the nose. May swell up in children.

ADIPOSE TISSUE A kind of connective tissue used for storing fat.

ADRENAL GLANDS Two glands situated above the kidneys which are responsible for the production of cortisone from their outer layers (the cortex) and adrenalin from their inner core (the medulla).

ADRENALIN The body's hormone of 'fight or flight'; stimulates heart, lungs, and other tissues for action. Produced by the adrenal medulla.

ALBUMIN A simple protein, manufactured in the liver and found in the blood plasma. It is both a food source for the tissues and a supplier of osmotic pressure to keep the blood fluid within the walls of the blood vessels themselves.

ALDOSTERONE A hormone produced by the adrenal cortex. It regulates excretion of salt by the kidneys, maintains a balance of salt and potassium, and plays a role in the body's use of carbohydrates.

ALLERGY Adverse reaction — such as wheezing or rashes — to a foreign substance which triggers the immune system. Usually the substance allergen is inhaled or contacts the skin. Food allergy also occurs.

ALVEOLI Tiny air sacs in the lungs which are surrounded by capillaries. It is here that the exchange of oxygen and carbon dioxide takes place.

ANTIBODY A substance carried dissolved in the blood which attaches itself to invading organisms (or other foreign substances) so helping the body to defend itself against infection.

AORTIC VALVE The valve which separates the aorta from the left ventricle. It allows blood to flow from the left ventricle to the aorta and thence into the tissues.

APOCRINE GLAND One of the sweat glands found in the armpits, groin and the areola of the breasts. These glands produce a thick milky substance and it is these glands upon which antiperspirant acts. (Compare eccrine gland.)

APPENDIX A narrow finger-shaped piece of intestine hanging from the caecum. It has no apparent use in the body (though it may have had in the past); it can become inflamed, necessitating removal.

AQUEOUS HUMOUR A watery fluid which fills the anterior chamber of the eye, between the cornea and the lens.

ARTERY Large blood vessels carrying oxygen-rich blood from the heart to the tissues (e.g. the aorta).

ATP Adenosine triphosphate. A high-energy phosphate compound produced by cells to provide power for the chemical reactions on which the cell depends. This ATP is stored in the cells until needed when it is broken down by the burning of glucose.

ATRIOVENTRICULAR NODE A node in the heart, at the junction of the atria and the ventricles. Signals the ventricles *not* to contract. This is part of the process which maintains a normal heartbeat pattern. (See Bundle of His and sinu-atrial node.)

ATRIUM The left and right atria are the two low pressure pumping chambers of the heart. They pump blood to their corresponding ventricle chambers.

AUTONOMIC NERVOUS SYSTEM Part of the nervous system which controls automatic functions, such as heartbeat and sweating. It consists of the sympathetic and parasympathetic nervous systems. Each of these separate systems is controlled by a special chemical 'messenger' or hormone; and they work by performance (e.g. one part controls inhaling, the other exhaling, together breathing).

BACTERIA Small single-celled organisms, some of which cause infection.

BARTHOLIN'S DUCT The duct from which is released the secretions of Bartholin's gland, the purpose of which is to lubricate the vagina.

BASAL GANGLIA Four masses of nerve cells deeply placed within the base of the brain.

BASAL METABOLIC RATE A measure of the basic level of the body's metabolic (chemical) processes. The rate is raised by thyroid over-activity and lowered by thyroid under-activity.

BICEPS The large flexor muscle at the front of the upper arm. Together with the triceps, it helps facilitate elbow and shoulder movement. (Note: the combination of biceps and triceps is what is known as 'antagonistic', that is they function by opposing one another.)

BILE Fluid produced by the liver that is stored in the gall bladder and enters the intestines through the bile duct.

BLADDER Urine produced in the kidneys is collected in the bladder which is voluntarily emptied. It lies in the pelvis.

BLOOD CLOTTING The vital mechanism whereby components of the blood solidify after any damage, so stopping bleeding.

BLOOD PRESSURE The pressure at which blood is carried in the arterial system.

BONE MARROW The soft red material in the centre of certain bones. It is in this red marrow that red blood cells, some white blood cells and platelets are manufactured.

BOWEL To the doctor, simply means another word for intestine. 'Opening the bowels' means passing faeces.

BRAIN STEM That area which links the brain with the spinal cord and comprises part of the hindbrain, all of the midbrain and part of the forebrain. It is here that all incoming stimuli are received and directed to the correct side of the brain for them to be analyzed and a response to be determined.

BROCA'S AREA The area of the brain to which deciphered speech is transmitted and where a reply is formed. From here a 'message' is sent to the face, via the motor cortex, which also stimulates the muscles of lips, tongue, jaw and throat to produce speech (in reply).

BRUNNER'S GLANDS Any of the small glands in the duodenum which secrete protective mucus and a powerful enzyme which breaks down protein.

BUNDLE OF HIS A very slim bundle of cardiac muscle that passes from the right atrium to the right and left ventricles, conducting the impulse to contract. This is part of the process which maintains a normal heartbeat pattern. (See atrioventricular node and sinu-atrial node.)

CAECUM The blind pouch from which the large intestine starts. The ileum, or last of the divisions of the small intestine, opens into the caecum. The appendix projects from it.

CALCANEUS A large bone that is part of the tarsus (instep). It is commonly called the 'heel' or 'heel bone'.

CALCIUM A mineral which is essential to give the hardness to bone. It is also carried dissolved in the blood, and it controls the way in which muscles contract.

CAPILLARY The tiny blood vessels that connect the arterioles (the ends of the arteries) to the venules (the ends of the veins), and so allow the contents of the blood to be passed through to the tissues.

CARBOHYDRATE One of the three basic food types. Carbohydrates are the sugars and starches (chemical combinations of sugars) found in cereals, bread, flour, potatoes.

CARBON DIOXIDE Oxygen is extracted from the air by the lungs and used to burn up food for energy. The waste product of this reaction is carbon dioxide which the lungs pass back into the air.

CAROTID ARTERY The artery which divides into right and left branches and carries blood to the head, one branch to the face and scalp, the other directly to the brain.

CARPALS The eight cube-like bones forming the 'hinge' at the wrist, between the bones of the forearms and the metacarpals of the hand itself.

CARTILAGE Gristly material attached to bone and making joint cavities. There are two free cartilages in the knee, which are easily damaged and which may need removal.

CELL The basic unit of the human body, and of all living things. Each cell contains a nucleus and protoplasm — the essential building material: the cell divides to build up tissues.

CEREBELLUM The part of the brain that is concerned with co-ordinating movement and maintaining equilibrium. It is situated at the back of the skull, beneath the cerebrum.

CEREBRAL CORTEX The outer layer of the brain.

CEREBROSPINAL FLUID Fluid that bathes and cushions the brain and spinal cord.

CEREBRUM The most highly developed and largest part of the brain. It is divided down the middle into two parts, known as the cerebral hemispheres.

CERVICAL SMEAR A method of scraping a few cells from the neck of the uterus for examination. Used to detect cancer. Commonly known as a 'pap smear' (after Dr Papanicolaou, the doctor from whose research the test was developed).

CERVIX The neck of the uterus. The central channel in the cervix dilates (opens) during labour to allow the birth of the baby.

CHOLESTEROL A fatty substance which is an essential part of the structure of cell walls. When present in the blood in excessive quantities, it is laid down in the walls of arteries causing atheroma.

CHROMOSOME One of a number of tiny rod-shaped bodies inside the cell nucleus that carry the genes — the hereditary determinants. There are 23 pairs of chromosomes plus an additional two sex-determining chromosomes.

CILIA Minute hairlike bodies within specialised cells (e.g. those cilia within the endolymph, or fluid, of the inner ear, which sense movement; or the cilia within the nose which trap dust particles).

CLAVICLE The bone which joins the scapula (shoulder blade) and the sternum (breast bone). Commonly called the 'collarbone'.

CLITORIS An extremely sensitive organ of the female genitals, consisting of spongy erectile tissue, and located at the juncture of the labia minora. Friction on the erect clitoris will usually lead to orgasm.

COAGULATION The process whereby blood solidifies to form a clot.

COCCYX The five small fused vertebrae at the base of the spinal column. Commonly called the 'tailbone', it is all that remains of the tail which has been lost through evolution.

COCHLEA The snail-shaped portion of the inner ear, which is filled with endolymph and lined with cilia, and through which sound waves are transmitted, via the cochleal nerve, to the brain where they are interpreted.

COLON The large intestine, a tube stretching from the end of the small intestine through to the rectum.

CONCEPTION The fertilization of the ovum (egg) by the sperm, leading to embryo formation.

CONJUNCTIVA The mucous membrane which lines the eyelid and continues over part of the eyeball.

CONNECTIVE TISSUE The basic 'cement and packaging' of the body, which holds the organs in place and fills spaces. Fibres of the protein collagen provide the strength, and the protein elastin provides stretchiness.

CORNEA The transparent 'front window' of the eye.

CORPUS LUTEUM When the ovary releases an egg in the middle of the menstrual cycle the corpus luteum is left at the site of release. It produces the hormone progesterone.

CORPUSCLE An old-fashioned word for a red or a white blood cell.

CORTISONE Hormone produced by the cortex (the part *around* the inner core) of the adrenal gland. It is essential for life and controls the body's response to stress.

COSTAL Of or relating to a rib or ribs. (E.g. intercostal spaces are those between the ribs.)

CRANIUM The part of the skull which encloses the brain. (The cranial cavity is one of the three main body cavities: compare with abdomen and thorax.)

CRYPTS OF LIEBERKÜHN Small projections within the duodenum which secrete digestive enzymes and alkaline juice to neutralize stomach acid.

DIABETES Failure of the hormone insulin to keep the blood sugar down. Leads to thirst and weight loss. Can be controlled by insulin injections, or in some cases by diet and medication.

DIAPHRAGM The sheet of muscle which forms a barrier between the contents of the chest and those of the abdomen.

DISC Flat circular body, consisting of a tough outer layer and an inner gelatinous core. The discs lie between each of the thoracic and lumbar vertebrae, which they cushion. They expand and contract as the spine moves, and can sometimes be jolted ('slip') out of place.

DNA (Deoxyribonucleic acid) The basic genetic material which is passed from generation to generation on the chromosomes. DNA is found in cell nuclei and controls protein manufacture in the cell.

DUODENUM The first 25cm (10in) of the small intestine as it leaves the stomach.

ECCRINE GLAND One of the sweat glands found all over the body (except the lips and part of the sexual organs). These glands are controlled by the central nervous system and some hormones, and so react not only to temperature change, but also to such things as excitement or the hot flush of the menopause.

ECZEMA A red, scaly, itchy skin rash. Childhood forms usually start behind the knees and in the elbow creases. Other forms may result from an allergy contact (dermatitis).

ELASTIC CARTILAGE Contains fibres of elastin as well as collagen (compare with fibrocartilage). It is strong but supple and forms the epiglottis, parts of the middle and outer ear, the Eustachian tube, and parts of the larynx.

EMBRYO The name given to the structure in the early stages of foetal development in the uterus (in the first trimester).

ENDOCRINE GLAND One of a number of ductless glands, scattered throughout the body, whose secretions pass directly into the bloodstream. The blood then transports the secretion to the organ they act upon. The endocrine glands (e.g. pituitary and thyroid glands) collectively form the endocrine, or hormone, system.

ENZYME Any one of many substances produced by the body which act as catalysts in vital processes, such as digestion. They may either break down large molecules into smaller ones, or utilize small molecules for growth, reproduction or defence against infection.

EPIDIDYMIS A mass of tubes located at the back of each testicle. It is here that new sperm, having been produced in the seminiferous tubules, gain maturity and motility (ability to move). These sperm are stored in the epididymis until just before ejaculation, when they travel, via the vas deferens, to the prostate gland where the sperm will be mixed with secretions to form the semen or seminal fluid. This fluid is then pushed out through the urethra.

EPIGLOTTIS A flap of tissue at the entrance to the larynx, or airway. When food is being swallowed this flap is pushed across the opening so that the food cannot be pushed down into the lungs, causing choking.

EUSTACHIAN TUBE: The tube that connects the middle ear (the part of the ear inside the ear drum) to the back of the throat. The tube allows the air pressure on both sides of the drum to equalize.

EXCRETION The removal of liquid and solid waste materials from the body.

EXOCRINE GLAND This type includes those glands which release their secretions to the surface of the body (e.g. sweat glands), or through the large ducts (e.g. the pancreas, which secretes substances into the small intestine).

EXTENSOR MUSCLE A muscle whose purpose is to extend or straighten a body part, such as a limb. E.g. triceps in the upper arm. (Compare with flexor muscle.)

FAECES The residue after the nutrient value of food has been absorbed by the small intestine. Water is absorbed in the colon and the faeces (stools, motions) are passed out through the anus.

FALLOPIAN TUBES (oviducts). The two tubes arising out of the uterus and ending near the ovary. Eggs produced in the ovary normally pass through the Fallopian tubes on their way to the uterus.

FAT One of the three basic food types: fat is, in fact, the most concentrated provider of energy and is stored in the body in the adipose tissue.

FEMORAL ARTERY The artery supplying blood to the thigh.

FEMUR The large bone of the upper leg, which articulates at the hip, in a ball and socket joint, and extends to the hinge joint at the knee. Commonly called the 'thigh bone', the femur is the longest and heaviest bone of the human body.

FERTILIZATION The process where a sperm enters an egg and fuses with it to make the embryo that will implant itself and develop in the uterus.

FIBROCARTILAGE Composed mainly of collagen fibres, making it tough and able to withstand compression. It is most plentiful in the cushioning discs between the spinal vertebrae, and it is also a tough form of connection between bones and ligaments.

FIBULA The long, very slender outer bone of the lower leg. Sometimes called the 'calf bone', it is the more delicate, and therefore more vulnerable, of the two lower leg bones.

FLEXOR MUSCLE A muscle whose purpose is to bend a body part, such as a limb. E.g. the biceps in the upper arm. (Compare with extensor muscle.)

FOETUS The name by which a developing being (in the uterus) is known, usually in the second and third trimesters. Before this it is an 'embryo'.

FONTANELLES The gaps between the developing bones of a baby's skull, covered by soft membranous tissue.

FORAMEN MAGNUM The hole at the base of the skull through which an outlet is provided for the spinal cord.

GALL BLADDER A sack-like organ attached to the liver which collects bile and then discharges it into the intestine in response to a fatty meal.

GAMMA GLOBULIN The gamma globulins are proteins which circulate in the blood carrying antibodies. Gamma globulin injections may be given to combat infections.

GANGLION A grouping of nerve cells. Also, a small cyst-like tumour, especially in the wrist or ankle.

GENES The minute segments of chromosomes that determine inherited characteristics — such as eye colour. Each characteristic is controlled by a pair of genes, one from each parent.

GENETICS The study of inherited characteristics. This includes the study of diseases which can be passed on from generation to generation.

GENITALS Part of the organs of reproduction (for example: the penis in the male; the clitoris in the female).

GLAND Any organ which produces a secretion. The endocrine glands secrete into the bloodstream, while other glands have more local effects.

GLUCOSE A simple sugar that is the main source of energy for the body's cells. It is extracted from starches and sweet foods.

GLUTEUS MAXIMUS The large major muscle (as opposed to the smaller gluteus minimus) of the buttocks.

GLYCOGEN A form of glucose which is stored in the liver and muscles and released as needed for energy.

GONAD One of the primary sex glands, which produce sex hormones and reproductive cells. In males, the gonads are the testes where testosterone and sperm are produced; in females, the ovaries where oestrogen and other hormones, as well as ova, or eggs, are produced.

HAEMOGLOBIN The red oxygen-carrying pigment in red blood cells.

HAMSTRING The group of muscles (semitendinosus, semi-membranosus and biceps femoris) at the back of the thigh. They straighten the leg at both the hip and the knee.

HEPATIC Of or relating to the liver. E.g. the hepatic artery delivers nutrients and oxygenated blood to the liver.

HEREDITY The passing of genetic information from parents to children.

HORMONES The chemical messengers of the body, hormones control the body's metabolic (chemical) processes. Carried in the blood.

HYALINE CARTILAGE A bluish-white translucent tissue. It forms the skeleton of the embryo and allows growth to full adult height, after which it is reduced to a thin layer on the ends of bones. It is also found in the nose, the trachea and bronchi.

HYMEN A thin, somewhat elastic and perforated membrane that partially covers the entrance to the vaginal canal. A traditional symbol of virginity, although its lack does not necessarily indicate intercourse has ever taken place.

HYPERTROPHY An enlargement of a part of the body. E.g. the greatly enlarged voluntary muscles of body builders. Involuntary muscles can also enlarge; if this happens in the muscle of the heart, special treatment will be required to prevent heart failure.

HYPOTHALAMUS The area at the base of the brain which controls many of the body's automatic and hormone-related activities.

ILEUM The lower part of the small intestine and the last part food passes through before it reaches the caecum, or blind pouch where the large intestine begins. Its main purpose is to absorb food so that it can pass, digested, to the liver.

ILIAC ARTERY The two large branches of the aorta (which divides approximately at midriff level) that supply blood to each of the lower extremities. It continues as the femoral and tibial arteries.

IMMUNE SYSTEM The complex system by means of which the body defends itself against infection.

INSULIN A hormone which is made in the pancreas and which lowers the level of sugar in the blood. Given by injection to treat diabetes, a condition in which too little insulin is produced.

INTESTINES The long continuous tube connecting the stomach to the anus. The first part (the small intestine) absorbs nutrients, while the second (the large intestine or colon) processes the waste.

JEJUNEM The part of the small intestine between the duodenum and the ileum. Its purpose is to allow passage of nutrients into the blood.

JUGULAR VEINS Two veins draining blood from the head. An accidentally cut jugular can allow air into the circulation and can, therefore, be fatal.

KERATIN The dead skin cells that make up the outer layers of the skin; it is shed in tiny scales. Hair and nails are a specialised form of keratin.

KETONES Acid waste products from the burning of fats by the body's cells. Ketones are produced in uncontrolled diabetes, since cells have to use fat instead of sugar as fuel.

KNEE JERK A reflex, where the knee muscles contract sharply to produce a kick as a result of being suddenly struck by a light blow with a tendon hammer.

LACHRYMAL GLANDS Small glands which produce a fluid to lubricate and cleanse the eye. The fluid emerges from ducts, commonly called the 'tear ducts'.

LARYNX The voice box, which contains the vocal cords.

LENS The soft, elastic, transparent part of the eye just behind the iris. Its purpose is the fine focusing of light rays.

LIGAMENT The strong fibrous cords which hold bones and joints together and also support the organs.

LIVER The largest gland of the body; situated in the upper right-hand corner of the abdomen just beneath the diaphragm; especially concerned with processing food for use by tissues.

LUMBAR Of or relating to the group of vertebrae between the thoracic vertebrae and the sacrum. (E.g. lumbar puncture, in which fluid is drawn from between vertebrae in this region.)

LUNULA The white crescent found towards the base of the fingernail.

LYMPHOCYTE One type of white blood cell found in the blood. Lymphocytes are also found in the lymph-vascular system where they control the body's immunity to disease.

LYMPH-VASCULAR SYSTEM A secondary circulation system that carries fats to the cells, collects and filters fluid from the tissues through lymph nodes, and is a central feature in the activity of the body's immune system.

MACROPHAGE A large white blood cell whose job it is to clear away debris (e.g. bits of bone) from healing wounds.

MANDIBLE The hinged part of the skull, forming the lower jaw. Its purpose is to allow movement so that food can be crushed.

MAXILLA The upper jaw in the skull.

MEDULLA OBLONGATA Stem-like lowest part of the brain where it merges with the spinal cord. Here, things vital to life, such as heart rate control, blood pressure maintenance, breathing and consciousness are controlled.

MEIOSIS A method of cell division in which chromosomes are duplicated, then they pair up and intertwine before pulling apart and dividing to produce sex cells containing half the information needed to produce a human being. The remaining half is supplied during fertilization.

MELANIN The pigment in the skin which gives skin its colour. A sun tan is brought about by an increase in the amount of melanin in the skin.

MEMBRANE Any thin sheet of tissue. The cells are surrounded by a wall or membrane whose chemical characteristics are central to the way they work.

MENARCHE The time when menstruation starts.

MENINGES The membranes which cover the brain (i.e. arachnoid, dura mater and pia mater) and the spinal cord. ('Meningitis' is an inflammation of the meninges.)

MENOPAUSE The cessation of menstruation known as the change of life.

MENSTRUATION The period of time during which the uterus sheds its lining and some blood each month during a woman's reproductive years.

METABOLISM The chemical processes by which the body works.

METACARPALS Five bones radiating out from the wrist. These bones lead to the phalanges which form the thumb and fingers on each hand.

MITOSIS A process of cell division in which pairs of chromosomes separate. Each half then divides into two identical parts which arrange themselves so that when the respective parts move to opposite ends of the cell and the cell divides into two, each new cell will contain all the genetic information necessary to replace or duplicate existing body cells.

MITRAL VALVE The valve on the left side of the heart which allows oxygenated blood to enter the left ventricle (from the left atrium). Its purpose is to prevent blood squirting back into the lungs when the left ventricle contracts.

MUCUS The semi-liquid substance that coats many of the internal membranes, so preventing both damage and infection.

MUSCLE Powerful tissues which are responsible for all movement. Voluntary muscle functions under conscious control; involuntary muscle discharges its functions independently.

MYELIN SHEATH The material which surrounds nerve fibres, and which insulates and protects them.

MYOFIBRIL A bundle of filaments within striated, or voluntary, muscle tissues. This bundle is made up of actin and myosin filaments, which consist of protein. Bundles of myofibrils are called 'muscle fibres'.

NERVES Bundles of specialised conducting tissue which carry messages to and from the brain. Sometimes though a disease is said to be due to 'nerves' when it is thought that it is primarily due to an emotional disturbance rather than a physical one.

NORADRENALIN A hormone produced by the adrenal medulla and which also makes up most of the chemical transmitter for sympathetic nerves. Among other things, it helps maintain even blood pressure.

NUTRITION Nourishment. Adequate nutrition ensures that the body receives the correct amount and type of food for growth and the maintenance of health.

OESOPHAGUS The gullet which leads from the mouth down through the chest to the stomach.

OESTROGEN One of the two important female hormones. Variations in oestrogen level occur during the monthly cycle and may explain many of the changes of mood which occur.

OPTIC NERVE The nerve that runs from the retina – the light-sensitive membrane – and carries messages to the brain.

ORGASM The climax of sexual intercourse (involving emission of semen in the male).

OSTEOBLAST A cell which produces bone.

OVARY The female organ where the eggs are made. The ovaries are found inside the abdomen at the ends of the Fallopian tubes (although they are not connected) which carry the eggs down to the uterus.

OVULATION The time at which the ovaries release an egg, usually in the middle of the menstrual cycle.

OXYGEN The gas which makes up about a fifth of the atmosphere. Life depends upon oxygen to burn up fuel and produce the energy that drives the body's processes. The lungs are responsible for absorbing it from the air and transferring it to the blood.

PALATE The roof of the mouth which is made up of the parts which separate the mouth from the nasal cavity. It consists of the hard palate and the soft palate.

PANCREAS The organ at the back of the abdomen responsible for producing many of the digestive juices. It is also a hormone gland which produces insulin.

PARASYMPATHETIC NERVOUS SYSTEM Part of the autonomic nervous system, controlled from the brain and the lower spinal cord, which interacts with the sympathetic nervous system (controlled from the spinal cord), to maintain a balance of the body's vital unconscious functions (e.g. breathing, digestion and heartbeat).

PARATHYROID GLANDS Four tiny glands just behind the thyroid glands and found just below the larynx. They play a major role in the level of calcium in the body which affects not only teeth and bones, but also nerves and muscles. The calcium levels are controlled by PTH, a hormone which is produced by the parathyroid glands.

PATELLA The slightly teardrop-shaped bone lying in front of and protecting the knee joint; commonly called the 'kneecap'.

PELVIS The basin-like structure formed by the ring of bones at the base of the torso and into which the legs are hinged. It consists of the sacrum and coccyx; the ilium (hip bone), containing the acetabulum, into which the femur slots; the ischium (base of the buttock); and the pubis, made up of the two pubic bones, joined by the disc of cartilage known as the interpubic disc.

PEPSIN A digestive enzyme, secreted by the mucous lining of the stomach, and whose purpose is to break down protein. It is the active constituent of the gastric juice, whose other part is hydrochloric acid.

PERCEPTION Information about the outside world is received by the organs of sense (especially the eyes and ears) and collated to build up a picture of the world. This process is called perception.

PERICARDIUM The fibrous membrane around the heart, which secretes a fluid for lubrication.

PERIODONTAL LIGAMENTS The fibres which anchor the teeth in place. They are connected to the cementum under the gum and the alveolar bone (part of the jaw) in which the teeth roots are fixed. These ligaments are elastic and cushion shock to a degree when the teeth are biting.

PERISTALSIS Wave-like, rhythmic muscular contractions that cause food to be pushed along through the body, during the digestive process.

PERITONEUM The smooth transparent layer of tissue which lines the abdomen and encloses the abdominal organs.

PINNA The external part of the ear whose purpose is to collect sound waves from the air and funnel them through into the ear canal.

PIRIFORMIS The muscle which runs under the gluteus maximus and minimus to join the femur to the sacrum, thus enabling sideways movement of the thigh.

PITUITARY A hormone gland, situated at the base of the brain, which controls the activity of many of the other glands in the body, as well as secreting hormones controlling growth and water balance.

PLACENTA The placenta is attached to the inside of the mother's uterus, and through it the foetus receives all its food and oxygen via the umbilical cord. Commonly called 'afterbirth'.

PLASMA The straw-coloured liquid part of the blood, consisting mainly of water, in which float, among other things, red and white blood cells and platelets.

PLATELETS The tiny cells in the blood which are essential for clotting.

PLEURA The thin membrane which lines lungs and the inner thoracic cavity and eases friction during breathing. ('Pleurisy' is inflammation of this pleural membrane).

PONS The roughly ovoid-shaped mass of nerve fibres at the base of the brain and top end of the medulla oblongata. It is here that stimuli are relayed from the cerebral cortex to the opposite side of the cerebellum.

PORTAL VEIN A large vein whose purpose it is to deliver blood to an area other than the heart. E.g. the hepatic portal vein transports blood from the organs of the digestive system (and the spleen) to the liver for processing.

POTASSIUM One of the most important of the body's minerals. The cells maintain a balance with potassium inside and sodium (salt) outside their walls.

PROSTAGLANDIN A substance produced by the body which causes muscles to contract, causing an increased susceptibility to feel pain. Painkillers (analgesics) act by inhibiting the production of prostaglandins.

PROSTATE GLAND The gland at the base of the bladder in males which is involved in semen production, and which may enlarge later in life and obstruct urine flow.

PROTEIN The substance which forms the basic building blocks of the body, protein is made from strings of amino acid molecules.

PUBERTY The stage during which the physical and emotional changes of sexual maturity take place.

PULSE The force of the heart's contractions is felt as a pressure wave that travels along arterial walls. The term generally refers to the pulsations of the radial artery.

RADIUS The long bone on the inside (at the wrist) of the lower arm, which articulates with the ulna at both wrist and elbow.

REFLEX The nervous system has many automatic responses to various sorts of stimulation; these are called reflexes. For example, when a muscle is stretched on being hit by a tendon hammer it automatically contracts.

REFLUX Where some fluid component of the body flows in the wrong direction. The reverse flow of acid from the stomach into the oesophagus is called oesophageal reflux.

RETINA The multi-layered, light-sensitive area of the eye which lines the entire curved surface at the back of the eyeball. It is made up of two different light-sensitive cells, rods and cones, which together interpret images.

SAC A pouch or soft-walled cavity (e.g. pericardial sac of the heart; alveoli, air sacs in the lungs; a sac caused by a cyst or tumour).

SACRUM The triangular bone at the back of the pelvis, formed by five fused vertebrae. It is located immediately above the coccyx, or tailbone, and below the five lumbar vertebrae of the spine.

SALIVA The fluid present in the mouth and secreted by the salivary glands.

SALT One of the body's basic requirements. The level of salt is critical in many of the body's chemical processes.

SCLERA The tough outer layer of the eyeball beginning around the cornea (at the front). This layer constitutes what is commonly called the 'white' of the eye.

SCROTUM The pouch which hangs outside the male body and is situated just behind the penis. It contains the testes.

SEBACEOUS GLANDS Glands in the skin which make sebum to keep the skin soft and supple.

SEBUM The grease produced by the sebaceous glands.

SECRETIN A hormone produced in the duodenum when food is present and which causes the nearby pancreas to produce digestive enzymes.

SECRETION Where a gland of any type produces (i.e. secretes) a substance (secretion) which works outside the gland itself.

SEMEN The fluid which is discharged by the male when he ejaculates. Contains sperm and secretions from other glands such as the prostate.

SEX HORMONES Hormones which control sexual functions. Testosterone is the main male hormone, while oestrogen and progesterone are both important in female sexual functions.

SINU-ATRIAL NODE Located in the right atrium, it passes impulses to both atria, causing them to contract. This is part of the process which maintains a normal heartbeat pattern. (See atrioventricular node and Bundle of His.)

SINUS Any of a number of cavities and/or channels for inflamed matter to pass through. Best known are the sinus cavities at the front of the skull, which help to cushion the impact of blows to the face. These sinuses also connect to the inside of the nose.

SMOOTH MUSCLE That muscle concerned with involuntary movement of internal organs. E.g. peristaltic waves in digestion that push food along.

SODIUM CHLORIDE Chemical name for common salt.

SOLAR PLEXUS Not a medical term; used to describe a general area at the top of the abdomen.

SPERM Fertilization of the female egg takes place when a sperm from the male fuses with it. Sperm are produced in the testes and emitted in the semen.

SPHINCTER A muscular ring around any tube which serves to close it off.

SPINAL CORD The cord of nervous tissue which runs down from the brain inside the central bony canal of the spine. All the nerves to the body below the neck branch off from the spinal cord.

SPLEEN An organ in the upper left-hand corner of the abdomen. The spleen is responsible for filtering worn-out blood cells.

STARCH The general term for carbohydrate foods which form the basis of the human diet.

STERNUM The large piece of cartilage at the front of the rib cage and to which all but the 11th and 12th (the lowest) ribs are attached. Commonly called the 'breastbone'.

STEROIDS Complex chemical molecules. The sex hormones and cortisone are steroids. Commonly the word is used to describe cortisone – produced by the adrenal glands – and the drugs which have a cortisone effect.

SUBCLAVIAN ARTERY Each of the two branches of the artery which supplies blood to the arms. One branch comes from the arch of the aorta; the other from the innominate artery. It continues as the brachial artery, subdividing into the radial and ulnar arteries.

SUBCUTANEOUS Simply means under the skin.

SUGAR Chemically, sugars are small carbohydrate molecules. Glucose is a sugar and it is the basic substance that the body's cells use for fuel.

SYMPATHETIC NERVOUS SYSTEM The part of the autonomic nervous system controlled from the spinal cord, which interacts with the parasympathetic nervous system (controlled from the brain and lower spinal cord), to maintain a balance of the body's vital unconscious activities (e.g. breathing, digestion and heartbeat).

TENDON The strong fibrous cords which bind muscles on to the bones and transmit the force of their contraction.

TENOSYNOVITIS Inflammation of the lubricated sheaths through which some tendons run, for example those running across the wrist.

TESTIS The male sexual organ responsible for the production of both sperm and male sex hormone. The two testes hang at the base of the abdomen in the scrotum.

TESTOSTERONE The male sex hormone, produced by the testes.

THORAX The part of the body between the abdomen and the neck. The thoracic cavity (compare with abdomen and cranium) is supported by the rib cage and intercostal muscles. It contains the heart and lungs.

THYMUS A small gland in the neck whose importance in controlling the body's immune system early in life has only recently been appreciated.

THYROID The gland in the neck whose hormone (thyroxine) is very important in controlling the overall use of energy by the body.

TIBIAL ARTERY The artery supplying blood to the lower leg. It is actually two-branched and a continuation of the femoral artery that divides in two approximately at the knee.

TONSILS Two patches of lymphoid tissue which lie at the back of the throat on either side. May swell when infected.

TRACHEA Commonly called the 'windpipe', this tube or passageway connects the lungs to the throat and thus to the outside of the body.

TRANSPLANT The transferring of any piece of living tissue from one location in the body to another. However, more usually used to refer to the transfer of organs from one individual to another.

TRICEPS The large extensor muscle at the back of the upper arm. Together with the biceps, it facilitates elbow and shoulder movement. (Compare with biceps).

ULNA The long bone of the lower arm, which is on the outside of the wrist where it meets the radius.

UMBILICAL CORD The life-line between mother and foetus which carries all the nutrients and oxygen that the foetus needs.

UMBILICUS The correct name for the depression (actually a scar) in the abdomen, left by the umbilical cord which attached the foetus during its development to the mother. It is commonly called the 'navel', 'tummy button' or 'belly button'.

UNCONSCIOUSNESS A state resembling sleep, from which people are unrousable.

URETER The tube which leads from each of the kidneys to the bladder.

URETHRA The tube which leads from the bladder and through which urine is voided.

URINE The product of the kidneys, urine contains many of the waste products accumulated in the body.

UTERUS The small pear-shaped organ located between the bladder and the rectum, and connected to the ovaries by the Fallopian tubes. If conception takes place, the foetus will be nurtured and develop within the uterus. If there is no pregnancy, the uterine lining (endometrium) will be shed during the monthly process of menstruation, together with a small amount of blood. The uterus was popularly called the 'womb'.

UVULA The bit of the soft palate hanging at the back of the mouth. It has no obvious function, but it is thought it plays a role in the prevention of choking.

VAGINA The female genital passage which leads to the uterus.

VAGINISMUS Spasm of the muscles surrounding the vagina — can cause pain and difficulty on intercourse.

VALVE A mechanism which only allows fluid to flow one way down a tube. The most important valves control blood flow in the heart.

VAS DEFERENS The tube that carries sperm from the testes to the urethra. It is the vas which is cut in a vasectomy, thus stopping the sperm from continuing their passage.

VEIN A blood vessel that carries blood back from the tissues to the heart.

VENA CAVA The large vein by which blood returns to the heart: from the body, via the inferior vena cava; and from the head, via the superior vena cava. The blood enters the right atrium of the heart.

VENTRICLE One of two such pumping chambers of the heart, each of which receives blood from its corresponding atrium. The left ventricle pumps freshly oxygenated blood back into the body, via the aorta; the right ventricle pumps blood, via the pulmonary artery, to the lungs where its oxygen will be renewed.

VITAMIN An essential nutrient that the body requires only in small quantities. Vitamins are required in many of the body's chemical (metabolic) processes.

VITREOUS HUMOUR The jelly-like substance which fills the main interior chamber of the eye, and which gives the eyeball its firm, rubbery texture.

VOLUNTARY MUSCLE Also called 'striated'. Controlled from the brain, this form of muscle acts by contracting and is responsible for all forms of movement.

VULVA The external female genital organs, including the area of the labia, the clitoris and the urethral opening. Vulvitis is an inflammation or infection of the vulva.

WERNICKE'S AREA The area of the brain where sound is deciphered. (Compare with Broca's Area.)

Index

Page numbers in *italics* refer to illustrations